California HMH SCIENCE DIMENSIONS™
Volume 2

Grade 8
Units 3–5

Watch the cover come alive as you explore the solar system.
Download the HMH Science Dimensions AR app available on Android or iOS devices.

This Write-In Book belongs to

_____

Teacher/Room

_____

Houghton Mifflin Harcourt™

Consulting Authors

Michael A. DiSpezio

Global Educator
North Falmouth,
Massachusetts

Michael DiSpezio has authored many HMH instructional programs for Science and Mathematics. He has also authored numerous trade books and multimedia programs on various topics and hosted dozens of studio and location broadcasts for various organizations in the United States and worldwide. Most recently, he has been working with educators to provide strategies for implementing the Next Generation Science Standards, particularly the Science and Engineering Practices, Crosscutting Concepts, and the use of Evidence Notebooks. To all his projects, he brings his extensive background in science, his expertise in classroom teaching at the elementary, middle, and high school levels, and his deep experience in producing interactive and engaging instructional materials.

Marjorie Frank

Science Writer and Content-Area Reading Specialist
Brooklyn, New York

An educator and linguist by training, a writer and poet by nature, Marjorie Frank has authored and designed a generation of instructional materials in all subject areas, including past HMH Science programs. Her other credits include authoring science issues of an award-winning children's magazine, writing game-based digital assessments, developing blended learning materials for young children, and serving as instructional designer and coauthor of pioneering school-to-work software. In addition, she has served on the adjunct faculty of Hunter, Manhattan, and Brooklyn Colleges, teaching courses in science methods, literacy, and writing. For *California HMH Science Dimensions™*, she has guided the development of our K–2 strands and our approach to making connections between NGSS and Common Core ELA/literacy standards.

Acknowledgments

Cover credits: (telescope) ©HMH; (Mars) ©Stocktrek Images, Inc./Alamy.

Section Header Master Art: (machinations) ©DNY59/E+/Getty Images; (rivers on top of Greenland ice sheet) ©Maria-José Viñas, NASA Earth Science News Team; (human cells, illustration) ©Sebastian Kaulitzki/Science Photo Library/Corbis; (waves) ©Alfred Pasieka/Science Source

Printed in the U.S.A.

ISBN 978-0-358-22124-1

3 4 5 6 7 8 9 10   0877   27 26 25 24 23 22 21

4500817312   B C D E F G

Michael R. Heithaus, PhD

Dean, College of Arts, Sciences & Education Professor, Department of Biological Sciences
Florida International University
Miami, Florida

Mike Heithaus joined the FIU Biology Department in 2003 and has served as Director of the Marine Sciences Program and Executive Director of the School of Environment, Arts, and Society, which brings together the natural and social sciences and humanities to develop solutions to today's environmental challenges. He now serves as Dean of the College of Arts, Sciences & Education. His research focuses on predator-prey interactions and the ecological importance of large marine species. He has helped to guide the development of Life Science content in *California HMH Science Dimensions™*, with a focus on strategies for teaching challenging content as well as the science and engineering practices of analyzing data and using computational thinking.

Bernadine Okoro

Access and Equity Consultant

S.T.E.M. Learning Advocate & Consultant
Washington, DC

Bernadine Okoro is a chemical engineer by training and a playwright, novelist, director, and actress by nature. Okoro went from working with patents and biotechnology to teaching in K–12 classrooms. A 12-year science educator and Albert Einstein Distinguished Fellow, Okoro was one of the original authors of the Next Generation Science Standards. As a member of the Diversity and Equity Team, her focus on Alternative Education and Community Schools and on Integrating Social-Emotional Learning and Brain-Based Learning into NGSS is the vehicle she uses as a pathway to support underserved groups from elementary school to adult education. An article and book reviewer for NSTA and other educational publishing companies, Okoro currently works as a S.T.E.M. Learning Advocate & Consultant.

Cary I. Sneider, PhD

Associate Research Professor
Portland State University
Portland, Oregon

While studying astrophysics at Harvard, Cary Sneider volunteered to teach in an Upward Bound program and discovered his real calling as a science teacher. After teaching middle and high school science in Maine, California, Costa Rica, and Micronesia, he settled for nearly three decades at Lawrence Hall of Science in Berkeley, California, where he developed skills in curriculum development and teacher education. Over his career, Cary directed more than 20 federal, state, and foundation grant projects and was a writing team leader for the Next Generation Science Standards. He has been instrumental in ensuring *California HMH Science Dimensions™* meets the high expectations of the NGSS and provides an effective three-dimensional learning experience for all students.

Program Advisors

Paul D. Asimow, PhD
Eleanor and John R. McMillan
Professor of Geology and
Geochemistry
California Institute of Technology
Pasadena, California

Joanne Bourgeois
Professor Emerita
Earth & Space Sciences
University of Washington
Seattle, WA

Dr. Eileen Cashman
Professor
Humboldt State University
Arcata, California

Elizabeth A. De Stasio, PhD
Raymond J. Herzog Professor of
Science
Lawrence University
Appleton, Wisconsin

Perry Donham, PhD
Lecturer
Boston University
Boston, Massachusetts

Shila Garg, PhD
Professor Emerita of Physics
Former Dean of Faculty & Provost
The College of Wooster
Wooster, Ohio

Tatiana A. Krivosheev, PhD
Professor of Physics
Clayton State University
Morrow, Georgia

Mark B. Moldwin, PhD
Professor of Space Sciences and
Engineering
University of Michigan
Ann Arbor, Michigan

Ross H. Nehm
Stony Brook University (SUNY)
Stony Brook, NY

Kelly Y. Neiles, PhD
Assistant Professor of Chemistry
St. Mary's College of Maryland
St. Mary's City, Maryland

John Nielsen-Gammon, PhD
Regents Professor
Department of Atmospheric
Sciences
Texas A&M University
College Station, Texas

Dr. Sten Odenwald
Astronomer
NASA Goddard Spaceflight Center
Greenbelt, Maryland

Bruce W. Schafer
Executive Director
Oregon Robotics Tournament &
Outreach Program
Beaverton, Oregon

Barry A. Van Deman
President and CEO
Museum of Life and Science
Durham, North Carolina

Kim Withers, PhD
Assistant Professor
Texas A&M University-Corpus
Christi
Corpus Christi, Texas

Adam D. Woods, PhD
Professor
California State University,
Fullerton
Fullerton, California

English Development Advisors

Mercy D. Momary
Local District Northwest
Los Angeles, California

Michelle Sullivan
Balboa Elementary
San Diego, California

Lab Safety Reviewer

Kenneth R. Roy, Ph.D.
Senior Lab Safety Compliance Consultant
National Safety Consultants, LLC
Vernon, Connecticut

Classroom Reviewers & Hands-On Activities Advisors

Julie Arreola
Sun Valley Magnet School
Sun Valley, California

Pamela Bluestein
Sycamore Canyon School
Newbury Park, California

Andrea Brown
HLPUSD Science & STEAM TOSA
Hacienda Heights, California

Stephanie Greene
Science Department Chair
Sun Valley Magnet School
Sun Valley, California

Rana Mujtaba Khan
Will Rogers High School
Van Nuys, California

Suzanne Kirkhope
Willow Elementary and Round
Meadow Elementary
Agoura Hills, California

George Kwong
Schafer Park Elementary
Hayward, California

Imelda Madrid
Bassett St. Elementary School
Lake Balboa, California

Susana Martinez O'Brien
Diocese of San Diego
San Diego, California

Craig Moss
Mt. Gleason Middle School
Sunland, California

Isabel Souto
Schafer Park Elementary
Hayward, California

Emily R.C.G. Williams
South Pasadena Middle School
South Pasadena, California

At a hydroelectric power plant, forces help convert the energy of falling water into electrical energy.

VOLUME 1

UNIT 2 Noncontact Forces 117

During thunderstorms, electric charges build up within clouds to produce spectacular lightning displays.

VOLUME 2

UNIT 3 Space Science 211

UNIT 4 Earth through Time 307

VOLUME 2
UNIT 5 Evolution and Biotechnology

391

VOLUME 3
UNIT 6 Waves

477

VOLUME 3

UNIT 7 Technology and Human Impact on Earth Systems

565

Ecosystem health and services are related to the biodiversity of the ecosystem.

Claims, Evidence, and Reasoning

Constructing an Argument

Constructing a strong argument is useful in science and engineering and in everyday life. A strong argument has three parts: a claim, evidence, and reasoning. Scientists and engineers use claims-evidence-reasoning arguments to communicate their explanations and solutions to others and to challenge or debate the conclusions of other scientists and engineers. The words *argue* and *argument* do not mean that scientists or engineers are fighting about something. Instead, this is a way to support a claim using evidence. Argumentation is a calm and rational way for people to examine all the facts and come to the best conclusion.

A **claim** is a statement that answers the question "What do you know?" A claim is a statement of your understanding of a phenomenon, answer to a question, or solution to a problem. A claim states what you think is true based on the information you have.

Evidence is any data that are related to your claim and answer the question "How do you know that?" These data may be from your own experiments and observations, reports by scientists or engineers, or other reliable data. Arguments made in science and engineering should be supported by empirical evidence. Empirical evidence is evidence that comes from observation or experiment.

Evidence used to support a claim should also be relevant and sufficient. Relevant evidence is evidence that is about the claim, and not about something else. Evidence is sufficient when there is enough evidence to fully support the claim.

Reasoning is the use of logical, analytical thought to form conclusions or inferences. Reasoning answers the question "Why does your evidence support your claim?" So, reasoning explains the relationship between your evidence and your claim. Reasoning might include a scientific law or principle that helps explain the relationship between the evidence and the claim.

Here is an example of a claims-evidence-reasoning argument.

Claim	Ice melts faster in the sun than it does in the shade.
Evidence	Two ice cubes of the same size were each placed in a plastic dish. One dish was placed on a wooden bench in the sun and one was placed on a different part of the same bench in the shade. The ice cube in the sun melted in 14 minutes and 32 seconds. The ice cube in the shade melted in 18 minutes and 15 seconds.
Reasoning	This experiment was designed so that the only variable that was different in the set-up of the two ice cubes was whether they were in the shade or in the sun. Because the ice cube in the sun melted almost 4 minutes faster than the one in the shade, this is sufficient evidence to say that ice melts faster in the sun than it does in the shade.

To summarize, a strong argument:

• presents a claim that is clear, logical, and well-defended
• supports the claim with empirical evidence that is sufficient and relevant
• includes reasons that make sense and are presented in a logical order

Constructing Your Own Argument

Now construct your own argument by recording a claim, evidence, and reasoning. With your teacher's permission, you can do an investigation to answer a question you have about how the world works. Or you can construct your argument based on observations you have already made about the world.

Claim	
Evidence	
Reasoning	

 For more information on claims, evidence, and reasoning, see the online **English Language Arts Handbook.**

Whether you are in the lab or in the field, you are responsible for your own safety and the safety of others. To fulfill these responsibilities and avoid accidents, be aware of the safety of your classmates as well as your own safety at all times. Take your lab work and fieldwork seriously, and behave appropriately. Elements of safety to keep in mind are shown below and on the following pages.

Safety in the Lab

☐ Be sure you understand the materials, your procedure, and the safety rules before you start an investigation in the lab.

☐ Know where to find and how to use fire extinguishers, eyewash stations, shower stations, and emergency power shutoffs.

☐ Use proper safety equipment. Always wear personal protective equipment, such as eye protection and gloves, when setting up labs, during labs, and when cleaning up.

☐ Do not begin until your teacher has told you to start. Follow directions.

☐ Keep the lab neat and uncluttered. Clean up when you are finished. Report all spills to your teacher immediately. Watch for slip/fall and trip/fall hazards.

☐ If you or another student is injured in any way, tell your teacher immediately, even if the injury seems minor.

☐ Do not take any food or drink into the lab. Never take any chemicals out of the lab.

Safety in the Field

☐ Be sure you understand the goal of your fieldwork and the proper way to carry out the investigation before you begin fieldwork.

☐ Use proper safety equipment and personal protective equipment, such as eye protection, that suits the terrain and the weather.

☐ Follow directions, including appropriate safety procedures as provided by your teacher.

☐ Do not approach or touch wild animals. Do not touch plants unless instructed by your teacher to do so. Leave natural areas as you found them.

☐ Stay with your group.

☐ Use proper accident procedures, and let your teacher know about a hazard in the environment or an accident immediately, even if the hazard or accident seems minor.

Safety Symbols

To highlight specific types of precautions, the following symbols are used throughout the lab program. Remember that no matter what safety symbols you see within each lab, all safety rules should be followed at all times.

Dress Code

- Wear safety goggles (or safety glasses as appropriate for the activity) at all times in the lab as directed. If chemicals get into your eye, flush your eyes immediately for a minimum of 15 minutes.
- Do not wear contact lenses in the lab.
- Do not look directly at the sun or any intense light source or laser.
- Wear appropriate protective non-latex gloves as directed.
- Wear an apron or lab coat at all times in the lab as directed.
- Tie back long hair, secure loose clothing, and remove loose jewelry. Remove acrylic nails when working with active flames.
- Do not wear open-toed shoes, sandals, or canvas shoes in the lab.

Glassware and Sharp Object Safety

- Do not use chipped or cracked glassware.
- Use heat-resistant glassware for heating or storing hot materials.
- Notify your teacher immediately if a piece of glass breaks.
- Use extreme care when handling any sharp or pointed instruments.
- Do not cut an object while holding the object unsupported in your hands. Place the object on a suitable cutting surface, and always cut in a direction away from your body.

Chemical Safety

- If a chemical gets on your skin, on your clothing, or in your eyes, rinse it immediately for a minimum of 15 minutes (using the shower, faucet, or eyewash station), and alert your teacher.
- Do not clean up spilled chemicals unless your teacher directs you to do so.
- Do not inhale any gas or vapor unless directed to do so by your teacher. If you are instructed to note the odor of a substance, wave the fumes toward your nose with your hand. This is called wafting. Never put your nose close to the source of the odor.
- Handle materials that emit vapors or gases in a well-ventilated area.
- Keep your hands away from your face while you are working on any activity.

Safety Symbols, continued

Electrical Safety

- Do not use equipment with frayed electrical cords or loose plugs.
- Do not use electrical equipment near water or when clothing or hands are wet.
- Hold the plug housing when you plug in or unplug equipment. Do not pull on the cord.
- Use only GFI-protected electrical receptacles.

Heating and Fire Safety

- Be aware of any source of flames, sparks, or heat (such as flames, heating coils, or hot plates) before working with any flammable substances.
- Know the location of the lab's fire extinguisher and fire-safety blankets.
- Know your school's fire-evacuation routes.
- If your clothing catches on fire, walk to the lab shower to put out the fire. Do not run.
- Never leave a hot plate unattended while it is turned on or while it is cooling.
- Use tongs or appropriately insulated holders when handling heated objects.
- Allow all equipment to cool before storing it.

Plant and Animal Safety

- Do not eat any part of a plant.
- Do not pick any wild plant unless your teacher instructs you to do so.
- Handle animals only as your teacher directs.
- Treat animals carefully and respectfully.
- Wash your hands thoroughly with soap and water after handling any plant or animal.

Cleanup

- Clean all work surfaces and protective equipment as directed by your teacher.
- Dispose of hazardous materials or sharp objects only as directed by your teacher.
- Wash your hands thoroughly with soap and water before you leave the lab or after any activity.

Student Safety Quiz

Circle the letter of the BEST answer.

1. Before starting an investigation or lab procedure, you should
   A. try an experiment of your own
   B. open all containers and packages
   C. read all directions and make sure you understand them
   D. handle all the equipment to become familiar with it

2. At the end of any activity you should
   A. wash your hands thoroughly with soap and water before leaving the lab
   B. cover your face with your hands
   C. put on your safety goggles
   D. leave hot plates switched on

3. If you get hurt or injured in any way, you should
   A. tell your teacher immediately
   B. find bandages or a first aid kit
   C. go to your principal's office
   D. get help after you finish the lab

4. If your glassware is chipped or broken, you should
   A. use it only for solid materials
   B. give it to your teacher for recycling or disposal
   C. put it back into the storage cabinet
   D. increase the damage so that it is obvious

5. If you have unused chemicals after finishing a procedure, you should
   A. pour them down a sink or drain
   B. mix them all together in a bucket
   C. put them back into their original containers
   D. dispose of them as directed by your teacher

6. If electrical equipment has a frayed cord, you should
   A. unplug the equipment by pulling the cord
   B. let the cord hang over the side of a counter or table
   C. tell your teacher about the problem immediately
   D. wrap tape around the cord to repair it

7. If you need to determine the odor of a chemical or a solution, you should
   A. use your hand to bring fumes from the container to your nose
   B. bring the container under your nose and inhale deeply
   C. tell your teacher immediately
   D. use odor-sensing equipment

8. When working with materials that might fly into the air and hurt someone's eye, you should wear
   A. goggles
   B. an apron
   C. gloves
   D. a hat

9. Before doing experiments involving a heat source, you should know the location of the
   A. door
   B. window
   C. fire extinguisher
   D. overhead lights

10. If you get chemicals in your eye you should
   A. wash your hands immediately
   B. put the lid back on the chemical container
   C. wait to see if your eye becomes irritated
   D. use the eyewash station right away, for a minimum of 15 minutes

> *Go online to view the Lab Safety Handbook for additional information.*

Space Science

How does gravity explain observations of patterns in space?

This shadow on Earth was cast during a solar eclipse in 2017. During a solar eclipse, the moon moves directly between Earth and the sun, casting a shadow on Earth.

You Solve It When Will an Eclipse Occur? Use a model of the Earth-sun-moon system to analyze patterns of past eclipses and predict when future eclipses will happen.

Go online and complete the You Solve It to explore ways to solve a real-world problem.

Build a Museum Model

The bright band of stars in this image is the Milky Way galaxy, which is home to Earth and our solar system.

A. Look at the photo. On a separate sheet of paper, write down as many different questions as you can about the photo.

B. **Discuss** With your class or a partner, share your questions. Record any additional questions generated in your discussion. Then choose the most important questions from the list that are related to the size and structure of the Milky Way galaxy. Write them below.

C. Choose a feature of the Milky Way galaxy to research. What feature will you research?

D. Use the information above, along with your research, to propose a model of the Milky Way galaxy for a museum or community park. Use the engineering design process to develop a proposal for your installation. Use the model to describe the scale of objects in the universe.

Discuss the next steps for your Unit Project with your teacher and go online to download the Unit Project Worksheet.

Language Development

Use the lessons in this unit to complete the network and expand your understanding of these key science concepts.

Similar term
Phrase
Cognate
Example
Definition

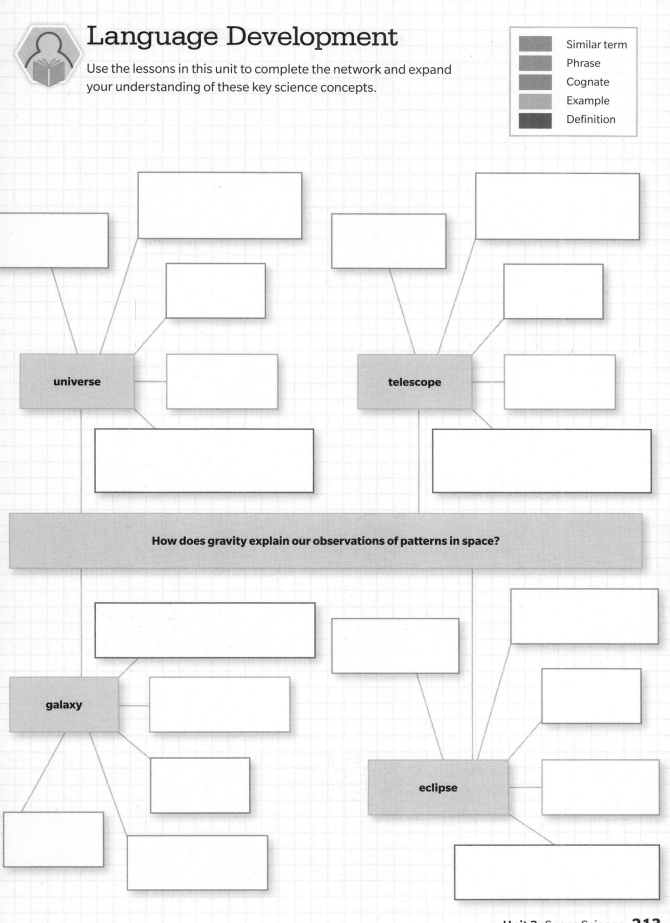

universe

telescope

How does gravity explain our observations of patterns in space?

galaxy

eclipse

Observations Provide Evidence for the Structure of the Solar System

The sun shines through the center gap in Stonehenge in England. This marks the summer solstice, the longest day of the year.

Explore First

Observing Earth's Rotation Place a pencil vertically in the ground where it can cast a shadow from the sun. Mark the spot where the pencil's shadow falls. Mark the shadow again in five minutes. Why has the position of the shadow changed?

Go online to view the digital version of the Hands-On Lab for this lesson and to download additional lab resources.

CAN YOU EXPLAIN IT?

What are "shooting stars"?

Explore Online

For thousands of years people have watched "shooting stars" streak across the sky. Showers of shooting stars occur at regular times each year. However, shooting stars do not follow the normal movement of stars through the night sky. They appear as a streak of light and disappear moments later.

1. Have you ever seen a shooting star or read about one in a poem or a book? How would you describe a shooting star?

2. What conditions are necessary to see a shooting star?

 EVIDENCE NOTEBOOK As you explore the lesson, gather evidence to help explain why shooting stars behave differently than other stars do.

Analyzing Patterns in the Sky

People have been observing patterns in the movements of the sun, moon, and stars for millenia and have used those observed patterns to develop models of our solar system. During the day, the sun appears to travel across the sky. Stars shine day and night, but you can only see them after the sun sets. Much like the sun during the day, the stars appear to move east to west during the night. The moon always rises along the eastern horizon, appears to travel across the sky, and sets along the western horizon. But the moon rises at different times during the month, in a regular pattern.

Although the sun is far away in space, it lights up Earth.

3. **Discuss** Look at the images. What patterns do you see in the apparent motion of objects in the sky? Describe any patterns you observe.

I don't really see a pattern but I think basically it goes around (the earth) and the sun stays in it's position and just repeats.

The Daily Path of the Sun, Moon, and Stars

In the morning, you can watch the sun rise on the eastern horizon. In the evening, you can look to the west to see the sun set on the western horizon.

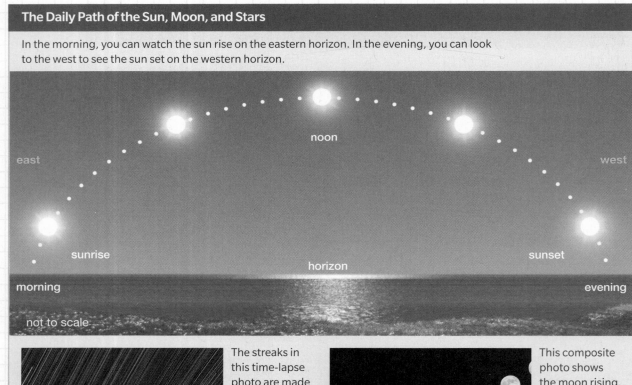

noon

east   west

sunrise   sunset

horizon

morning   evening

not to scale

The streaks in this time-lapse photo are made as stars move across the sky during the night.

This composite photo shows the moon rising. The sun, stars, and the moon move from east to west across the sky.

Hands-On Lab
Model the Apparent Motion of the Sun

You will model the Earth-sun system to develop an explanation for night and day and the apparent motion of the sun in the sky.

MATERIALS
- ball, styrene, on a stick
- lamp with removable shade
- markers
- tape

Procedure

STEP 1 **Act** Work with a partner. Choose who will play the part of the sun and who will play Earth. Write *sun* on one piece of paper and *Earth* on another, and tape the labels to each actor. Stand facing each other. Discuss how the motion of the sun or Earth can result in periods of daytime and nighttime on Earth.

STEP 2 **Act** If you are the actor playing Earth, stand facing the sun. Slowly turn in a circle toward your left. Keep your head in line with your body. Your head is representing Earth. Say *night* when you can no longer see the sun and say *day* when you first see the sun again. Take turns being Earth and the sun. NOTE: Turning toward the left models Earth's counterclockwise movement as you are looking down at the North Pole.

STEP 3 Now use the lamp and foam ball to make a model that explains day and night. Write *Earth* on the tape and put the label around the center of the ball. Hold the ball in front of the lamp and turn the stick toward the left.

Analysis

STEP 4 When I was playing Earth and could see the sun, my face represented the part of Earth that was experiencing day / night.

When I could not see the sun, it was day / night.

When I first saw the sun, it was sunrise / sunset.

When I last saw the sun, it was sunrise / sunset.

It was morning / noon / midnight when I was directly facing the sun.

STEP 5 Think about a compass. If you are facing south, your right shoulder is west and your left shoulder is east. In what direction did you first see the sun in the morning? As you turned, in what direction did the sun seem to move throughout the day? (Imagine that you are always facing south even as you turn. This would represent a stationary observer on the rotating Earth.)

STEP 6 Based on your observations, why does the sun appear to move across the sky?

Earth's Rotation

When you spin around in one place, you are modeling Earth's rotation. You are on Earth, so you do not feel it turning, but you experience the rotation in other ways.

Earth's Rotation Explains the Path of the Sun

The apparent motion of the sun, including daytime and nighttime, is caused by Earth's rotation. A day on Earth is 24 hours because Earth completes one full rotation during that time. As Earth spins, different parts of Earth face the sun. It is daytime when an area faces toward the sun and nighttime when it faces away from the sun.

If you were looking down on Earth from the North Pole, it would rotate counterclockwise. Therefore, on Earth, the eastern horizon turns toward the sun first in the morning. Throughout the day, the sun appears to move from east to west as Earth rotates. The way the sun appears to move always follows the same pattern, rising in the east, moving in an arc across the sky from east to west, and setting in the west.

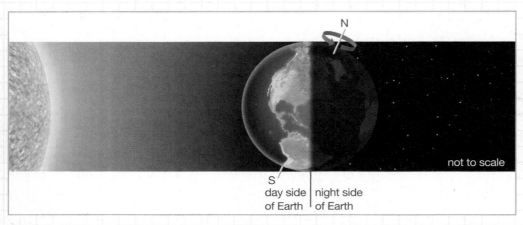

Stars are visible at night on the side of Earth facing away from the sun.

N

S
day side | night side
of Earth | of Earth

not to scale

Earth's Rotation Explains the Path of the Stars

During the daytime, the sun is so bright that you cannot see other stars. Look at the diagram. The area of Earth that is experiencing nighttime faces away from the sun, so you are able to see the stars. As with the sun, the stars appear to move from east to west as Earth rotates. Throughout the night, different stars rise and set. The stars rise and become visible over the horizon as Earth rotates. For example, the constellation Orion comes into view in the eastern night sky around 9 p.m. in late November in the Northern Hemisphere. As Earth spins, Orion appears to move westward. Orion is at its highest point in the sky around midnight. Then Orion continues toward the west, where it sets.

4. How does the daily cycle of daytime and nighttime depend on Earth's rotation?

   A. The sun rises in the west and sets in the east because Earth rotates west to east.

   B. It is morning on the part of Earth that is facing into the sun and evening on the part that is facing away from the sun.

   C. The Northern Hemisphere experiences daytime while the Southern Hemisphere experiences nighttime because Earth rotates around its axis.

EVIDENCE NOTEBOOK

5. Do shooting stars match any of the observed patterns in apparent motion of other objects in the sky? Record your evidence.

   I'm not sure but since the earth rotates the stars rotate as well.

6. Stars appear to move because Earth spins toward the ~~east~~ / west. On the same day, people who live in the eastern United States see the same / ~~different~~ stars in the night sky as those who live at the same latitude in the western United States.

Earth's Rotation Explains the Path of the Moon

The moon also appears to move east to west in the sky as Earth rotates. However, the motion of the moon is a bit different than the motion of the sun and the stars. The moon's orbit causes it to rise slightly later each day, but the timing of the moon's rising and setting is predictable. The moon also appears to slowly move eastward with respect to the background of stars. In addition, the moon is visible sometimes during the day. Although Earth's rotation explains the moon's daily rising and setting pattern, the moon's overall apparent motion is also affected by other factors.

7. Why are the patterns of movement of the sun, stars, and the moon across Earth's sky similar? *They are similar since the earth is rotating not the sun or the whole galaxy.*

Do the Math
Analyze Star Motion

8. Polaris is also called the *North Star* because Earth's North Pole points toward it. As Earth rotates, other stars seem to spin around Polaris in a counterclockwise direction. In one day, the stars will make one complete circle (360°) around Polaris. Compare the positions of the constellations in the two diagrams. Calculate how many hours have passed between the first and second diagrams.

I think 1 hour. I caculated it by how it just changed one time and not like more than one time.

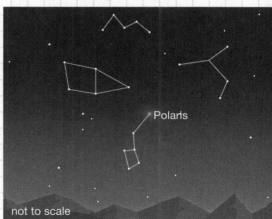

not to scale

Seasonal Star Patterns

Earth's place in its orbit affects which stars can be seen during different seasons. The location of stars in the night sky changes as Earth moves along its orbit. During the year, you will be able to see all the stars visible from one specific place on Earth.

On a given day, you will only be able to see the stars that are in the opposite direction of the sun. The stars seen from the Northern Hemisphere may be different from the stars seen from the Southern Hemisphere. If you are on the North or South Pole, the stars will appear to rotate around a point directly above your head because of Earth's rotation. The sky seen from the North Pole is completely different from the sky seen from the South Pole. As you move from the North Pole toward the South Pole, the sky will change. The sky seen by someone in Florida may have some of the same stars in the sky seen by someone in Brazil, but the whole pattern of stars seen is not the same.

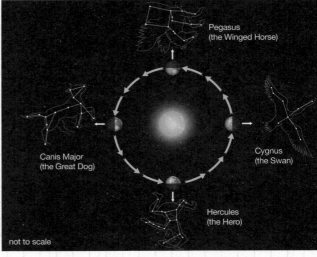

Different stars are seen from Earth at different times of the year. For example, Cygnus is seen in the night sky of the Northern Hemisphere in summer.

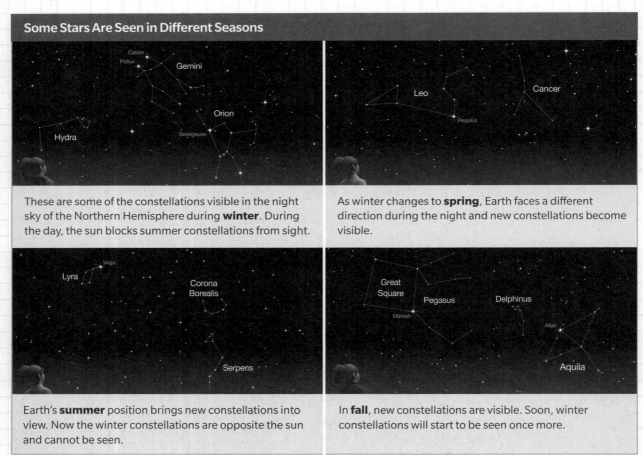

Some Stars Are Seen in Different Seasons

These are some of the constellations visible in the night sky of the Northern Hemisphere during **winter**. During the day, the sun blocks summer constellations from sight.

As winter changes to **spring**, Earth faces a different direction during the night and new constellations become visible.

Earth's **summer** position brings new constellations into view. Now the winter constellations are opposite the sun and cannot be seen.

In **fall**, new constellations are visible. Soon, winter constellations will start to be seen once more.

9. **Discuss** If you were an ancient astronomer who observed the seasonal changes in stars, what questions might you ask or what other observations would you want to make before constructing an explanation for this observation?

I think I would ask questions on how the stars make an object or a kind of animal like clouds. stars are like rocks but how come they're bright & shing?

The Wandering Stars

To ancient astronomers, some stars did not appear to behave like the other stars. They would rise and set along with the rest of the stars. However, when observed over several weeks, they appeared to change their location among the other stars. Greek astronomers called those bodies *astéres planétai*, or "wandering stars." They are the planets we can easily see from Earth: Mercury, Venus, Mars, Jupiter, and Saturn. As planets moved across the sky, they traveled at different speeds. Sometimes, a planet would catch up to and pass another object that appeared to move more slowly. As they moved, planets appeared to pass in front of or behind the sun. Occasionally, they would pass behind, but never in front of the moon. When plotted on a sky chart for days or weeks, some planets' paths through the sky appeared to loop or move backward. This reverse motion puzzled astronomers. They struggled to construct an explanation for this phenomenon.

Language SmArts
Interpret Words and Visuals

Term	Root meanings
retrograde	Latin roots: *retro-* means "backward" and *gradi* means "to walk or step"
transit	Latin root: *transire* means "to cross"

10. Look at the terms and the meanings of their root words. Then create a label for each image by matching the term to the correct image.

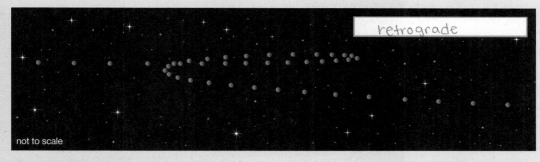

retrograde

not to scale

Mars appears to move backward or have a looping path as its movement is viewed from Earth over several weeks.

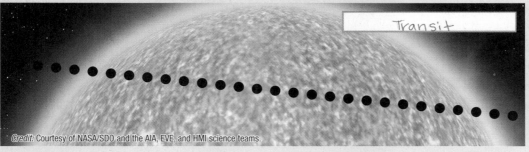

Transit

Credit: Courtesy of NASA/SDO and the AIA, EVE, and HMI science teams.

This composite image shows Venus as it passes in front of the sun. The dark circles represent the positions of Venus over several hours.

11. From Earth, the moon is seen to transit in front of both the sun and Venus. Venus transits across the sun but never across the moon. List the three bodies described in order of increasing distance from Earth. Explain your thinking.

the Three bodies are I think called astéres planétai, or "wandering stars" as well. Also retrograde and transit. Which is "to cross" and "backword" also gradi means to "walk or step".

Developing Models of the Solar System

Early Models of the Solar System

Early astronomers developed models of the solar system based on what they knew. Because objects in the sky appeared to circle Earth, many astronomers placed Earth at the center of the model. The Greek philosopher Aristotle (384–322 BCE) developed a model that had a fixed, non-moving Earth as the center of the universe. He proposed that all other bodies in the sky—including the moon, the sun, the planets, and the stars—moved around Earth. Aristotle claimed that all objects in the sky moved along regular, perfectly circular paths. This *geocentric*, or Earth-centered model explained why objects in the sky appear to revolve around Earth on regular paths. It explained why Earth appears—to someone on Earth's surface—to be unmoving. It also explained why Venus or Mercury would transit in front of the sun, and why any of the planets would pass behind, but never in front of the moon.

12. Which of the following observations support Aristotle's geocentric model? Select all statements that apply.

A. The sun, moon, and stars appear to follow a circular path through the sky.

B. The sun and moon appear to be the same size and brightness as the stars.

C. The sun, moon, and stars seem to move at the same rate across the sky.

D. For people on Earth, the planet does not feel like it is moving.

E. Some planets appear to cross between the sun and Earth.

F. Some planets appear to pass behind and beyond the sun.

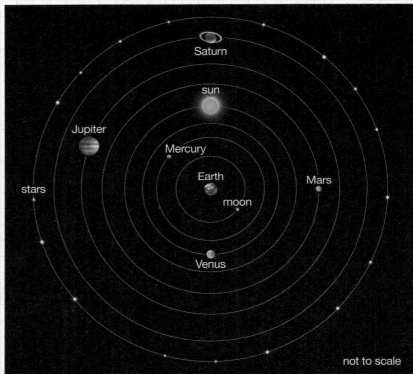

In Aristotle's model of the universe, the planets, sun, moon, and stars all revolved around a fixed, non-moving Earth.

13. What would Aristotle's geocentric model predict about the brightness of the planets when viewed from Earth? What about the stars? Explain your reasoning.

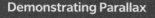

Demonstrating Parallax

Hold your thumb a few inches from your nose. Look at your thumb with one eye closed. Then switch which eye is open and which eye is closed. Your thumb will appear to shift position.

Parallax and Geocentrism

To understand another argument for the geocentric model, it is important to understand a phenomenon called parallax. **Parallax** is the apparent shift in position of an object when it is viewed from different points. As an example, look at the photos that demonstrate parallax. Parallax can be used to measure the distance to an object based on the size of the apparent shift in position when the object is viewed from two places. The bigger the apparent shift in position is, the closer the object is to the viewer.

The stars and constellations do not appear to change positions relative to each other when viewed from Earth with an unaided eye. Astronomers reasoned that this fact indicated that either the stars are extremely far away or they are all the same distance from Earth. Aristotle's geocentric model proposed that the stars were fixed in position on a sphere that orbited Earth. This explanation fit the evidence, so it was accepted by other astronomers.

Ptolemy Answers the Retrograde Motion Problem

Aristotle's model failed to explain retrograde motion of planets or strange phenomena like shooting stars or comets. About 400 years after Artistotle, Claudius Ptolemy improved Aristotle's model by explaining retrograde motion. He claimed that planets moved in small circles, called *epicycles,* along their orbits around Earth. As the planets moved on these epicycles, they sometimes appeared to move backward. Ptolemy's geocentric model was accepted by most scientists for about 1,000 years.

14. Why would solving retrograde motion improve Aristotle's model?

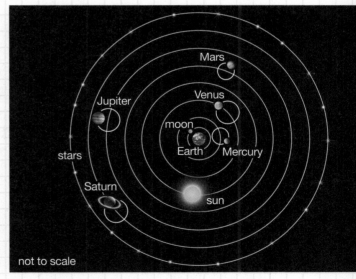

Ptolemy's geocentric model used epicycles to explain retrograde motion.

Hands-On Lab
Investigate Parallax

Use parallax to compare the relative distances between objects.

Procedure

STEP 1 Place the table about 2 m from the wall. Tape the meterstick to the table so that the 100 cm mark is closest to the wall.

STEP 2 Place the pushpin into the meterstick at 100 cm. Sit or kneel on the side of the table farthest from the wall. Place the tip of your nose on the 0 cm end of the meterstick. Make sure you are positioned so that your eyes are evenly spaced on opposite sides of the meterstick.

STEP 3 Without moving your head, close your right eye. Tell your partner where the pin appears against the background. He or she will mark that point on the wall with a labeled sticky note.

STEP 4 Without moving your head, switch your open and closed eyes. Tell your partner where the pin appears against the background. He or she will mark that point with a labeled sticky note.

STEP 5 Repeat Steps 4–6 with the pushpin at 75 cm, 50 cm, and 25 cm. Make sure your head is in the same position, with the tip of your nose on the 0 cm end, for all four placements of the pushpin.

MATERIALS
- markers (4 colors)
- meterstick
- pushpin (at least 10 mm tall)
- sticky notes
- stool or chair
- table
- tape

Analysis

STEP 6 What pattern did you see between the distance between the pin and your nose and the distance between the apparent positions of the pin when viewed with alternating eyes?

STEP 7 Stars do not appear to change position in relation to other stars when viewed from two locations on Earth's surface. How do you think this evidence supported ancient astronomers' belief in early geocentric models?

Analyze Data That Do Not Fit the Model

Aristotle's and Ptolemy's models included stars and planets that moved at a constant rate. The stars did not change their relative positions or brightnesses. These models explained events that fit a pattern. However, ancient astronomers from around the world recorded some events that did not appear to fit the observed patterns of motion of objects in the sky. Resolving these events with existing models of the universe became a challenge for all astronomers.

Observed phenomenon	Description
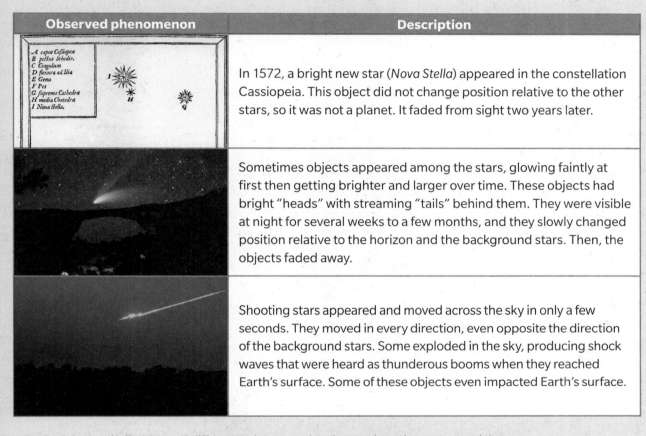	In 1572, a bright new star (*Nova Stella*) appeared in the constellation Cassiopeia. This object did not change position relative to the other stars, so it was not a planet. It faded from sight two years later.
	Sometimes objects appeared among the stars, glowing faintly at first then getting brighter and larger over time. These objects had bright "heads" with streaming "tails" behind them. They were visible at night for several weeks to a few months, and they slowly changed position relative to the horizon and the background stars. Then, the objects faded away.
	Shooting stars appeared and moved across the sky in only a few seconds. They moved in every direction, even opposite the direction of the background stars. Some exploded in the sky, producing shock waves that were heard as thunderous booms when they reached Earth's surface. Some of these objects even impacted Earth's surface.

15. Explain the similarities and differences between the observations that supported the geocentric models of the solar system and the phenomena described in the table.

_____

_____

16. Imagine that a small, bright object appeared in the sky, moved along with a nearby constellation, and then disappeared a year later. Scientists in China, Persia, Europe, and Central America observed the event. How close to Earth did this phenomenon most likely occur? How do you know?

_____

_____

 EVIDENCE NOTEBOOK

17. How close to Earth must shooting stars be, and what does this mean about what causes them? Record your evidence.

Incorporating New Discoveries

Despite the widespread acceptance of the geocentric model, astronomers continued to gather data and refine the model. Many Indian and Arab astronomers made great advances in mathematical models that explained the movements of objects in the solar system. In 1543, a scientist named Nicolaus Copernicus used their calculations to propose a new model of the solar system: one with the sun at the center. Copernicus's *heliocentric*, or sun-centered model explained retrograde motion in a simpler way. It placed the sun at the center and arranged the planets around the sun based on how quickly each planet orbits the sun. It takes Earth about 365.25 days, or about one year, to orbit the sun.

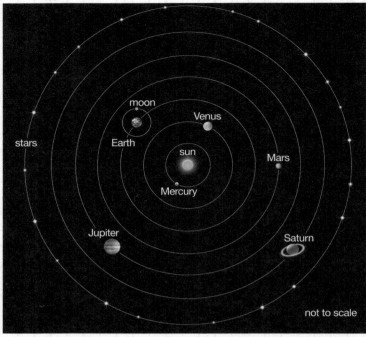

Copernicus's heliocentric model of the solar system put each planet, including Earth, in orbit around the sun. The moon orbited Earth.

18. Using the word bank, complete the Venn diagram by entering the claims made by each scientist.

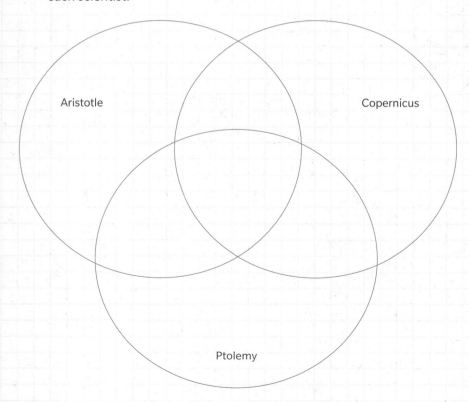

WORD BANK
- sun orbits Earth
- moon orbits Earth
- other planets orbit Earth
- Earth orbits sun
- other planets orbit sun
- sun at center
- Earth at center
- explains retrograde motion
- explains movements of sun and moon
- planets move in epicycles

19. Why might scientists favor Copernicus's heliocentric model over Ptolemy's geocentric model?

Revising and Expanding the Model

In the late 1500s, Danish scientist Tycho Brahe built huge instruments that allowed him to take extremely precise measurements of stars and planets. His assistant, Johannes Kepler, used Brahe's data to calculate the shapes of planetary orbits. By suggesting that planets have elliptical, or oval-shaped, orbits rather than circular orbits, Kepler was able to explain complex planetary motions. These new findings helped convince scientists that Earth and the other planets revolve around the sun.

20. The immense size of the instruments used by Tycho Brahe allowed him to construct an accurate mathematical / physical model of the solar system. The advantage of such precise measurements was that they allowed Brahe to make observations / predictions about the future positions of the stars and planets.

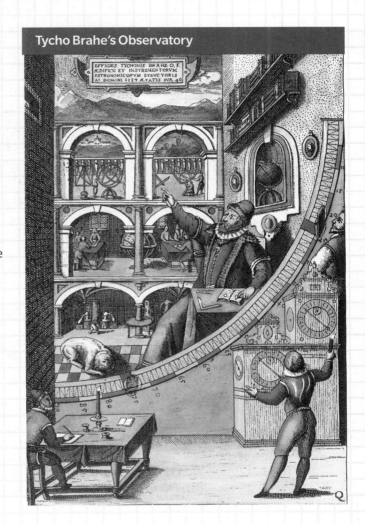

Tycho Brahe's Observatory

New Technology Led to New Discoveries

As Kepler was publishing his work, revolutionary technologies were being developed. In Italy, Galileo Galilei combined two magnifying lenses to make the first telescope in 1609. A **telescope** is an instrument that collects and concentrates light from distant objects to make the objects appear larger or brighter. Early telescopes magnified objects by only three to 30 times. But that small amount had a huge effect on astronomy.

   Galileo's observations through his telescopes revealed details of planets and moons that changed centuries of scientific thought. He noticed that the surface of Earth's moon was rugged, not smooth. He observed sunspots on the sun and identified the phases of Venus. He also saw four small objects moving around Jupiter. These moons of Jupiter provided further evidence that objects could orbit bodies other than Earth.

Analyze the Movement of Jupiter's Moons

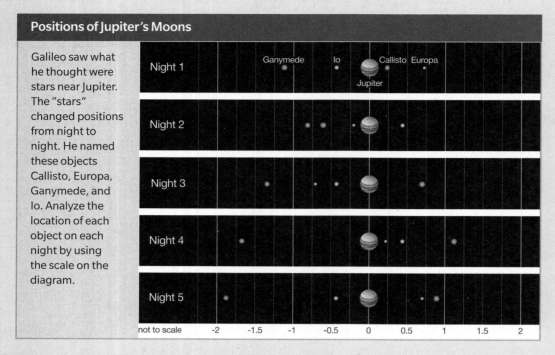

Positions of Jupiter's Moons

Galileo saw what he thought were stars near Jupiter. The "stars" changed positions from night to night. He named these objects Callisto, Europa, Ganymede, and Io. Analyze the location of each object on each night by using the scale on the diagram.

Night 1 — Ganymede, Io, Jupiter, Callisto, Europa

Night 2

Night 3

Night 4

Night 5

not to scale   -2   -1.5   -1   -0.5   0   0.5   1   1.5   2

21. Look at the diagram. Which moon appeared to move the fastest? Which moon appeared to move the slowest? Explain your reasoning.

22. Use the scale on the diagram to determine the maximum distance each object travels away from Jupiter. Place that number in the center column of the chart. Then rank the objects in order of increasing distance from Jupiter.

Object	Maximum distance from Jupiter on the scale	Rank by distance from Jupiter (1= closest and 4 = farthest)
Callisto		
Europa		
Ganymede		
Io		

Exploring the Structure of the Solar System

Astronomers eventually accepted the heliocentric model as the best fit to all the evidence. The development of improved telescopes and space probes has helped astronomers continue to refine our understanding of all the bodies of the solar system.

23. Which of the following lines of evidence support the heliocentric model of the solar system? Select all statements that apply.

   A. The observation that Jupiter has moons that orbit around it.

   B. The discovery that the moon circles around Earth in the same direction that Earth rotates.

   C. The observation that the stars do not appear to change positions relative to each other when viewed from two distant places on Earth.

   D. The discovery that planets move in small circles, called epicycles.

   E. The calculation that planets have elliptical, or oval-shaped, orbits rather than circular orbits.

The planets do not emit light. They reflect light from the sun. Some planets in the solar system are easy to find among the many stars in the night sky. This photo shows Venus, Mars, and Jupiter over Utah.

A Growing Family of Objects

Advancements in telescopes occurred quickly over the 300 to 400 years after Galileo first invented them. Each advancement allowed scientists to see farther or with greater clarity and detail. Scientists collected data and used mathematical modeling to discover and describe new planets, moons, and numerous smaller objects in the solar system. All of these objects are influenced by the sun's gravity, which keeps the objects in motion around the sun.

More Than Planets Orbit the Sun

Mathematical models predicted that planets should exist beyond the orbit of Saturn and between Mars and Jupiter. One model was based on the pattern of planetary distances from the sun. Scientists used telescopes to look for these predicted objects. In 1801, a small, round object was discovered between the orbits of Mars and Jupiter. This object, named Ceres, was not a planet. It was the first object identified in the asteroid belt and is now considered a dwarf planet. The planet Neptune was discovered in 1846, the planet Uranus was discovered in 1871, and the dwarf planet Pluto was discovered in 1930.

24. New technologies, such as *astrolabes / telescopes*, allowed astronomers to see dim or distant objects in space. The development of new technology is *necessary / unnecessary* to the advancement of science. Scientists must *consider / disregard* new evidence as they propose explanations for observed phenomena.

EVIDENCE NOTEBOOK

25. Use the following information about small bodies in the solar system to record evidence that might help you identify the source of shooting stars.

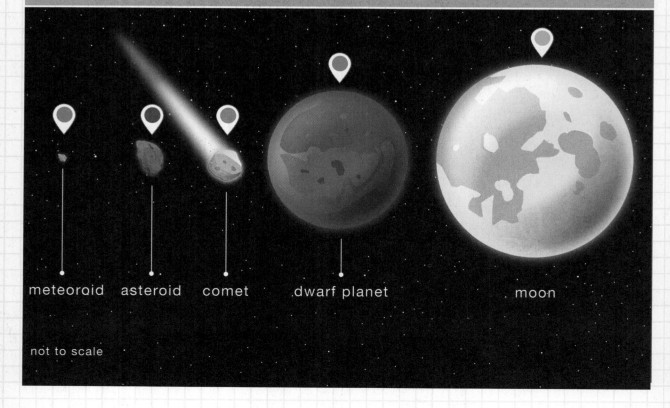

Small Bodies in the Solar System

Sizes of moons and dwarf planets in this illustration are relative and not to scale. The smaller objects, such as meteoroids, would be invisible at that scale, so they are shown in an enlarged view.

meteoroid   asteroid   comet   dwarf planet   moon

not to scale

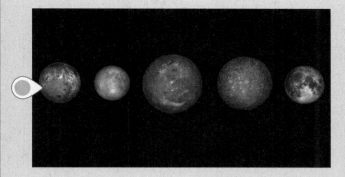

Moons are bodies that orbit larger bodies such as planets, dwarf planets, or asteroids. Moons do not orbit the sun. Some moons are round, such as Earth's moon. Many moons are not round and may be asteroids or other space debris that are captured by the gravity of the larger body they orbit.

Dwarf planets are similar to planets. They orbit the sun, and they are massive enough to be roughly spherical. However, dwarf planets are not large enough to have cleared their orbit of other large objects. Most dwarf planets are in areas that are surrounded by many small and large objects, such as asteroids and other dwarf planets.

Comets are small bodies of ice, rock, and dust. They follow highly elliptical orbits around the sun. As a comet passes close to the sun, gas and dust break off of the comet and form tails. They have not cleared their orbits and may collide with larger objects.

Asteroids are small, irregularly shaped rocky and metallic bodies. They range from the size of a car to several kilometers across. Although most asteroids orbit the sun in the asteroid belt (between the orbits of Mars and Jupiter), some travel through space on elliptical orbits like comets. They cross the orbits of other bodies, including Earth.

Meteoroids are small, rocky or metallic bodies. They may be debris left over from when the solar system formed. They may also break off of comets or asteroids. If a meteoroid enters Earth's atmosphere, it burns up. The short, bright streak of light is called a *meteor*.

Compare and Categorize Solar System Objects

Objects in our solar system are categorized according to their observable characteristics. For example, astronomers use size, shape, and orbit to classify objects. Planets are spherical and are held in orbit around the sun by the sun's gravitational pull on them. Moons may be spherical or irregular, and they orbit larger bodies, such as planets, dwarf planets, or asteroids. Knowing the characteristics of space objects helps astronomers classify new objects that are discovered.

Observed Objects in the Solar System				
Body	Shape	Orbits	Orbited by	Orbit cleared
Ceres	sphere	sun	––	No
Ida	irregular	sun	Dactyl	No
Mercury	sphere	sun	––	Yes
Neptune	sphere	sun	14 bodies	Yes
Phobos	irregular	Mars	––	––
Pluto	sphere	sun	Charon	No
Titan	sphere	Saturn	––	––
Vesta	irregular	sun	––	No

26. Identify whether each object listed is a planet, dwarf planet, asteroid, or moon. Write the name of each object in the correct column.

Planets	Dwarf planets	Moons	Asteroids

WORD BANK
- Ceres
- Ida
- Mercury
- Neptune
- Phobos
- Pluto
- Titan
- Vesta

27. What information helped you sort the objects into categories?

Continue Your Exploration

Name: _____   Date: _____

Check out the path below or go online to choose one of the other paths shown.

| Exploring the Outer Solar System | • **People in Science**
 • **Reflecting and Refracting Telescopes**
 • **Hands-On Labs** 🖐
 • **Propose Your Own Path** | *Go online to choose one of these other paths* |

The sun's gravity holds many objects in orbit. In addition to the planets, smaller objects are found in different parts of the solar system. The asteroid belt between Mars and Jupiter holds hundreds of thousands of objects. These range in size from small specks of dust to the dwarf planet Ceres. Beyond the orbit of the most distant planet, Neptune, is the Kuiper Belt. This ring of rocky and icy bodies is many times larger than the asteroid belt between Mars and Jupiter. The Kuiper Belt includes Pluto and several other icy dwarf planets. Far beyond the Kuiper Belt lies the Oort cloud, a collection of trillions of icy bodies left over from the formation of the solar system.

A number of uncrewed spacecraft have been sent to explore objects in the outer solar system. These space probes carry instruments that can take images and make measurements and send them back to Earth by radio. It would take too much energy to send a spacecraft directly to another solar system object. Instead, spacecraft use the gravitational fields of the sun and the planets to accelerate and change course. These gravity assist maneuvers requiring careful timing to make sure that the spacecraft approaches a planet at just the right time and at the right speed to accurately change course to the next planet it was designed to fly by.

The *New Horizons* spacecraft was launched in 2006 with the goal of exploring the outer solar system. In July 2015, *New Horizons* flew by the dwarf planet Pluto. The spacecraft is now on a path to fly by objects in the Kuiper Belt.

There have been several successful missions to the outer solar system. The spacecraft have returned valuable information that continues to be used by scientists to understand the structure and early formation of the solar system.

1. Why is it useful to send uncrewed spacecraft to explore distant parts of the solar system?

Continue Your Exploration

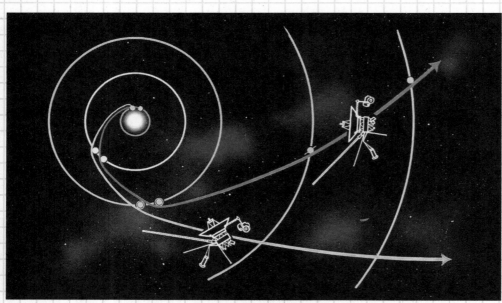

The spacecraft Voyager 1 and Voyager 2 both started from Earth, but their flight paths were very different.

2. What caused the flight paths of Voyager 1 and Voyager 2 to differ?

3. Why is it important for the scientists and engineers who plan uncrewed missions to accurately know the masses and the paths of the planets the spacecraft will visit?

4. **Collaborate** Work with a partner to create a poster that describes the mission of another uncrewed space probe. Include information about what the probe was designed to study and how it relayed that information to Earth. Include some kind of labeled diagram on your poster.

Can You Explain It?

Name: _____   **Date:** _____

What are "shooting stars"?

Explore Online

EVIDENCE NOTEBOOK

Refer to the notes in your Evidence Notebook to help you construct an explanation for what causes shooting stars.

1. State your claim. Make sure your claim fully explains what causes shooting stars.

2. Summarize the evidence you have gathered to support your claim and explain your reasoning.

Checkpoints

Answer the following questions to check your understanding of the lesson.

Use the photo to answer question 3.

3. The photo shows a *meteoroid / comet*. These objects move in *circular / elliptical* orbits around the sun.

4. Which of the following is a characteristic of all planets?

   A. a highly elliptical orbit

   B. a rocky or metallic body

   C. a spherical shape

5. How did our changing understanding of the solar system relate to the cumulative nature of scientific discovery? Select all that apply.

   A. Scientists favored the simplest model that explained observations.

   B. Scientists adopted new models to account for new observations.

   C. Observations that did not fit a model could be ignored.

   D. Observations improved as new technologies become available.

6. The appearance of different constellations in the night sky during the year provide evidence for which of the following?

   A. that the stars move around Earth

   B. that Earth moves around the sun

   C. that the moon moves around Earth

   D. that the sun moves around Earth

Use the diagram to answer question 7.

7. Which statement is demonstrated by this model?

   A. The same stars are visible all year long.

   B. The sun orbits Earth once every year.

   C. The moon rises and sets at the same time every day.

   D. Earth and the moon rotate in the same direction that they orbit.

not to scale

8. How can models help us understand the apparent motion of the sun, the moon, and the stars in the sky? Select all that apply.

   A. Models can be used to make predictions.

   B. Models can be used to explain events.

   C. Models can be used to describe events.

   D. Models can be used to make observations.

Interactive Review

Complete this section to review the main concepts of the lesson.

The sun, stars, and moon appear to move across the sky from east to west on a daily basis.

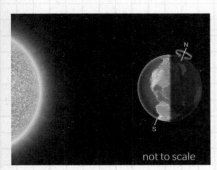

not to scale

A. How did the apparent motions of planets set those objects apart from other stars when observed by ancient astronomers?

Early astronomers developed models of the solar system to explain their observations of the apparent movements of the sun and the planets.

B. Explain why observations of comets and shooting stars presented challenges to ancient astronomers using Ptolemy's model to explain the solar system.

Copernicus's heliocentric model and the invention of telescopes changed and expanded scientists' understanding of the solar system.

not to scale

C. How did the telescope bring about changes in astronomy?

Advances in technology have allowed scientists to understand more about the smaller objects that are found in the solar system.

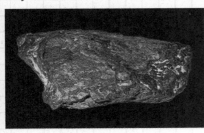

D. Explain how objects in the solar system are classified.

Case Study: Explaining Eclipses and Lunar Phases

The moon sometimes appears orange as it rises. When the moon is near the horizon, the bending of light in the atmosphere can also distort the moon's shape.

Explore First

Simulating an Eclipse Hold a ball at arm's length. With your other hand, hold a coin between your eyes and the ball. Close one eye, and move the coin back and forth until it blocks your view of the ball. Why are you able to block your view of the ball with the much smaller coin?

CAN YOU EXPLAIN IT?

Why can we see the moon at night and also during the day?

At night, the moon is the biggest, brightest object in the sky. If you look closely, you may also be able to see the moon during the day when the sun is also out. These photographs were taken about 2 weeks apart.

1. How is the moon similar and different in the two photos?

2. Do you think the shape of the moon would appear to be different if photos were taken a few hours later than the photos shown here? Explain your reasoning.

3. Do you think the shape of the moon would appear to be different if photos were taken one week later than the photos shown here? Explain your reasoning.

 EVIDENCE NOTEBOOK As you explore the lesson, gather evidence to help explain why we see the moon at night and also during the day.

Analyzing Moon Phases

Because it is so close, the moon is the brightest body in the night sky as seen from Earth. The light we see from the moon is reflected sunlight. The sun always lights half of the moon, and the other half is always dark. From Earth, the moon does not always appear the same. The moon's appearance changes from a totally dark disk to a fully lit disk and back again over the course of a month. These images show a pattern of change in the moon's appearance called the moon's phases. A **phase** is the change in the sunlit area of one celestial body, such as the moon, as seen from another celestial body, such as Earth.

The moon's changing appearance in the sky is shown in these images, taken about four days apart over the period of one month.

4. Does the fraction of the moon that receives sunlight ever change? Explain your reasoning.

   No, because it's honestly probably always going to stay how it is and basically stay in its orbit

The Moon Orbits Earth

Earth rotates on its axis once every 24 hours, which explains the pattern of sunrise and sunset, or day and night. Like the sun, the moon always rises along the eastern horizon and sets along the western horizon. The moon is visible for about twelve hours at a time.

   The same side of the moon always faces Earth. This happens because the moon's orbit and the time the moon takes to rotate on its axis are the same—about 27 days. However, the moon takes slightly longer—29.5 days—to complete one cycle of phases. Because Earth is also moving in its orbit around the sun as the moon orbits Earth, after 27 days, Earth and the moon have changed position with respect to the sun. Therefore, the moon must travel a little longer than 27 days before it is directly between the sun and Earth, where the cycle of phases begins again. This pattern can be observed as the moon rises and sets about 50 minutes later each day.

EVIDENCE NOTEBOOK

5. If the moon is lit by the sun, why can you still see it after sunset? Record your evidence. *I think since the moon stays in it's spot and I think yeah just stays.*

Hands-On Lab
Model Moon Phases

You will model the Earth-sun-moon system to develop an explanation for the changing appearance of the moon as seen from Earth.

MATERIALS
- ball, styrene, on a stick
- lamp with removable shade
- markers
- tape

Procedure

STEP 1 Continue working with your partner. The lamp (sun) should be placed at eye level. Use the marker and tape to label the polystyrene ball as *moon*.

STEP 2 **Act** Have the person playing Earth face the sun (the lamp). The other partner stands next to the sun, facing Earth. Earth holds the moon at arm's length so the moon is between Earth and the sun, then raises the moon so that the moon is slightly higher than his or her head. Record your observations of how much of the moon appears to be lit. Each partner records his or her observations in the appropriate column of the table.

STEP 3 **Act** Keeping the moon held in the same position at arm's length, Earth slowly turns in a circle toward the left, stopping at each quarter turn. At each stop, the partners each record their observations of how much of the moon appears to be lit.

STEP 4 **Act** Switch roles and repeat STEPS 2 and 3, completing the table by recording your observations from the other perspective, from either Earth or next to the sun.

Orientation of Earth	Appearance of the moon from Earth	Appearance of the moon from the sun
Facing the sun	0%	100%
1st quarter turn	50%	100%
2nd quarter turn (facing away from the sun)	100%	100%
3rd quarter turn	50%	100%

Analysis

STEP 5 What is being modeled by the ball when the person playing Earth is turning in a circle?

    A. Earth's rotation

    B. the moon's rotation

    C. Earth's orbit around the sun

    (**D.**) the moon's orbit around Earth

STEP 6 When I was playing Earth, the shape of the fraction of the moon that appeared lit ~~changed~~ / stayed the same.

When I was facing the sun, the moon appeared to be completely ~~dark~~ / lit.
When I was facing away from the sun, the moon appeared to be completely dark / (lit.)

When I was observing the moon from the sun, the fraction of the moon that was lit changed / was always one half.

STEP 7 **Language SmArts** Compare the information that you have read so far in the text with what you observed in the experiment. Write an explanation for why the phases of the moon occur. Give examples from the model to support your explanation. As the moon orbits the Earth, we see different amounts of the bright side of the moon from Earth.

The Moon's Monthly Cycle of Lunar Phases

The phases of the moon depend on the relative positions of Earth, the sun, and the moon as these objects move in space. When the moon is dark, or in the new moon phase, the moon is between Earth and the sun, and the unlit portion of the moon is facing Earth. As the moon moves around Earth, sunlight makes a sliver of the moon's edge visible. When less than half of the moon is visible, the phase is called a crescent, and when the lit portion of the moon is getting larger, the moon is said to be waxing. The outward curve of a crescent moon faces toward the sun. Over the course of a few nights, the thickness of the crescent will grow until after a week, the moon will appear half lit. This is the first quarter phase. During the waxing gibbous phase, the lighted portion of the moon's surface will continue to grow until it reaches a fully lit disk, or full moon.

After the full moon, the moon will enter the waning gibbous phase, in which the size of the lit disk will slowly begin to decrease. The side of the moon that was originally lit in the first crescent phase will be dark. About three weeks after the new moon, or one week after the full moon, the moon will be in the third quarter phase and will appear half lit. As the moon gets closer to its starting position between the sun and Earth, it will appear as a thin crescent again. As the moon moves back between Earth and the sun, the new moon begins the cycle over.

Phases of the Moon

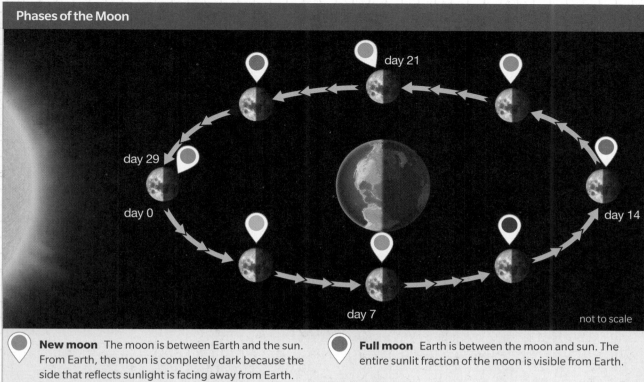

day 21

day 29

day 0

day 14

day 7

not to scale

New moon The moon is between Earth and the sun. From Earth, the moon is completely dark because the side that reflects sunlight is facing away from Earth.

Waxing crescent A thin sliver of the moon becomes visible and continues to grow. *Waxing* means the part of the moon that appears lit is getting larger.

First quarter From Earth's Northern Hemisphere, the right half of the moon appears half lit.

Waxing gibbous The sunlit fraction of the moon that is visible from Earth continues to increase.

Full moon Earth is between the moon and sun. The entire sunlit fraction of the moon is visible from Earth.

Waning gibbous The sunlit fraction of the moon that is visible from Earth decreases. *Waning* means that the part of the moon that appears lit is getting smaller.

Third quarter From Earth's Northern Hemisphere, the left half of the moon appears lit.

Waning crescent The visible fraction of the sunlit moon continues to decrease.

Phases of the Moon Observed from Earth

6. Write the missing labels for the phases of the moon. Some labels may be used more than once.

- full moon
- new moon
- waning
- waxing

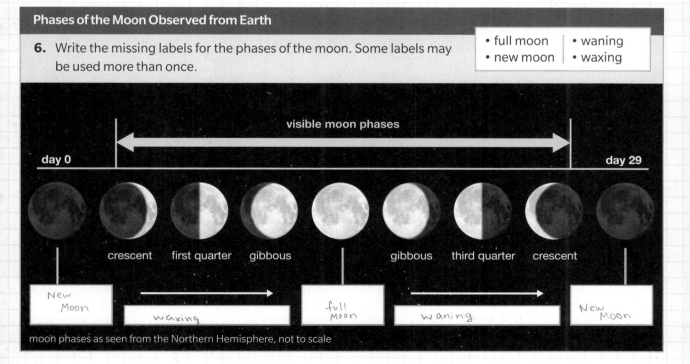

visible moon phases

day 0

day 29

crescent   first quarter   gibbous   gibbous   third quarter   crescent

New Moon

waxing

full Moon

waning

New Moon

moon phases as seen from the Northern Hemisphere, not to scale

7. During a (full) new moon, Earth is between the sun and the moon. So, all of the sunlit part of the moon is visible from Earth. The moon's sunlit half, which is its (day) night side, faces Earth's day /(night) side. That is always the case for a full moon.

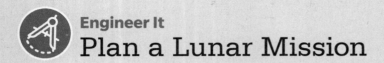

Engineer It
Plan a Lunar Mission

You are planning an expedition to the moon in which astronauts will stay on the moon for four days to collect samples and data. You want them to land on the part of the moon that is lit by the sun so they can see their surroundings. While on the moon, astronauts need to use radio waves to communicate with Earth, and for the radio waves to reach Earth, your transmitter must be pointed toward Earth. Because the same side of the moon always faces toward Earth, and phases of the moon are predictable, you can choose the best location and time for the trip years before launch.

8. During which phase(s) and where on the moon would you want to land? Explain your reasoning and draw a diagram to illustrate and justify your choice.

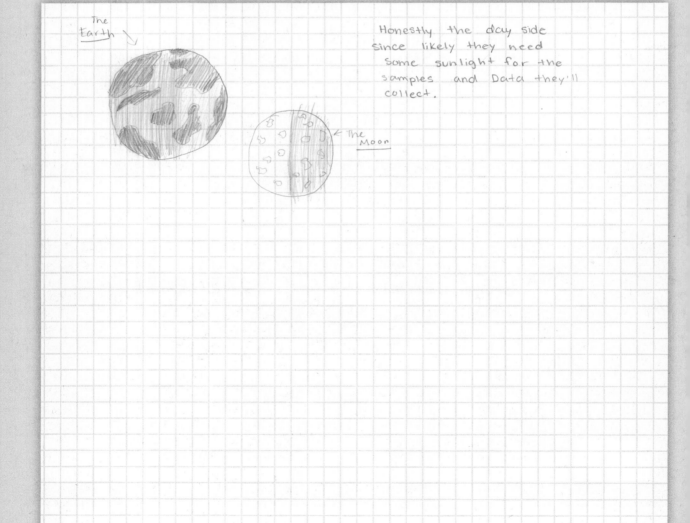

Exploring Eclipses

You can make shadow puppets, such as the one in the photo, using a flashlight and your hands. You can also use paper cutouts to make shadows. Moving the cutout or your hands makes the shadow move.

9. In the photo, why does the shadow of a dog's head form on the wall behind the hand?

because the shape of the hand, and because the light is infront of the hand, so the front of the hand blocks the light and makes the dogs head from behind technically.

You can make a shadow puppet of a dog's head using your hand and a light source.

Eclipses

Earth and the moon block the light from the sun and form shadows behind them in space. Sometimes, the moon moves into Earth's shadow or Earth moves into the moon's shadow. Both events are called an *eclipse*. An **eclipse** happens when the shadow of one celestial body falls on another. Both solar and lunar eclipses, shown in the photos below, occur in the Earth-sun-moon system. During a *solar eclipse*, the shadow of the moon falls on Earth. During a *lunar eclipse*, the shadow of Earth falls on the moon. Eclipses can be explained by laws that describe the movements of Earth, the moon, and the sun. These laws can be used to make accurate predictions about when future eclipses will occur.

A solar eclipse: from Earth, we can see the moon come between Earth and the sun.

A lunar eclipse: from Earth, we can see the shadow of Earth falling on the moon.

10. Use what you see in the photos to explain how shadows are formed during a solar eclipse and a lunar eclipse. Include the sun, moon, and Earth in your explanations.

A solar Eclipse is formed on how the moon is blocking the sun and the moon moving it's way infront of the sun.

A lunar Eclipse is also formed based on the earth going infront of the moon and reflecting its shadow.

Model Solar and Lunar Eclipses

You will model the Earth-sun-moon system to develop an explanation for solar and lunar eclipses.

MATERIALS
- lamp with removable shade
- moon model from previous activity

Procedure and Analysis

STEP 1 Continue working with your partner. The lamp (sun) should be placed at eye level. One partner plays Earth first, completing STEPS 2–4. Then switch roles and have the other partner play Earth. Each partner records his or her own observations.

STEP 2 **Act** The partner playing Earth faces the sun. Earth holds the moon at arm's length so the moon and the sun are in a straight line with the moon directly between Earth and the sun.

STEP 3 **Act** Earth closes one eye and slowly turns toward the left. As you turn, stop when your view of the moon is completely covered in shadow. Record your observations of the alignment of the Earth-sun-moon system and what you see from Earth.

STEP 4 **Act** Earth continues to turn left. Stop when you notice that the moon blocks your view of the sun. Record your observations.

STEP 5 A solar eclipse happens when the moon casts a shadow on ~~Earth~~/ the sun. I modeled a solar eclipse when my head /~~the ball~~ blocked the light of the sun and cast a shadow on ~~my head~~/ the ball. A lunar eclipse happens when Earth casts a shadow on the ~~moon~~/ sun . I modeled a lunar eclipse when ~~my head~~/ the ball blocked the light of the sun and cast a shadow on my head /~~the ball~~.

STEP 6 If time allows, repeat STEPS 2–4, this time holding the moon slightly above your head. What differences do you see?

In the Shadow of the Moon

Solar eclipses occur when the moon moves between the sun and Earth and the moon blocks some sunlight from reaching Earth. The shadow that extends behind the moon has two cone-shaped parts, modeled in the photo. The darker, inner shadow is the *umbra*, and the lighter, larger shadow is the *penumbra*.

At least two solar eclipses occur every year, but, as the diagram shows, the moon's shadow does not completely cover Earth. Only a small area is covered by the shadow, which is why not everyone on Earth can see every solar eclipse. To see a solar eclipse, you must be in the moon's shadow. The dark umbra covers an even smaller area than the larger penumbra. As an area of Earth passes through the umbra, the sun appears to be totally eclipsed. The sun briefly "goes dark," for a few minutes at most, but it may seem like nighttime until that area of Earth moves out of the moon's shadow.

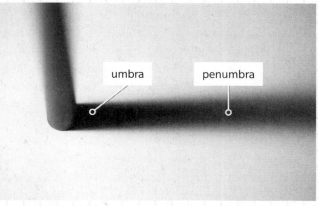

The umbra is the darkest part of a shadow. The penumbra is the lighter part of a shadow.

A Solar Eclipse

The moon casts a shadow on an area of Earth during a solar eclipse. The umbra is the smaller, darker part of the shadow. The umbra is surrounded by the lighter penumbra.

During a solar eclipse, the shadow of the moon falls on Earth.

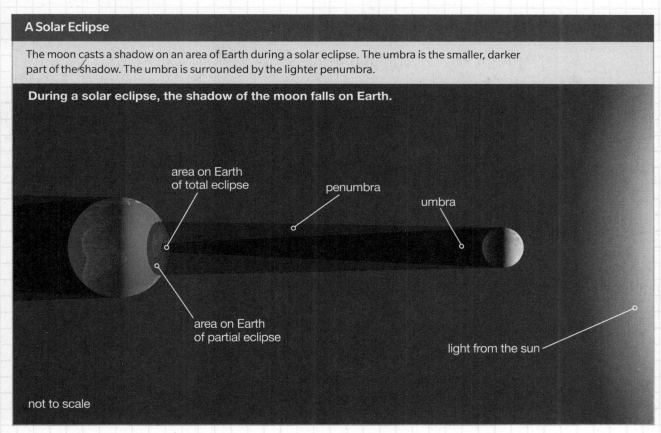

area on Earth of total eclipse

penumbra

umbra

area on Earth of partial eclipse

light from the sun

not to scale

11. Why can solar eclipses be observed only on certain parts of Earth? Circle all that apply.

(A.) The moon is smaller than Earth.

(B.) Half of Earth is facing away from the sun and cannot see the moon's shadow.

(C.) Sunlight in areas outside of the umbra and penumbra is not blocked by the moon.

D. Solar eclipses occur only once every few years.

Types of Solar Eclipses

There are three types of solar eclipses. A *total solar eclipse* occurs when the sun appears to be completely blocked except for a bright halo of light. A total eclipse happens only when the moon, sun, and Earth are in a straight line, with the moon directly between the sun and Earth. When a total eclipse of the sun occurs, only people who observe from the umbra will see the total eclipse. People who observe from the penumbra will see a *partial solar eclipse*, because from their point of view, the moon only blocks part of the sun's light. An *annular solar eclipse* also occurs when all three bodies are in a straight line. However, the moon is farther away from Earth, because its orbit is elliptical and the umbra shadow does not quite reach Earth. So, the moon does not completely cover the sun. The sun's outer edges can be seen as a ring of light around the darker center during an annular eclipse.

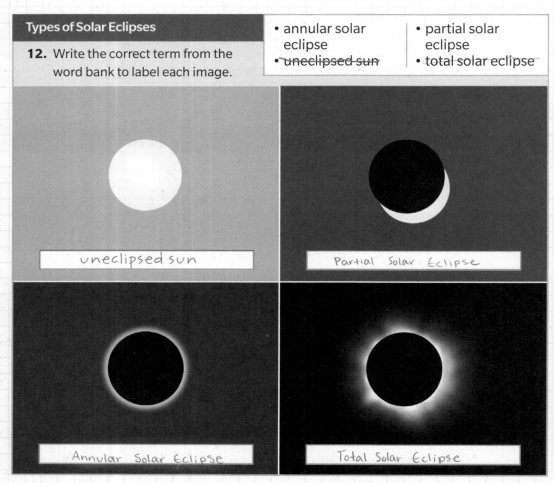

Types of Solar Eclipses

12. Write the correct term from the word bank to label each image.

- annular solar eclipse
- ~~uneclipsed sun~~
- partial solar eclipse
- ~~total solar eclipse~~

uneclipsed sun

Partial Solar Eclipse

Annular Solar Eclipse

Total Solar Eclipse

In the Shadow of Earth

During a lunar eclipse, Earth is between the moon and the sun. Because Earth is so much bigger than the moon, Earth's shadow covers the entire moon when they are aligned. As the diagram of a lunar eclipse shows, Earth's shadow also has an umbra and penumbra. Remember, the moon reflects sunlight, so when Earth blocks sunlight from reaching the moon, the moon appears dark. Instead of being totally dark, the moon often appears to be a rusty red color because Earth's atmosphere bends some sunlight into the shadow. Everyone who is on the night side of Earth can see a lunar eclipse.

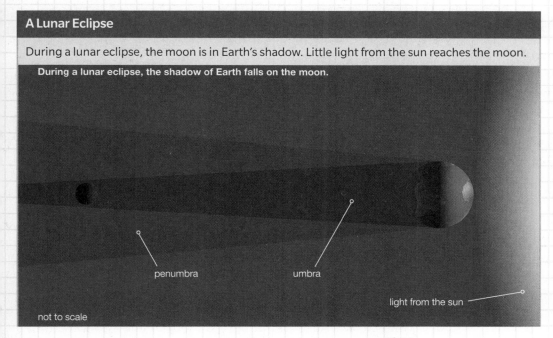

A Lunar Eclipse

During a lunar eclipse, the moon is in Earth's shadow. Little light from the sun reaches the moon.

During a lunar eclipse, the shadow of Earth falls on the moon.

penumbra

umbra

light from the sun

not to scale

13. Analyze the image. The moon will always be new when a ~~lunar~~/ solar eclipse happens. During a lunar eclipse, the moon will be ~~new~~ / (full.)

Types of Lunar Eclipses

During a lunar eclipse, the moon may appear totally or partially dark depending on where it passes through Earth's shadow. The composite photo shows multiple images of the moon taken over about three and a half hours during a *total lunar eclipse*, which occurs when the whole moon passes through Earth's umbra. During a *partial lunar eclipse*, only part of the moon passes through the umbra. The part of the moon that passes through Earth's shadow becomes dark. There is one more type of lunar eclipse— the *penumbral lunar eclipse*, which occurs when the moon passes through the penumbra. While total and partial eclipses are easy to observe, penumbral eclipses are difficult to see. The penumbra is a lighter shadow, and sunlight still reaches the moon when it passes through this part of Earth's shadow.

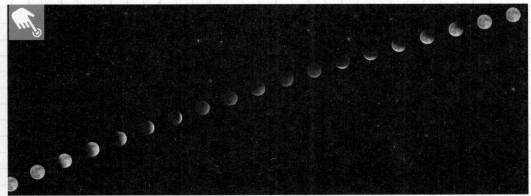

As the moon passes through Earth's umbra, more of it becomes dark. It turns a reddish-orange instead of being totally dark because Earth's atmosphere bends sunlight into the shadow.

14. Write total, partial, or penumbral to complete the paragraph.

If the entire moon passes through the part of Earth's shadow called the umbra, a ___total___ lunar eclipse will occur. If the moon passes only through the penumbra, a ___partial___ lunar eclipse will occur.

Timing of Eclipses

Every time the moon orbits Earth, the moon comes between the sun and Earth, and Earth comes between the moon and the sun. Yet, eclipses do not occur every time the moon orbits Earth. To understand why, you need to think of space in three dimensions. Think of the sun and Earth's nearly circular orbit around the sun in a flat plane. The moon's orbit is not in the same plane, although it may appear that way in many two-dimensional diagrams. The moon's orbit is actually tilted about 5° to the Earth-sun plane as the diagram shows. Because of this tilted orbit, the moon is usually above or below Earth during its orbit instead of being aligned in the same plane as Earth and the sun. So, the moon and Earth usually do not pass through each other's shadows.

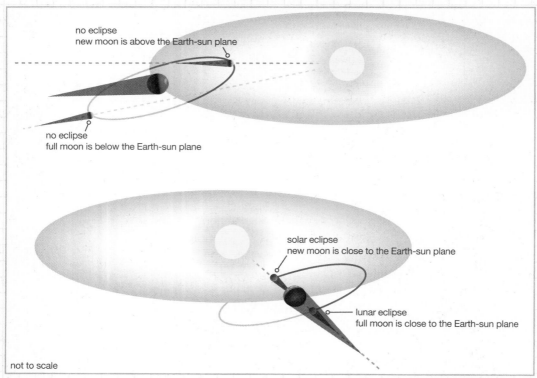

no eclipse
new moon is above the Earth-sun plane

no eclipse
full moon is below the Earth-sun plane

solar eclipse
new moon is close to the Earth-sun plane

lunar eclipse
full moon is close to the Earth-sun plane

not to scale

The moon spends half its time above the Earth-sun plane and half its time below this plane. The moon only passes through Earth's shadow when it is in the same plane as Earth and the sun. Similarly, the moon must be in the same plane as Earth and the sun in order to cause a solar eclipse.

 EVIDENCE NOTEBOOK

15. An eclipse season is a period of about a month when a lunar or solar eclipse is likely to occur. Two eclipse seasons occur each year. What is the location of the moon in its orbit during an eclipse season? Record your evidence.

Eclipses and the Moon's Orbit

16. Because its orbit is tilted with respect to the Earth-sun plane, the moon spends most of its time either above or below the plane. How many times would the moon cross through the Earth-sun plane each time it orbits Earth? Explain.

> It will cross two times I think since it is close or something.

Name: _____   Date: _____

Check out the path below or go online to choose one of the other paths shown.

People in Science

- **Using Shadows and Shades**
- **Hands-On Labs** 🖐
- **Propose Your Own Path**

Go online to choose one of these other paths.

Leon Foucault, Physicist

By 1850, it was widely accepted that Earth rotates on its axis. But a French physicist, Leon Foucault (FOO•koh), was the first person to design an instrument that demonstrated Earth's rotation.

Foucault realized that he could show Earth's rotation using a carefully designed pendulum. A pendulum is an object that hangs from a fixed point and can swing freely. Once the object is released, it swings back and forth. Foucault used a 67-meter-long wire and designed the pendulum so that it could swing in any direction. He hung his first pendulum from the Paris Observatory in 1851. The swinging pendulum appeared to gradually change its direction of swing over the course of a day. This change in direction was evidence that Earth is rotating.

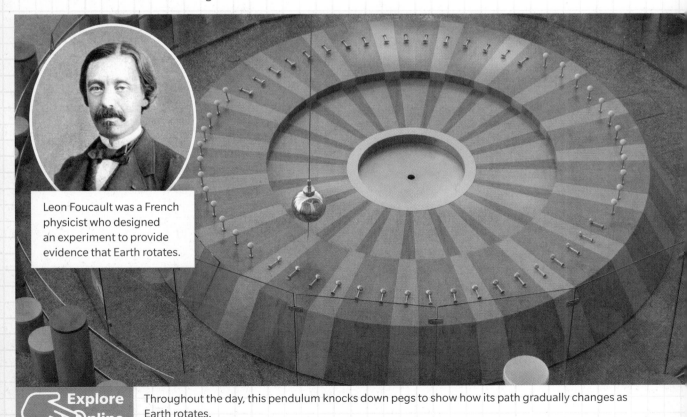

Leon Foucault was a French physicist who designed an experiment to provide evidence that Earth rotates.

Explore Online Throughout the day, this pendulum knocks down pegs to show how its path gradually changes as Earth rotates.

Continue Your Exploration

1. Why was it necessary for Foucault's pendulum to swing freely in all directions in order for it to demonstrate that Earth rotates?

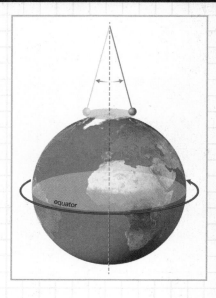

2. How does the explanation for the way Foucault's pendulum appears to move relate to the explanation for why the sun, moon, and stars appear to circle Earth every 24 hours?

3. **Do the Math** Locations other than the North and South Poles move in a circle around Earth's axis as Earth rotates. Because of this motion, Foucault's pendulum does not complete a full circle in one day. For example, it only turns 270° in one day in Paris. How many hours would it take to complete one full circle (360°) in Paris?

   A. 11

   B. 18

   C. 27

   D. 32

4. **Collaborate** With a group, prepare a multimedia presentation to explain how Foucault's pendulum works. Consider including videos or demonstrations.

Can You Explain It?

Name: _____   Date: _____

Why can we see the moon at night and also during the day?

EVIDENCE NOTEBOOK

Refer to the notes in your Evidence Notebook to help you construct an explanation for why the moon is visible at night and during the day.

1. State your claim. Make sure your claim fully explains why you can see the moon during the daytime and the nighttime.

2. Summarize the evidence you have gathered to support your claim and explain your reasoning.

Checkpoints

Answer the following questions to check your understanding of the lesson. Use the images to answer Questions 3–4.

3. Why does the annular eclipse in the top image appear to be different from the total eclipse in the bottom image?

    A. In the top image the moon is farther away from Earth.

    B. In the top image the moon is closer to Earth.

    C. In the bottom image the moon does not completely cover the sun.

    D. In the bottom image the moon is not directly between Earth and the sun.

4. In August 2017, a total solar eclipse was visible from the United States. A total solar eclipse happens when Earth / the moon moves directly in front of the moon / sun. A total solar eclipse can be seen from everywhere / a narrow path on Earth. The bottom image was seen from the umbra / penumbra during the eclipse.

Use the photos to answer Questions 5–6.

5. Why is the moon's appearance different in the two photos? Circle all that apply.

    A. The sun was at a different point in its orbit when each photo was taken.

    B. The top photo shows an eclipse during a full moon, and the bottom photo shows the moon during a different phase.

    C. The moon in the bottom photo occurs about once every month.

    D. The moon in the top photo occurs only when the moon is in Earth's shadow.

6. The moon in the bottom photo is in its third quarter. How will the moon look after it moves another quarter of the way through its orbit?

    A. The same as it looks in the photo.

    B. The full circle of the moon will be lit.

    C. The moon will be completely dark.

    D. The quarter moon will be lit on the other side.

Interactive Review

Complete this section to review the main concepts of the lesson.

The moon goes through a pattern of phases over a period of 29.5 days. Phases change as the fraction of the sunlit area of the moon that is visible from Earth changes.

A. About how much time passed between these two images of the moon? Use evidence and reasoning to support your claim.

Eclipses happen when Earth is in the shadow of the moon or the moon is in the shadow of Earth.

B. Explain the difference between a partial solar eclipse and a total solar eclipse.

The Solar System Formed from Colliding Matter

Scientists use technology to understand the events that formed the solar system billions of years ago.

Explore First

Modeling the Formation of Planets Place small pieces of clay on a table top. Roll another larger lump of clay over the smaller pieces until they all stick to the larger lump of clay. What has happened to the size of the larger piece of clay? How do you explain any difference you see?

Go online to view the digital version of
the Hands-On Lab for this lesson and to
download additional lab resources.

CAN YOU EXPLAIN IT?

Why do all the planets in the solar system orbit the sun in the same direction?

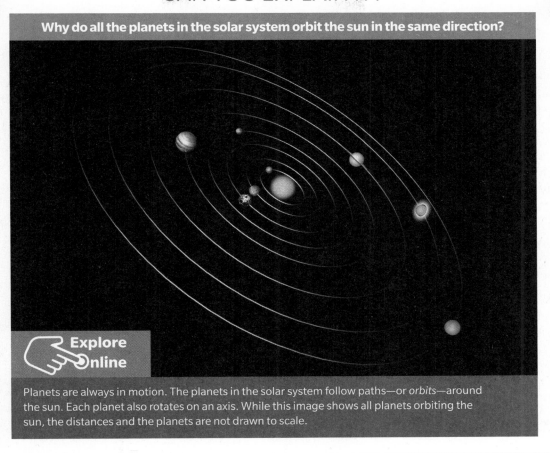

Explore Online

Planets are always in motion. The planets in the solar system follow paths—or *orbits*—around
the sun. Each planet also rotates on an axis. While this image shows all planets orbiting the
sun, the distances and the planets are not drawn to scale.

1. Why do planets move around the sun?

2. How could the movement of the planets in the solar system be used as evidence for
how the solar system formed?

 EVIDENCE NOTEBOOK As you explore the lesson, gather evidence to explain
why all planets in the solar system orbit the sun in the same direction.

Exploring Gravity in the Solar System

Gravity in the Solar System

An object's mass determines the strength of its gravitational field. The gravitational fields of stars are very strong and extend far into space. As a result, a star influences the motion of other objects around it. Gravity is always attractive, and the strength of a gravitational field decreases as the distance between objects increases. The law of universal gravitation is written mathematically as:

$$F = \frac{G(m_1 \times m_2)}{d^2}$$

In this equation, F is the force of gravity, G is the gravitational constant, m stands for masses of the objects, and d stands for distance between them. The force of gravity between two objects is proportional to the masses of the two objects and inversely proportional to the square of the distance between them.

Planet	Mass (kg)	Mass relative to Earth	Distance from sun (millions of km)	Distance from sun relative to Earth
Sun	1.9×10^{30}	333,000	–	–
Mercury	3.3×10^{23}	0.06	58	0.39
Venus	4.9×10^{24}	0.8	108	0.72
Earth	5.9×10^{24}	1	150	1
Mars	6.4×10^{23}	0.1	228	1.5
Jupiter	11.9×10^{27}	318	778	5.2
Saturn	5.7×10^{26}	95	1,433	9.6
Uranus	8.7×10^{25}	15	2,872	19
Neptune	1.0×10^{26}	17	4,495	30

3. Analyze the data in the table. How does the gravitational force between the sun and Mercury compare to the gravitational force between the sun and Jupiter?

Gravity and the Sun

The sun is an average-sized star, yet it is large enough to contain 1.3 million Earth-sized planets! This large volume is filled with hot, churning hydrogen and helium, as well as trace amounts of many other elements such as oxygen, carbon, and iron. The sun is the largest single object in the solar system. Although it has one-fourth the density of Earth, it is so large that it has 333,000 times more mass. The sun lies at the center of the solar system, producing a massive gravitational field in all directions. All of the objects in the solar system are held in orbit by the gravitational pull between themselves and the sun.

4. Look at the photos. What pattern(s) do you see between the mass of an object and its shape? Why do you think this is?

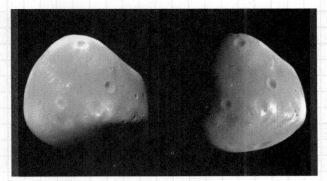

The moon Deimos has a mass of 1.4762×10^{15} kg.

Gravity and the Shape of Objects in the Solar System

Not all of the objects in the solar system have the same shape. Although the planets are all spherical, many of the smaller objects are not. The shapes of the objects in the solar system are related to their mass. The more massive an object is, the more spherical shape it has. The shapes of objects in the solar system can provide evidence for how the solar system formed.

The moon Phobos has a mass of 10.6×10^{15} kg.

When two objects in the solar system interact, each object exerts a gravitational force on the other object. As long as they are not touching, the objects have potential energy. Some of this potential energy will be transformed into thermal energy if one object collides with another object. This thermal energy can cause an object to melt or partially melt.

Once an object in space melts or partially melts, the matter becomes more fluid and can change shape. The matter at the center attracts the matter at the outer surface of the body. The matter flows so that it can come as close to the center of the body as possible. The shape that forms when every particle is as close to the center as every other particle is a sphere. Therefore, gravity pulls the material in the object into a more spherical shape. The more massive an object is, the stronger its gravitational field will be, and the more spherical it will become.

The asteroid Vesta has a mass 2.59076×10^{20} kg.

5. Look at the photos. Which of these objects probably had the greatest amount of thermal energy during its formation?

The dwarf planet Ceres has a mass of 9.39×10^{20} kg.

Gravity and the Composition of Planets

The planets are the next largest objects in the solar system, after the sun. The planets can be divided into two groups that relate to their positions and compositions. The inner, or terrestrial, planets—Mercury, Venus, Earth, and Mars—are small, rocky, and dense. These planets have solid surfaces. Below the surfaces of the terrestrial planets are layers of solid and molten rock and metals. At the center of each terrestrial planet is a dense solid core composed of iron and nickel.

The outer planets—gas giants Jupiter and Saturn and ice giants Uranus and Neptune—are larger, icy or gaseous, and less dense. The giant planets do not have solid, rocky surfaces. The outer layers of the these planets are composed of liquids, ices, and gases. These planets do have dense, solid cores, but their cores are composed of rock and ice instead of metal.

The planets are very different from one another but also have some similarities. The layers of each planet increase in density toward the center of the planet. On Earth, the solid iron and nickel core is four times as dense as the rocky surface we are familiar with. The pattern we see in the layers of all the planets is evidence that the planets were all molten at one time in their past.

This layered density pattern found in each planet is similar to the density pattern seen in the solar system as a whole. The denser material is generally found in the planets closer to the sun. The less dense material is generally found in the planets farther from the sun. However, although the inner planets are denser, most of the mass that makes up the planets in the solar system is in the giant outer planets.

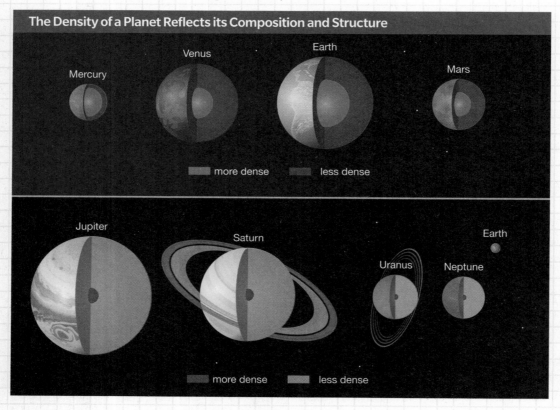

The Density of a Planet Reflects its Composition and Structure

Mercury   Venus   Earth   Mars

more dense   less dense

Jupiter   Saturn   Uranus   Neptune   Earth

more dense   less dense

6. When these terrestrial planets formed, more dense / less dense materials stayed near the surface. Within the solar system, a similar / different pattern occurred. The inner terrestrial planets are more dense / less dense, and the outer gas giant planets are more dense / less dense.

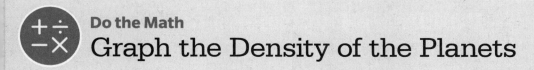

Do the Math

Graph the Density of the Planets

7. In the space provided, make a bar graph to compare the densities of the planets.

8. The density of liquid water is 1.0 g/cm³, the density of rock is 2.7 g/cm³, the density of iron is 7.9 g/cm³. Add this information to your graph.

9. Are the densities of the planets roughly proportional to their diameters? Use evidence to support your claim.

_____

_____

_____

_____

_____

Planet	Density (g/cm³)	Diameter (km)
Mercury	5.4	4,879
Venus	5.2	12,104
Earth	5.5	12,756
Mars	3.9	6,792
Jupiter	1.3	142,984
Saturn	0.68	120,536
Uranus	1.3	51,118
Neptune	1.6	49,528

10. How does the graph you made help you visualize the different types of materials that make up the planets?

_____

_____

_____

_____

_____

Building a Hypothesis of How the Solar System Formed

Ancient astronomers used observations of the sky to develop the first models of Earth in space. Similarly, modern astronomers use observations and evidence to model the formation of the solar system.

11. **Discuss** With a partner, make a list of questions about how the solar system formed. What mechanisms or processes would you want to explore in order to develop a hypothesis about the formation of the solar system?

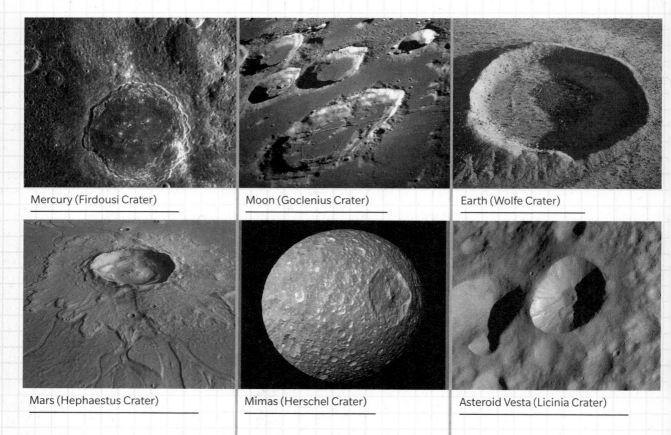

Mercury (Firdousi Crater)

Moon (Goclenius Crater)

Earth (Wolfe Crater)

Mars (Hephaestus Crater)

Mimas (Herschel Crater)

Asteroid Vesta (Licinia Crater)

Collisions as Evidence of the Early Solar System

Impact craters are evidence that collisions have occurred between objects in space. Impact craters on the moons, planets, and asteroids in the solar system vary in size, shape, and age. The sizes and shapes of impact craters differ based on the mass and speed of the bodies that collide. The angle at which an object strikes a surface can affect the shape of a crater. Although the moon and other objects in the solar system show a record of many impacts, there are very few impact craters remaining on Earth's surface. Most impact craters on Earth have been weathered and eroded. However, all impact craters are evidence that matter collided as bodies of different sizes, compositions, and speeds moved through their orbits around the sun.

12. Why are impact craters evident on terrestrial objects but not on outer planets?

Kant's Nebular Hypothesis

In the mid-1700s, Immanuel Kant developed the *nebular hypothesis* of the origin of the solar system. He proposed that matter in the solar system began as separate particles. This cloud of dust and gas from which the planets and sun formed is now known as the **solar nebula.** Kant suggested that attractive forces between the particles caused them to collide and join together, forming larger clumps. As the clumps increased in size, their gravitational fields increased in strength, and they attracted even more particles. The sun formed at the middle of the cloud of particles, where the attractive forces were the greatest. The remaining particles joined with the larger masses until the planets were formed. The large mass of the sun and the gravitational attraction between the planets and the sun kept the planets in orbit around the sun. Kant's hypothesis explained the process in which matter in the solar system went from an unordered state to a structured system with distinct bodies orbiting the sun in a predictable pattern. While Kant's nebular hypothesis described the formation of the solar system, it did not explain several characteristics of the solar system. For example, his hypothesis did not explain why all planets orbit the sun in the same direction or why the planets orbit the sun in roughly the same plane.

13. **Draw** Storyboards can be drawn to illustrate the steps in a sequence. Use the space below to draw a storyboard that explains Kant's nebular hypothesis. Write a caption to support the art you make.

14. **Discuss** According to current criteria, a space object is classified as a planet if it (1) orbits a star, (2) is large enough to have a nearly spherical shape, and (3) has "cleared the neighborhood" around its orbit. The orbital path of a planet is cleared when smaller masses are attracted to and combine with the planet or are pushed to a different orbit. How are Kant's hypothesis and impact craters related to the classification of an object as a planet?

Laplace Refines Kant's Model

About 40 years after Kant's work became known, Pierre-Simon Laplace used mathematics to refine the nebular hypothesis. Laplace suggested that after forming in a collapsing cloud of dust and gas, the sun cooled and became more compact in size. This made the sun rotate more quickly. In the same way, ice skaters spin faster when they draw their arms into their bodies. For both the sun and the ice skater, the rotational speed increases as mass moves toward the center of the object.

Dust and gas were pushed outward while the sun's gravity pulled matter inward toward the sun. The constant push and pull flattened the cloud into a large disk. Scientists refer to these disks of matter as **protoplanetary disks.** The prefix "proto-" means "earliest" in Greek. The disk rotated around the sun, and material in the disk formed concentric rings of debris. Matter collided and fused in the rings, eventually forming the planets.

The ice skater begins to spin with her arms extended and her leg out. As she contracts her mass by bringing her arms and leg inward, she spins faster.

15. Which of the following are explained by Laplace's hypothesis of how the solar system formed? Circle all that apply.

   A. All planets orbit the sun in the same direction.

   B. Planets are dense collections of rock and gas with strong gravitational fields.

   C. Planets spin on their axes at the same rates.

   D. The orbital paths of the planets are in about the same plane.

Laplace's Hypothesis of Solar System Formation

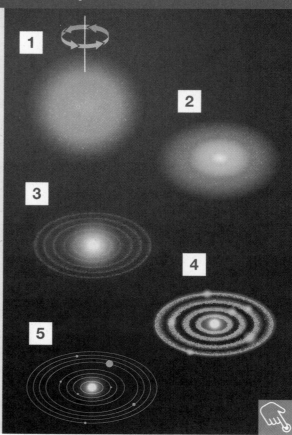

(1) A slowly rotating cloud of dust and gas **(2)** begins to condense, causing it to spin faster. The sun forms at the center of the cloud. **(3)** The cloud flattens into the shape of a disk, and rings of debris form in a plane. **(4)** Materials in each ring collide and clump together due to gravity, **(5)** forming planets and the solar system.

Model Nebular Disk Formation

You will construct a model of nebular disk formation that is consistent with Laplace's hypothesis of solar system formation. Identify similarities and differences between the model and the formation of star systems in space.

MATERIALS
- dowel rod, long and thin
- drawing compass
- glue
- hole punch
- pencil
- ruler
- scissors
- tag board

Procedure

STEP 1 Use the compass to draw three separate circles on the tag board. Make one circle 3 cm in diameter. Make two circles 4 cm in diameter. Cut out the circles carefully using scissors.

STEP 2 Punch a hole in the center of each circle. For the 3 cm circle and one 4 cm circle, the hole should be just big enough to fit snugly over the dowel rod. For the other 4 cm circle, the hole should be slightly larger so that the circle can slide freely over the dowel.

STEP 3 Cut eight strips of tag board that are 1.25 cm wide by 30 cm long.

STEP 4 Glue one end of each strip to the 4 cm circle that fits snugly over the dowel. Pinch and hold in place for 30–60 seconds. Space the strips evenly around the circle. Slide this circle over the dowel and glue it in place about 3 cm from the top of the dowel. Next, slide the 3 cm circle over the bottom of the dowel and glue it in position about 12 cm below the first circle. Give the glue time to dry.

STEP 5 Slide the remaining 4 cm circle over the bottom of the dowel. Glue the loose end of each strip to this circle, making sure the strips are evenly spaced. When the dowel is held upright, this circle should hang below the others and slide freely.

STEP 6 Hold the dowel upright between the palms of your hands. Predict what will happen when you spin the dowel by moving it between your palms. Record your prediction.

Cut along the lines to form the strips for the sphere.

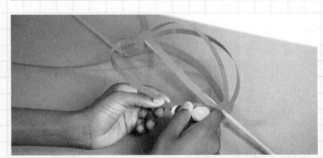

Glue the strips to the top and bottom tag board circles. Measure distances carefully.

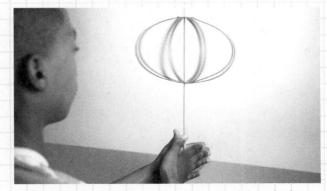

Roll the dowel between both palms to control the spinning. Spin the dowel as fast as you can.

Analysis

STEP 7 Describe what you saw when you spun the dowel.

STEP 8 How does this model relate to the formation of the solar system? Include similarities and differences between the model and the formation of the solar system as described by Pierre-Simon Laplace.

EVIDENCE NOTEBOOK

16. Imagine the figure skater as the sun and imagine that she was holding a ball in her outstretched hand. How would the motions relate to the orbital direction of the planets? Record your evidence.

Engineer It
Evaluate the Effect of Gravity

The planets are natural satellites that orbit the sun. The moon is a natural satellite that orbits Earth. Many artificial satellites also orbit Earth. Gravity keeps satellites in orbit around Earth, moons in orbit around planets, and planets and other objects in orbit around the sun. The organization of matter we observe on Earth, in the solar system, and in the universe would not exist without gravity.

17. What would happen to the satellites in orbit around Earth without gravity?

_____
_____
_____
_____

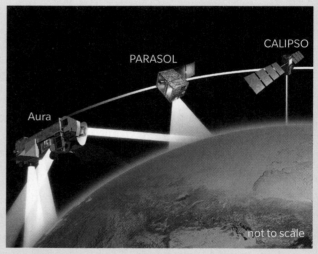
These satellites orbit Earth on a specific path and collect data related to climate change.

18. Brainstorm ways gravity could affect a space probe launched from Earth that is intended to travel to and orbit Jupiter. Why is it necessary to consider gravity when launching a spacecraft or putting a spacecraft into orbit?

_____
_____
_____

Gathering Data on the Formation of Star Systems

In order to understand what is happening in a protoplanetary disk, astronomers develop models based on observations. Gravity plays an important role in the formation of a star system, and the models are based on this. This drawing is based on a model of star system formation. According to this model, the central star is surrounded by a large rotating disk of gas and dust. The central star is pulling in material from the outer disk. The arms of dust and gas form a bridge across the disk. Other material in the disk is forming clumps that will eventually form planets. By developing models like this one, astronomers are able to infer how the star system probably formed.

19. If this star system formed similarly to the solar system, would you expect the star to be stationary or spinning? What about the planets? Use evidence and reasoning to support your claim.

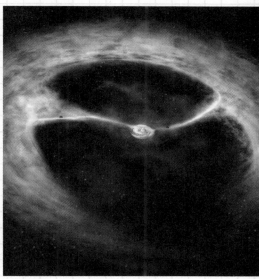

This artist's drawing shows a new star system forming in the disk surrounding a young star.

Evidence of How Star Systems Form

Observations of processes and relationships within our solar system provide evidence for how other star systems may form. Because physical laws are likely the same in other star systems, the way the star and planets in a distant system move can be calculated from how our sun and planets move. These illustrations show the changing positions of sunspots. Sunspots are dark patches that appear temporarily on the sun's surface.

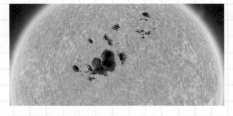

20. What do you know about the sun's motion based on the nebular hypothesis model?

    A. The sun and planets both move on the same orbital paths.

    B. The sun rotates in the same direction as planets move around the sun.

    C. The faster the sun moves, the faster the planets travel in their orbits.

    D. There is no relationship between planetary movement and the sun.

21. These images show the position of spots on the surface of the sun over a 1-week period. Based on these images, what conclusion could you draw?

Direct Observation of Star System Formation

The primary source of evidence supporting the hypothesis that the solar system formed from the solar nebula is the observation of similar processes occurring elsewhere in space. By using telescope technology, scientists can observe the formation of stars inside clouds of gas and dust. They can capture images of young stars surrounded by disks of debris. Some telescopes collect electromagnetic radiation, such as x-rays, radio waves, gamma rays, and infrared light, to produce images of developing stars and their surroundings.

In recent years, astronomers and engineers have worked together to find evidence for the nebular hypothesis by looking for places elsewhere in the universe where new star systems are forming. Observing these events is expensive. To share the costs and equipment, international science groups worked together to build the Atacama Large Millimeter Array (ALMA). ALMA is a series of 66 radio telescope dishes. The dishes work together to detect clouds of gas and dust like the solar nebula and other signs of star system formation such as protoplanetary disks. One of these disks that has been detected about 450 light-years away is shown in the illustration.

Stars, and perhaps star systems, are forming within the Horsehead Nebula.

This illustration shows a protoplanetary disk. Objects like this can be observed using the Atacama Large Millimeter Array.

22. What stages of the nebular hypothesis do the images above represent? How do you know? Record your claim, evidence, and reasoning.

Computer Modeling and Simulations

Space telescopes do not provide images like those taken with a typical camera. The telescopes collect data, which are translated into an image by a computer. Sometimes artists or a computer program add color to these images. This helps people visualize the object or event being studied. Computers can also model phenomena in space. Models allow scientists to use physical and chemical laws to simulate events that are occurring in space. For example, scientists have modeled the formation of the solar system, the interaction between black holes, and even the collision of a planet and an asteroid.

Explore Online

This computer model shows dense areas of gas as bright areas in the cloud around a forming star.

23. Astronomers use ~~models / experiments~~ to represent space events that they cannot see directly or that occur over a long time span. Using ~~computer models / current data / both models and data~~ makes it possible to simulate the formation of the solar system. Computers allow scientists to perform investigations in ~~accelerated / real~~ time frames.

24. Language SmArts | Write an Adventure Story You may have heard or read fictional stories about people exploring space. Write a story about space travelers exploring a distant solar system that is just beginning to form. You may include an illustration that clarifies important details in your story. Present your story and illustration to a classmate.

Additional Support for the Nebular Hypothesis

Several lines of evidence support the nebular hypothesis. These include the growing number of observations of forming star systems and the observation that the sun rotates in the same direction and plane in which the planets revolve. Other evidence supporting the nebular hypothesis includes computer models that also explain why the inner planets of the solar system are composed of rock and metal, while the outer planets are icy and gaseous. The evidence in support of the nebular hypothesis is so strong that the work of planetary astronomers today is to explain the details of how the solar system went from a cloud of gas and dust to the planets and other bodies seen today.

The Life Cycle of Stars

By observing many stars at different stages, scientists have confirmed that stars follow a predictable life cycle. Stars form in nebulae that are dense and cold. When a nebula collapses, the temperature and pressure increase over time as particles in the nebula collide and clump together. A protostar forms at the center of the nebula, surrounded by gaseous and rocky debris.

Once the protostar becomes very hot (10 million °C), it becomes a young star. The fusion of hydrogen into helium in the star generates large amounts of thermal energy and light. As the young star warms, the core contracts and begins to spin. At this stage, the debris held by the star's gravity flattens into a protoplanetary disk. The early stages of planet formation occur in the bulging disk of matter surrounding the young star. As the smaller particles are pulled toward the larger clumps, their kinetic energy increases and their potential energy decreases. When the particles collide, the kinetic energy transforms into thermal energy. Gravity pulls the partially molten material into a spherical shape.

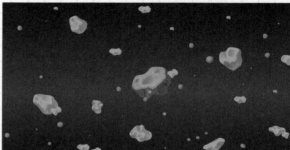

Particles collect into clumps. The process increases in speed as the clumps get larger and the gravitational attraction increases.

Scientists have observed different stages of this process in many places throughout space. The results of computer modeling also support this part of the nebular hypothesis.

25. If you sprinkle iron filings in a ring and then drag a magnet through the filings, the magnet will collect a cluster of filings. How is this a model for what happens in a protoplanetary disk?

   A. The magnet moves in an orbit in the same way that planets orbit the sun.

   B. As they move, the magnet and clumps of planetary matter both collect iron because of magnetism.

   C. The magnet collects iron filings as it moves around the ring just as a new planet collects smaller masses due to its strong gravitational pull as it orbits its star.

   D. As they move, the magnet and clumps of planetary matter both collect matter due to their mass and gravity.

26. How does the magnet model differ from what occurs in a protoplanetary disk?

The Composition of the Planets

The temperature near the center of a protoplanetary disk would be very hot. Only elements that are solid at high temperatures would be able to form a solid planet near the center of the disk. This is why the terrestrial planets in the inner solar system consist of elements with high melting points. The outer planets in the solar system consist of elements with lower melting points, such as hydrogen, because those planets formed farther from the center of the disk.

Meteorites collected on Earth also provide evidence of how small bodies formed in the protoplanetary disk. These small, rocky bodies formed at the same time as the planets and are considered "left-over" fragments from the formation of the solar system.

The distance between the planets are not to scale.

The difference in composition between the solar system's terrestrial planets and gas and ice giants provides evidence supporting the nebular hypothesis.

The Orbits of Planets

Humans have directly observed and mapped the movements of planets and other objects in the night sky for thousands of years. These observations show that the planets move across the sky in a narrow band. This suggests that the planets are arranged in a disk shape around the sun. Scientists also observed that all of the planets orbit the sun in the same direction, which is also the same direction in which the sun spins on its axis. These observations support the idea that the planets formed as part of a spinning protoplanetary disk.

 EVIDENCE NOTEBOOK

27. If the planets did not form as part of a protoplanetary disk, how might their path across the sky differ from what is observed? Record your evidence.

The Nebular Theory

Astronomers have gathered enough evidence about the nebular hypothesis to conclude that it is highly likely to be an accurate description of how the solar system must have formed. So it is now widely accepted as a theory that explains how planets form in some detail. According to the nebular theory, gravitational disturbances caused a large cloud of gas and dust in a nebula to collapse into a space the size of the solar system. The particles in the cloud collided and joined to form larger particles with more gravity. As a result of the collisions within the cloud, the nebula became very hot and began to spin. The collapsing and spinning caused the cloud to flatten into a disk shape. The hot, dense center of the cloud became the sun. The rest of the material formed concentric rings around the sun. The rings of material rotated in the same direction that the sun rotated. The observed pattern is that a nebula produces multiple stars, and there seems to be gas and dust that doesn't get incorporated into a new star system but remains in the nebula.

The other seven planets in the solar system will be visible from Earth at the same time on May 6, 2492. This image shows how the planets will be aligned, based on a computer simulation. Notice how the planets are arranged in a narrow band.

Observations, Evidence, and Predictions

28. Imagine you are an astronomer who has discovered a star with a system of planets. Based on the nebular theory, what predictions can you make about the composition and movements of the planets? Use evidence to support your claim.

_____

_____

_____

_____

_____

_____

Continue Your Exploration

Name: _____   Date: _____

Check out the path below or go online to choose one of the other paths shown.

Careers in Science

- **Structure of Other Star Systems**
- **Hands-On Labs** ✋
- **Propose Your Own Path**

Go online to choose one of these other paths.

Conceptual Space Artist

Imagine using art and science together to inspire people and help them visualize things that we cannot see from Earth. This is what conceptual space artists do every day at the National Aeronautics and Space Administration (NASA). Scientists use various instruments to study objects and events in space. Many of these instruments do not produce normal images. Instead, they collect data in various forms, including series of numbers or simple bands of colored light. Conceptual space artists use this information to produce graphics and illustrations. This career requires an art background and the ability to use complex computer programs. The drawings and diagrams made by space artists help scientists and laypeople better understand space phenomena.

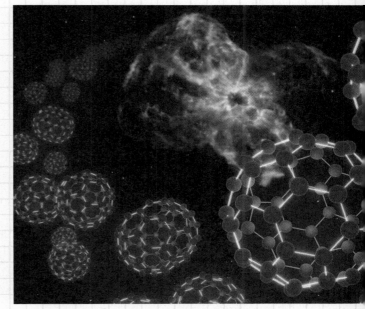

A space artist illustrated carbon spheres exiting a young nebula. Each carbon sphere has 60 carbon atoms arranged in a pattern similar to a soccer ball's.

This space artist's drawing shows what it might look like to watch three suns rising above the horizon from a moon that orbits HD188553 Ab, a large gaseous planet. It is based on data gathered by NASA's Keck telescope.

Continue Your Exploration

1. How is conceptual art different from a photograph?

2. Why are conceptual space artists important for astronomers and the public?

3. What is another example of a profession that translates scientific or professional information for a general audience?

4. Collaborate Working in a small group, select one type of space object (a star, nebula, galaxy, supernova, planet, or moon) and create a poster presenting the works of various conceptual space artists. Label each image with the title, artist's name (if available), the distance between the object and Earth, and the technology that provided data for the art.

Can You Explain It?

Name: _____

Date: _____

Why do all the planets in the solar system orbit the sun in the same direction?

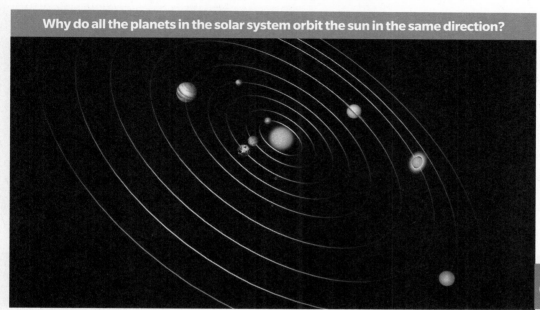

Explore Online

EVIDENCE NOTEBOOK
Refer to the notes in your Evidence Notebook to help you construct an explanation for why all the planets orbit the sun in the same direction.

1. State your claim. Make sure your claim fully explains why all the planets in the solar system orbit the sun in the same direction.

2. Summarize the evidence you have gathered to support your claim and explain your reasoning.

Checkpoints

Answer the following questions to check your understanding of the lesson.

Use the illustration to answer Questions 3–4.

3. Which of these is most likely the next stage after the one shown in the illustration?

   A. a new star forms

   B. the cloud of dust and gas begins to spin

   C. planets develop with individual orbits

   D. the disk flattens with the star at the center

4. When a new star contracts / expands, it begins to slow down / spin . As a result, the surrounding dust and gases compress into a sphere / disk.

Use the illustration to answer Questions 5–6.

5. Which stages involve the collision and clumping of matter in the nebula? Circle all that apply.

   A. stage 1

   B. stage 2

   C. stage 3

   D. stage 4

6. What evidence supporting the nebular hypothesis is shown?

   A. composition of the planets

   B. composition of the sun

   C. revolving disk of dust and gas

   D. density of the planets

---

7. Why are there two different types of planets in the solar system?

   A. The amount of material available to form planets was greater in the outer reaches of the protoplanetary disk.

   B. Rocky material could not collect and form planets beyond the asteroid belt.

   C. The nebular cloud from which the solar system formed had very little gas.

   D. The sun's heat allowed only rocky planets to form in the inner portion of the solar system.

Interactive Review

Complete this section to review the main concepts of the lesson.

Gravity played an important role in the shape and composition of the objects in the solar system.

A. Why is the density pattern seen in the layers inside the planets similar to the density pattern seen in the solar system?

The nebular hypothesis of solar system formation explains how the solar system formed from the gas and dust of a nebula and why all planets orbit the sun in the same direction.

B. How was the nebular hypothesis of solar system formation refined to account for the motion of the planets?

Scientists have gathered a variety of evidence to support the nebular hypothesis, including observations of distant star systems and the composition of the planets.

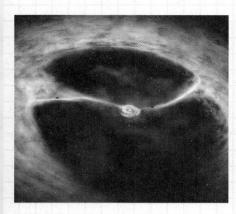

C. What lines of evidence support the nebular theory of solar system formation?

The Solar System and Galaxies Can Be Modeled

This photo shows a star forming near the edge of the Milky Way galaxy. It was taken by the Hubble Space Telescope.

Explore First

Building a Scale Model Use simple materials, such as drinking straws, craft sticks, and tape, to build a simple scale model of your classroom. How many times smaller is your model than your actual classroom? Compare your model to the models built by your classmates. Are they all built to the same scale?

Go online to view the digital version of the Hands-On Lab for this lesson and to download additional lab resources.

CAN YOU EXPLAIN IT?

How can we make a model of the Milky Way galaxy that shows Earth's location?

Earth is a small planet close to one star, the sun. The sun is one of billions of stars in the Milky Way galaxy. This is an artist's conception of how the Milky Way would look from a distance.

1. If you were standing on a sidewalk, how could you figure out where you are in a city without using a map?

2. How would a map of a galaxy be different from a map of a city?

 EVIDENCE NOTEBOOK As you explore this lesson, gather evidence to explain how scientists determine Earth's location within the Milky Way galaxy.

Modeling the Solar System

Mathematical modeling is important in determining the structure of the solar system. One important part of mathematical modeling is scale. *Scale* is the mathematical relationship between the measurements or distances in a model and the actual measurements or distances of an object or system. It is difficult to imagine distances as large as those in space. Scale provides a way to compare such distances accurately.

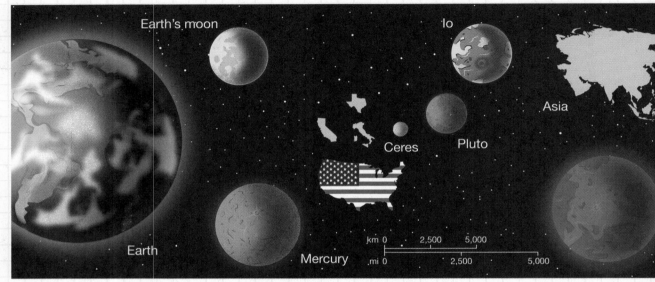

Scale lets us compare familiar objects and distances to astronomical objects and distances. For example, the diameter of Mercury is about the distance across the United States, and the diameter of Mars is about the distance across the continent of Asia.

3. Identify at least three ways scale could help someone understand the solar system.

Size and Distance in the Solar System

Models compare various characteristics of different objects. There are many ways to model the solar system. A physical model or a visual model, such as a drawing or map, could show the structure of the solar system. A mathematical model or a computer model could describe how objects in the solar system move.

Some models are made to scale. Some are not. Both scale and not-to-scale models can be useful. The type of model used depends on what information needs to be shown and how that information is being presented. Some aspects of the solar system are difficult to show with scale models. It is easy to make a scale model of the size of the sun and planets. Adding small asteroids and space dust to that scale model is more challenging. Modeling the huge distances between objects in space is also difficult.

Hands-On Lab
Model the Solar System

Scientists measure distances inside the solar system using kilometers or astronomical units. One **astronomical unit** (AU) is the average distance from the sun to Earth, about 150 million km. Create a scale model of the sun and planets and the distances between them.

Procedure and Analysis (Part 1)

STEP 1 Look at the table called *Solar System Objects*. The table lists the diameter (in km) of the sun and each planet. Use the numbers 1–9 to rank the sun and planets in order from the largest to the smallest.

STEP 2 Look at the objects available for your model. Compare their relative sizes. Predict which objects could be used to represent the sun and each planet in a scale model of the solar system. Write your responses in the table.

STEP 3 Measure and record the diameter of each object.

Solar System Objects				
Solar system object	Diameter (km)	Relative size (biggest = 1, smallest = 9)	Representative object in model	Diameter of object (cm)
Sun	1,392,000	1		
Mercury	4,879	9		
Venus	12,104			
Earth	12,756			
Mars	6,792			
Jupiter	142,984			
Saturn	120,536			
Uranus	51,118			
Neptune	49,528			

STEP 4 The dwarf planet Ceres has a diameter of 930 km. Analyze the scale properties of the objects in your model to determine which object would best represent Ceres in the model: a pinhead (1 mm), a baseball (75 mm), a grain of salt (0.3 mm), or a table tennis ball (30 mm). Explain your reasoning.

Procedure and Analysis (Part 2)

STEP 1 To use the same scale for distance in the solar system as you used for size, find the distance of 1 AU at this scale. Remember that the sun is 1,392,000 km in diameter and 1 AU (Earth's distance from the sun) is about 150,000,000 km. Divide the distance of 1 AU in km by the diameter of the sun in km to find out how many solar diameters are in one AU. Then multiply by the diameter of the model sun (in cm) to see how far 1 AU should be in the model.

$$\frac{1 \text{ AU (in km)}}{\text{sun's diameter (in km)}} \times \text{model sun diameter (in cm)} = \text{length of 1 AU in model}$$

STEP 2 Divide the answer in cm by 100 to get the answer in meters. The meter is a convenient unit; one meter is about the length of one very long stride.

STEP 3 Fill in the table below to show how far from the sun each planet should be placed in your model. Round answers to the nearest meter.

Approximate Distances from the Sun to the Planets			
Solar system object	Distance from sun (km)	Distance from sun (AU)	Distance from sun in model (m)
Mercury	58,000,000	0.4	
Venus	108,000,000	0.7	
Earth	150,000,000	1.0	
Mars	228,000,000	1.5	
Jupiter	778,000,000	5.2	
Saturn	1,433,000,000	9.5	
Uranus	2,872,000,000	19	
Neptune	4,495,000,000	30	

STEP 4 Place the model sun in one corner of the room. Place as many planets as you can the correct distance from the sun, using the same scale for distance as for size. How many planets will fit in your classroom?

STEP 5 Some people have said that "There is a huge amount of space in space!" What do you think they mean by that?

STEP 6 **Engineer It** Is it possible for one model to accurately show both the size of the planets and sun and the distance between the planets and sun? On a separate sheet of paper, describe the trade-offs between developing a model that illustrates both accurately and developing a model that illustrates only one of the measurements accurately.

Do the Math
Calculate Scale as a Ratio

Scale is often expressed as a ratio. A ratio is a way of comparing the relationship of quantity, amount, or size between two numbers. For example, the solar system has eight planets and one star (the sun). Thus, the ratio of planets to stars in the solar system is 8 to 1, or 8:1.

To calculate the scale of a model of the solar system, divide the actual size of a body by the size of the object that represents that same body in the model. The same process can be used to determine the scale for distances. The answer will be a ratio of the units in the model to the actual units. This is commonly expressed as "1" (unit in the model) to "X" (actual units) or "1:X." For example, the miniature town is built on a scale of 1:25. In other words, every 1 m in the model equals 25 m in the real town.

Scale, expressed as a ratio, can be used to make detailed models. The miniature town in this photo was built to scale with the real town. Every streetlight, tree, and building is exactly in proportion with its real-life counterpart.

---

4. Find the scale ratio that you used to model the solar system. Remember that 1 AU is about 150,000,000 kilometers, which is represented by 22 meters in the model. What is the scale of the model represented by a ratio?

5. How does using ratios or other mathematical comparisons help scientists communicate information?

Modeling the Milky Way

Our galaxy, the Milky Way, is just one out of billions of galaxies. A **galaxy** is a large collection of stars, gas, and dust that is held together by gravity. Most of the Milky Way is not visible when we observe space. Over time, astronomers developed technologies that expanded our ability to observe objects in space. Telescopes and space probes can be used to collect data and give us a much better understanding of our galaxy. These data also expand our understanding of the size of our galaxy compared to the surrounding universe. The **universe** includes space and all of the energy and matter within it.

The Milky Way is easier to see from remote areas. City lights interfere with light from space.

6. **Discuss** How do scientific discovery and technology influence each other?

The Milky Way in the Night Sky

For much of human history, the Milky Way was a mystery. Some civilizations thought it was a flowing river. Others thought it was milk spilled by gods that lived far above Earth. Greek philosophers debated whether it was a band of faint stars or something glowing within Earth's atmosphere. When Persian astronomers observed that larger bodies (planets) would pass in front of the glowing band, they theorized that the Milky Way was a collection of many distant stars. However, without the ability to distinguish individual stars within the band, they could not confirm this hypothesis.

The Milky Way galaxy can be seen only in a very clear and dark sky and appears as a hazy band of clouds.

The Milky Way through a Telescope

When Galileo Galilei first used a telescope to observe the Milky Way in the early 1600s, he described the Milky Way as a collection of "innumerable stars distributed in clusters." Later, astronomers made observations of the Milky Way from different locations on Earth. Over time, it became clear that the Milky Way surrounds Earth and the sun. Our solar system is a part of the Milky Way, not located outside of it.

7. Based on the photos of the Milky Way and the understanding that our solar system is located inside, not outside, the galaxy, what might be the shape of the Milky Way?

   A. sphere

   B. disk

   C. cube

8. What evidence did you use to infer a shape for the Milky Way galaxy?

Galileo Galilei used a telescope to distinguish individual stars within the Milky Way.

View of a Bicycle Tire from Different Locations

If you look from the center of a bicycle wheel to the rim, the tire appears to be a line extending across your field of view. This is how we see the Milky Way from Earth.

If you look at a spinning tire from a point outside the wheel, more of the tire may be visible. This is how we would view the Milky Way from outside of the galaxy.

The Shape of the Milky Way

In the late 1700s, astronomer William Herschel and his sister Caroline made a map of the Milky Way galaxy. The Herschels estimated distances to different stars using relative brightness. They reasoned that bright stars are closer to Earth and that dim stars are farther from Earth. The Herschels correctly described the Milky Way galaxy as a giant disk with stars orbiting its center. Because dim stars appeared to be equally distant from Earth, William Herschel placed our sun at the galaxy's center. William Herschel's placement of our sun was incorrect because huge clouds of dust in space make it difficult to see the most distant stars.

Determine Your Location within a Field of Objects

You will record observations of a group of objects from a single location, looking in four different directions. You will analyze a set of similar observations to determine the location of the observer.

MATERIALS
- pencil
- sheets of paper to crumple into balls
- sheets of paper for drawing

Procedure

STEP 1 As a class, crumple about 50 sheets of paper into different-sized balls. Scatter the balls of paper inside a large circle on the floor. The balls should be distributed randomly inside the circle and not in an orderly pattern.

STEP 2 Choose an observation point within the circle (there should be balls in all directions around you). Observe the locations of the balls around you, sitting or bending down so that the balls are as close to eye level as possible.

STEP 3 Look toward the front of the class and make a sketch (on a fresh sheet of paper) of how the balls in your field of view are distributed. Make a note of the direction that you are looking. Then turn 90° and make another sketch. Repeat until you have drawings facing four directions. When finished, you should have four separate sketches, each drawn on a separate sheet of paper.

Analysis

STEP 4 Exchange sketches with a partner. Compare your partner's sketches with the balls in the circle. Based on your partner's sketches, try to determine the point from which your partner's observations were made. Explain how you determined from which location the observations were made.

STEP 5 How well could this observation method be used to determine where our solar system is located within the Milky Way galaxy?

Earth's Place in the Milky Way

In the early 1900s, Harlow Shapley used telescopes to view large groups of stars called *globular clusters*. All of the globular clusters that Shapley observed were arranged in a large, spherical shape. This sphere, composed of many globular clusters, seemed to be centered around a point in space far from Earth. Shapley reasoned that these globular clusters were gathered in a spherical shape because they orbit the gravitational center of the Milky Way galaxy. Shapley could view evidence of the galaxy's center through a telescope, so he concluded that our solar system must lie outside the center. Although the Milky Way is indeed a disk, as the Herschels determined, our sun is not at its center. The gravitational forces from the center of the Milky Way attract stars and stellar systems and cause them to orbit around the more massive center of the galaxy. Shapley's data provided strong evidence that our solar system is located far from the galaxy's center.

 EVIDENCE NOTEBOOK

9. How might knowing Earth's position relative to the center of the Milky Way help you make a map of the Milky Way? Record your evidence.

Analyze Dark Portions of Space

When you look at the night sky, there are many dark patches, even in portions of the Milky Way.

10. In addition to globular clusters, which can contain as many as 100,000 stars, Shapley saw areas in space that did not seem to have any stars. Given that telescopes had already been used to find stars in areas of the night sky that previously appeared empty, which of the following statements are most likely to be true? Choose all that apply.

   A. These dark portions contain no stars.

   B. These dark portions contain stars that were too dim for Shapley's telescope to see.

   C. There might be matter such as dust blocking the light from stars.

11. What questions do you have about dark portions of the night sky?

_____

_____

_____

_____

Analyzing Other Galaxies

Outer space is filled with many different sources of light. In the daytime, sunlight fills the sky and hides most of the other sources of light. At night, however, you can see the moon, hundreds or thousands of stars, and several planets. If you are lucky, you might even see a comet or a streaking meteor.

The round points of light in this photograph are stars. Some of the stars appear to be much brighter than others. The brighter stars may be closer to Earth, or they may simply be hotter and bigger.

12. As you examine the photo, are there any light sources that stand out in comparison to the others? If so, what makes them different?

Unexplained Light Sources

While observing the night sky, many astronomers noticed light sources that looked very different from stars. These objects often appeared larger than stars and, unlike stars, seemed to have fuzzy edges. Some astronomers thought the unknown objects might be clouds of gas inside the Milky Way galaxy. Others thought they might be very large groups of stars, either inside the Milky Way or beyond it. The blurry patch of light that you can see in the photo is one of these light sources, named Andromeda.

Galaxies beyond the Milky Way

In the years following the observation of fuzzy, unexplained light sources, engineers designed larger telescopes for use in research. Large telescopes capture more light than small telescopes do. Capturing more light allows the telescope to produce more detailed images of distant objects. This is very similar to the way people can see the details of objects more clearly in bright light than they can in dim light.

In 1919, astronomer Edwin Hubble used what was then the largest telescope in the world to photograph a blurry patch of light known as Andromeda. When Hubble examined the new photographs carefully, he identified faint, individual stars. His discovery led to more questions. How many more stars might be a part of Andromeda? Why were so many stars clustered together? Was Andromeda within the Milky Way galaxy? Hubble would continue to gather data and work collaboratively with other scientists to determine the answers to these questions.

Large telescopes built in the 1900s were much more powerful than earlier telescopes. Edwin Hubble took this photograph of Andromeda using one of these more powerful telescopes.

 13. Language SmArts What evidence might be needed to determine if a blurry patch of light is located within the Milky Way galaxy or beyond it? Construct a written argument, including claims and reasoning, to present your ideas.

 EVIDENCE NOTEBOOK

14. How would the ability to observe other galaxies help in generating models of the Milky Way galaxy? Record your evidence.

Galaxies Are Defined by Their Shape

Edwin Hubble determined that Andromeda was another galaxy outside of the Milky Way. In the 1920s, Hubble began to classify the galaxies that he was discovering based on their shapes. Gravity plays an important role in the shapes of galaxies. There are four types of galaxies.

15. In a spiral galaxy, a larger, central core of stars will exert a *strong / weak* gravitational pull on stars in the arms of the galaxy. The stars in a *spiral / elliptical* galaxy orbit in the same plane around the galaxy's center.

Four Types of Galaxies

Elliptical galaxies contain older stars and very little dust and gas. Elliptical galaxies have very bright centers. Some elliptical galaxies are sphere-shaped, while others are more elongated. The stars in these galaxies do not rotate around the galaxy's center in the same plane.

Most galaxies are spiral galaxies. Spiral galaxies contain dust and gas as well as stars. Spiral galaxies have a bulge at the center and very distinct spiral arms. The massive central core of stars exerts a strong gravitational pull on the stars rotating in roughly the same plane around it in the spiral arms.

Barred spiral galaxies are similar in composition to spiral galaxies but have very distinct bars that extend from the center to the spiral arms. The bar shape may be a result of the complex gravitational interactions between stars orbiting the central core. The Milky Way is classified as a barred spiral.

Irregular galaxies are galaxies that don't fit into any other class. Irregular galaxies lack a large center with a strong gravitational field. The matter in irregular galaxies does not form a defined shape and may contain a relatively large amount of dust and gas.

Gravity Pulls Galaxies Together

Gravity does not just affect the stars, dust, and gas inside galaxies. Gravity also causes galaxies to interact with one another. Galaxies are massive and so the gravitational pull they have on each other can be large depending on how far apart they are from each other.

Galaxies form clusters that can contain thousands of galaxies held together by gravity. The Milky Way has two small galaxies orbiting it and is one of a cluster of over 30 galaxies called the Local Group. Most galaxy clusters are moving away from each other, but some galaxies within each cluster may collide.

Galaxy collisions are common in the universe but take millions of years to take place. If one or both of the galaxies is massive enough, they may join together to form a new, larger galaxy. If the galaxies are moving fast enough to overcome the gravitational forces, they may pass through each other.

Galaxy cluster Abell 370 contains hundreds of galaxies held together by gravity.

Explore Online

Colliding galaxies NGC 6050 and IC 1179 are 450 million light years away in the Hercules Galaxy Cluster.

16. How can galaxies exert such a strong gravitational pull on each other when they are millions of light years from each other?

Engineer It
Measure Distances Using Brightness

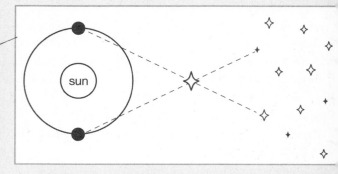

One way to measure the distance to a star is to use the parallax method. Hold your thumb up in front of your face. Close your right eye. Then close your left eye instead. Your thumb will seem to jump when you switch eyes. The closer your thumb is to your face, the bigger the jump will be. Now, imagine that the distance between your eyes is the diameter of Earth's orbit. You can record the position of a star in the sky and then record the position of the star again when Earth is on the other side of its orbit. The star will appear to be in a different place in the sky. This change in the star's position allows astronomers to calculate the star's distance from Earth. This method becomes less accurate the farther stars are from Earth. Astronomers also tried to use the brightness of stars to determine their distance from Earth, but this method had its own problems.

17. Look at the photo of the light bulb. Can you tell how far the light is from the camera? What are some factors that limit your ability to tell how far away objects are?

18. The light on the left is about 30 centimeters from the camera. The light on the right is about 100 centimeters from the camera. You can easily tell that these lights are at different distances because of the table. However, imagine that these lights were two stars that seemed equally bright in the night sky. What else would you need to know to determine which light was farther away?

A Universe Full of Galaxies

Edwin Hubble could not use parallax to measure the distance to the dim stars in Andromeda because they were too far away. However, astronomer Henrietta Leavitt had recently discovered Cepheid variable stars. Over regular time intervals, the brightness of a Cepheid variable star changes. Leavitt measured the distances to close Cepheid variable stars. She discovered that the brightest stars took a longer time to change in brightness, while the brightness of the dimmer stars changed more quickly.

Cepheid variable stars grow brighter and dimmer over time. This behavior gives astronomers a way to calculate how much light the star is producing.

Hubble identified several Cepheid variable stars within Andromeda. He observed these stars over time and determined how quickly each star's brightness changed. Then Hubble was able to use his observations and Leavitt's studies to determine how much light these stars were actually producing. Once Hubble knew how much light each star was producing and how bright each star appeared to him, he was able to determine how far away the stars were. He realized that they were very far away! That discovery provided strong evidence that Andromeda is outside the Milky Way and was, in fact, a galaxy itself.

19. Scientists observe that natural systems display order and consistency. How does this idea relate to Hubble's use of Cepheid variable stars to calculate the distance between Earth and the Andromeda galaxy?

Explain the Value of Measuring Distances between Objects in Space

20. Recall the example of making a map of a city. How could knowing the distance between you and big buildings or other landmarks in the city help you make a map of your city? Would the same strategies work for larger areas such as a state?

21. How does measuring the distances to stars help you figure out where you are in the universe?

Modeling Scales in the Universe

Since Hubble first found evidence that there were other galaxies, our ability to study the universe has greatly improved. Modern telescopes, including some that observe from outside Earth's atmosphere, provide more detail than Hubble's photographs did. Scientists have developed new methods to measure the distance and speed of objects farther away than Andromeda. Our models of the universe have become more accurate over the last hundred years.

22. After astronomers learned techniques for measuring distances to the planets and the sun, our understanding of the solar system grew. What might be some similar ways in which improved measurements and data collection would affect our view of the universe?

The Whirlpool Galaxy is about 23 million light-years away from the Milky Way. There are many galaxies that are even farther away than this.

The Size of the Milky Way

The Milky Way galaxy is so large that it is almost impossible to imagine its size. To describe the size of galaxies, astronomers needed a new unit of measurement. Astronomers often measure distances in *light-years*. A **light-year** is the distance that light travels in a vacuum in one year. Because light travels about 300,000 kilometers every second, a light-year is a very long distance. A light-year is 9.5×10^{12} km. The Milky Way galaxy measures about 100,000 light-years across. So it would take 100,000 years for light to travel from one side of the Milky Way to the other. That means that light from a star on one side of the galaxy could not be seen on the other side until 100,000 years after the light was produced. And there are galaxies even larger than the Milky Way.

EVIDENCE NOTEBOOK

23. How does knowing the distance across the Milky Way help to model the galaxy? Record your evidence.

Do the Math
Model the Scale of the Milky Way

The Milky Way galaxy is immense. It is so large that it is hard to describe. Knowing that it measures 100,000 light-years across gives the size a number, but does not really describe the scale. One way to imagine its size is to compare the Milky Way galaxy to our solar system. When numbers of very different sizes are compared, the difference in size can be described using the term *order of magnitude*. If there is a one-order-of-magnitude difference, one measurement is 10 times as large as the other. If there is a two-orders-of-magnitude difference, the larger number is 10 × 10, or 100 times as large.

24. To compare numbers that differ by more than one order of magnitude, it is often easier to use exponents. An exponent tells how many times a number is multiplied by itself. For example, 100 can be represented as 10^2 or as 10 × 10. The number 1,000 can be represented as 10^3 or as 10 × 10 × 10. Each time the exponent is increased, the number is multiplied by itself again.

_____ can be represented as 10^5 or as 10 × 10 × 10 × 10 × 10.

25. When you read numbers that use exponents, you will notice that a small change in the exponent can indicate a large difference in scale. For example, the thickness of a brick is about 80 millimeters (mm). This number can be written as $8 × 10^1$ mm. The tallest building in the world, the Burj Khalifa, is about 800 meters tall. This height is 800,000, or $8 × 10^5$, mm. How many bricks would there be in a stack of bricks as tall as the Burj Khalifa?

A. 1,000 (3 orders of magnitude)

B. 10,000 (4 orders of magnitude)

C. 100,000 (5 orders of magnitude)

26. The diameter of our solar system is approximately $3 × 10^{10}$ km. The diameter of the Milky Way galaxy is about $9 × 10^{17}$ km. Based on those measurements, the diameter of the galaxy is 30,000,000 times as big as our solar system's diameter, or about _____ orders of magnitude larger.

Stars and Planets in the Milky Way

It is impossible to count all of the stars in the Milky Way. In some areas, there are so many stars that they cannot be seen individually from Earth. Other stars are blocked by clouds of dust. Some stars are not bright enough to see even with our most powerful telescopes. Based on the stars they can observe, astronomers estimate that there are about one hundred billion, or 10^{11}, stars in the Milky Way. If even a small fraction of those stars have planets orbiting them, there would likely be billions of planets in our galaxy.

27. Write The number of stars in the Milky Way is enormous. On a separate sheet of paper, write how you would explain this number to another person. Write about comparisons that you could make to other examples of large numbers.

28. This photograph, known as the eXtreme Deep Field (XDF), shows the Hubble Space Telescope's observations of a tiny section of space. The section is so small that it is similar to looking at the sky through a drinking straw. Thousands of galaxies were recorded. What does this tell you about the number of galaxies that exist in the universe?

The XDF photo was made using photographs taken over a period of ten years by the Hubble Space Telescope. It shows a tiny section of the distant universe and contains thousands of galaxies.

Galaxies

Based on data such as the Hubble eXtreme Deep Field photograph, scientists estimate that there are tens of billions of galaxies in the universe. One of the closest galaxies is the Andromeda galaxy, which is about 3 million light-years from Earth. The most distant galaxies are more than 10 billion light-years away.

The eXtreme Deep Field (XDF) photo shows a portion of the sky that is much smaller than the area taken up by the moon.

Explore Data Collection

29. When astronomers such as Leavitt and Hubble were observing the brightness of stars, they had to manually adjust their telescopes and take images over long periods of time. Modern research telescopes are controlled by computers. What are some ways that being able to control a telescope with a computer might allow us to gather more data about objects in space? Choose all that apply.

   A. Computers are able to control the telescopes with more precision than humans.

   B. Computers can understand the data better than human observers.

   C. Computers can adjust the telescope to take images of an exact location many times.

   D. Computers can process data faster than humans.

Continue Your Exploration

Name: _____   Date: _____

Check out the path below or go online to choose one of the other paths shown.

The Kepler Mission

- • **Contributions of Arab and Indian Astronomers**
- • **Other Galaxies**
- • **Hands-On Labs** 🖐
- • **Propose Your Own Path**

Go online to choose one of these other paths.

The Kepler Mission is NASA's first exploratory data collection mission that is specifically designed to find Earth-sized planets. From its orbit around the sun, the Kepler observatory measures the light coming from distant stars. As it constantly observes more than 100,000 stars for years at a time, the Kepler instruments can detect small changes in a star's brightness. These changes can indicate that a planet is orbiting the star.

1. Astronomers use the Kepler observatory to search the areas around stars for planets that are similar to Earth. As a planet passes in front of its star, the brightness of the starlight reaching the telescope changes. How might the change in the brightness of a star give information about how large a planet is?

The Kepler observatory was launched in 2009 and orbits Earth. It collects data from space and sends it back to Earth.

Continue Your Exploration

2. Which statements describe limitations that could affect the ability of the Kepler observatory to measure the size of a planet? Circle all that apply.

   A. Only planets that move in front of a star can be measured by this method.

   B. Different stars are located at different distances from Earth.

   C. Stars do not all have the same diameter.

   D. Some stars' brightness can vary over time.

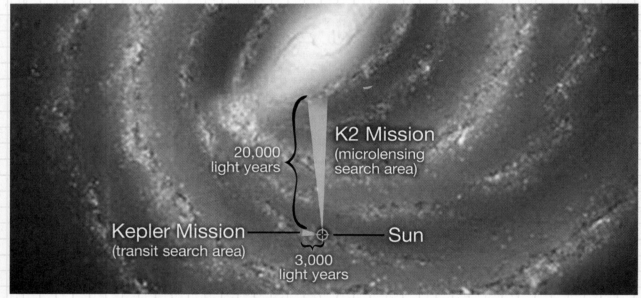

The Kepler observatory was originally used to search for planets that were less than 3,000 light-years from Earth. Under the K2 mission, it was used to search for planets up to 20,000 light-years away.

3. The Kepler observatory observes only a tiny portion of the night sky, as shown in the image. Even so, it has detected thousands of planets. What does this tell you about the number of planets in the Milky Way galaxy?

4. **Collaborate** Research and summarize some of the recent discoveries that have been made using the Kepler observatory. Research and define what the habitable zone is. Explain how the habitable zone relates to the Kepler observatory's mission.

Can You Explain It?

Name: _____ **Date:** _____

How can we make a model of the Milky Way galaxy that shows Earth's location?

EVIDENCE NOTEBOOK

Refer to the notes in your Evidence Notebook to help you construct an explanation for how scientists model Earth within the Milky Way galaxy.

1. State your claim. Make sure your claim fully explains how Earth's location in relation to the rest of the Milky Way can be determined.

2. Summarize the evidence you have gathered to support your claim and explain your reasoning.

Checkpoints

Answer the following questions to check your understanding of the lesson.

Use the photo to answer Question 3.

3. If an observer looked out from a planet near the center of this galaxy, what would it look like to that observer?

   A. a broad band of stars forming a ring around the planet

   B. a sphere of stars evenly spread in every direction

   C. a spiral shape with arms reaching out from a center

   D. a band of stars in one direction, with fewer stars in other directions

4. A model solar system is built to a scale of $1 : 7.0 \times 10^9$. This means that every 1 m in the _model / solar system_ equals 7.0×10^9 m in the _model / solar system_.

5. Astronomers use _parallax / Cepheid variable stars_ to measure distances between the Milky Way and other _galaxies / star systems_.

Use the photo to answer Question 6.

6. Most of the points of light in the photo are likely _stars / galaxies_. The larger, bright object toward the center of the photo could possibly be a _galaxy / universe_ because of its fuzzier edges. To definitively tell what this object is, you would need to identify stars inside the light and measure how _bright / far away_ those stars are.

7. Two stars on opposite sides of the night sky appear very different. One star is very bright and can be seen before the sky is completely dark. The other can barely be seen on a dark night. Which of the following could be a reason that these two stars have different apparent brightnesses? Select all that apply.

   A. The brighter star emits much more light than the dimmer star does.

   B. A planet orbiting the dimmer star blocks most of its light.

   C. The brighter star is much closer to Earth than the dimmer star is.

   D. Clouds of dust block some of the light from the dimmer star.

Interactive Review

Complete this section to review the main concepts of the lesson.

A scale model can be used to compare the sizes and distances between objects in space.

A. Explain how using scale helps scientists model different sizes or distances in the solar system.

The Milky Way galaxy is a large group of stars that includes our sun.

B. What observations provide evidence for our current understanding of the Milky Way's shape?

There are many other galaxies beyond the Milky Way. Other galaxies have different shapes due to how they formed.

C. What evidence can be used to show that galaxies other than the Milky Way exist?

Our sun is one of many billions of stars in the Milky Way, which is one of many billions of galaxies in the universe.

D. Explain why using measurements such as the light-year becomes necessary when discussing distances in the universe.

Choose one of the activities to explore how this unit connects to other topics.

☐ People in Science

Annie Easley, Computer Scientist Annie Easley grew up in Birmingham, Alabama. In 1955, Easley began to work as a "human computer," solving difficult computations for researchers. Machines eventually replaced human computers, but she adapted to the new technology. Easley became a computer programmer and worked on various NASA programs. In 1977, she graduated from Cleveland State University with a degree in Mathematics.

Research how mathematics and computers are related and create a short presentation on your findings.

☐ Physical Science Connection

Structure of Other Solar Systems Until recently, astronomers expected that other planetary systems would be similar to our solar system. They expected to find small, rocky inner planets and large, gas giant planets farther from the center. However, some distant planetary systems that have been recently discovered include such anomalies as "Super-Jupiters" close to the central sun.

Research current hypotheses about how extrasolar planetary systems form. Describe how these systems inform our understanding of our own solar system and galaxy. Make a multimedia presentation to share what you learned with your class.

☐ Math Connection

Leap Year Archaeological discoveries, such as this ancient Egyptian calendar carved on a stone wall, show that, even thousands of years ago, various cultures tracked time by using calendars.

A leap year is a year that contains one extra calendar day on February 29th. In the Gregorian calendar, most years that are multiples of four are leap years. Research the history behind leap years and determine why we add a day to our calendar every four years. Find out when and how the need for a leap year was first calculated and why the leap year system works. Write a short essay of your findings about leap years and present it to the class.

Name: _____   Date: _____

Complete this review to check your understanding of the unit.

Use the diagram to answer Questions 1–4.

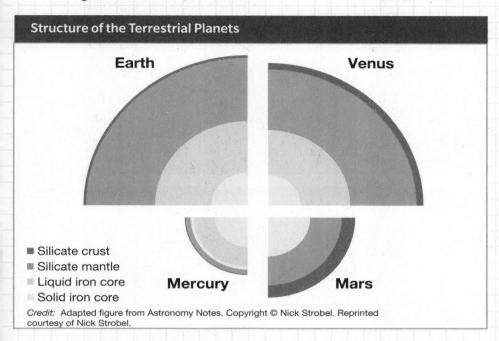

Structure of the Terrestrial Planets

Earth   Venus

Mercury   Mars

- ▪ Silicate crust
- ▪ Silicate mantle
- ▫ Liquid iron core
- ▫ Solid iron core

Credit: Adapted figure from Astronomy Notes. Copyright © Nick Strobel. Reprinted courtesy of Nick Strobel.

1. Compare the internal structures of the terrestrial planets. How do the scales of the internal layers of the planets compare?

2. Compare the diameters of the terrestrial planets. How do the relative sizes of the planets compare?

3. Compare the layers of the terrestrial planets. What role did density play in the structure of the terrestrial planets?

4. Compare the pattern that occurred during the formation of the terrestrial planets with the pattern that occurred during the formation of the solar system. How are these patterns similar?

Use the images to answer Questions 5–8.

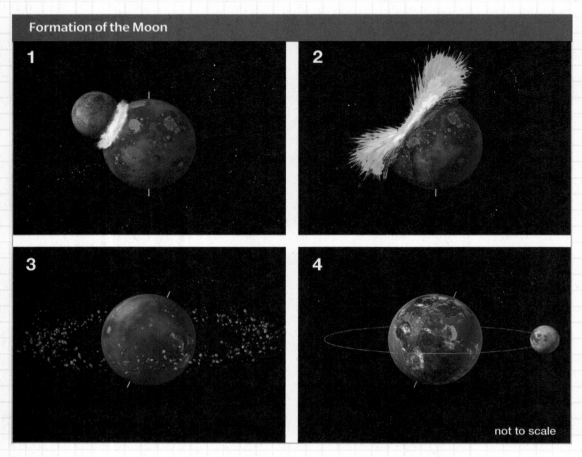

Formation of the Moon

1

2

3

4

not to scale

5. What forces were acting on Earth and on the impacting object before they collided?

6. What role did gravity play in the formation of the moon?

7. How is the formation of the moon around Earth similar to the formation of Earth around the sun? How is it different?

8. Why does the moon orbit Earth in the same direction that Earth orbits the sun?

Name: Date:

What role does gravity play in a lunar landing?

An understanding of gravity has played an important role in the space program and in the lunar landings. You have been invited to participate in the Constellation Program, which aims to have another lunar landing and "sustained human presence" in space in the future. Learn about the space program and how they rely on an understanding of gravity to plan missions and outposts in space. You will focus on how gravity affects sending people and materials into space and landing people and materials safely on other bodies. You will also learn about how changes in gravity affect the human body.

Constellation Mission Diagram

This diagram shows a proposed Constellation mission to land on the moon and includes the outbound and inbound trajectories and landing areas.

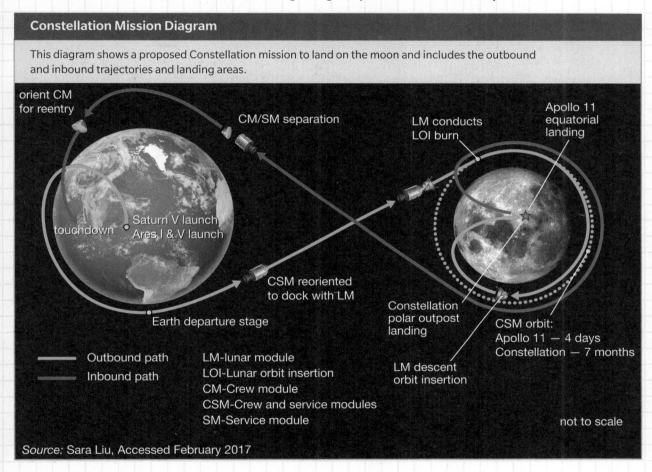

Source: Sara Liu, Accessed February 2017

The steps below will help guide your research and help you write a proposal.

1. **Ask a Question** Develop questions you will need to answer to write a proposal for sending a crewed spacecraft to the moon to develop a colony. Think about how gravity plays a role in what items are brought into space, how people and the spaceships move around, and the structure of the spaceship.

2. **Conduct Research** Research answers to the relevant questions using multiple sources, including NASA and the Constellation Program, as resources. Think about answers to how gravity affects people's bodies, supplies for travel, and spacecraft movement.

3. **Evaluate Data** Analyze your research to identify important variables that you need to consider in your proposal. Include a list of ways that you will address gravity in your plan.

4. **Write a Proposal** Based on your research, construct a written proposal for sending a crewed spacecraft to the moon to develop a colony. Describe how your proposal is supported by evidence.

5. **Communicate** Present your recommendation about a lunar colony to the class.

✓ **Self-Check**

	I identified and accounted for the role gravity plays in sending people into space and landing them back on Earth or another body in space.
	I researched the Constellation Program and how the space program relies on an understanding of gravity in space.
	I constructed a written proposal for sending a crewed spacecraft to the moon to develop a colony.
	My proposal and recommendation were clearly communicated to others.

Earth through Time

How do patterns in the rock record provide evidence for the history of Earth and life on Earth?

Paleontologists chip away at a rock face in the Republic of Madagascar. They are searching for fossils of organisms that lived during earlier time periods in Earth's history.

You Solve It   Is Antibiotic Use Related to Antibiotic Resistance in *E. coli*?

Analyze geographic data on antibiotic prescriptions and antibiotic resistance to see if there is a relationship between the data sets.

Go online and complete the You Solve It to explore ways to solve a real-world problem.

Construct a Family Tree

Sea otters (left) and badgers (right) belong to a family of carnivores called mustelids.

A. Look at the photos. On a separate sheet of paper, write down as many different questions as you can about the photos.

B. **Discuss** With your class or a partner, share your questions. Record any additional questions generated in your discussion. Then choose the most important questions from the list that are related to the anatomical similarities and differences between these two animals. Write them below.

C. Choose an animal to research in order to construct its "family tree." Here's a list of animals you can consider:

Dogs
Foxes
Tigers
Gorillas

D. Use the information above, along with your research, to create a diagram or timeline that shows how the animal you chose is related to other animals.

 *Discuss the next steps for your Unit Project with your teacher and go online to download the Unit Project Worksheet.*

Language Development

Use the lessons in this unit to complete the network and expand your understanding of these key concepts.

	Similar term
	Phrase
	Cognate
	Example
	Definition

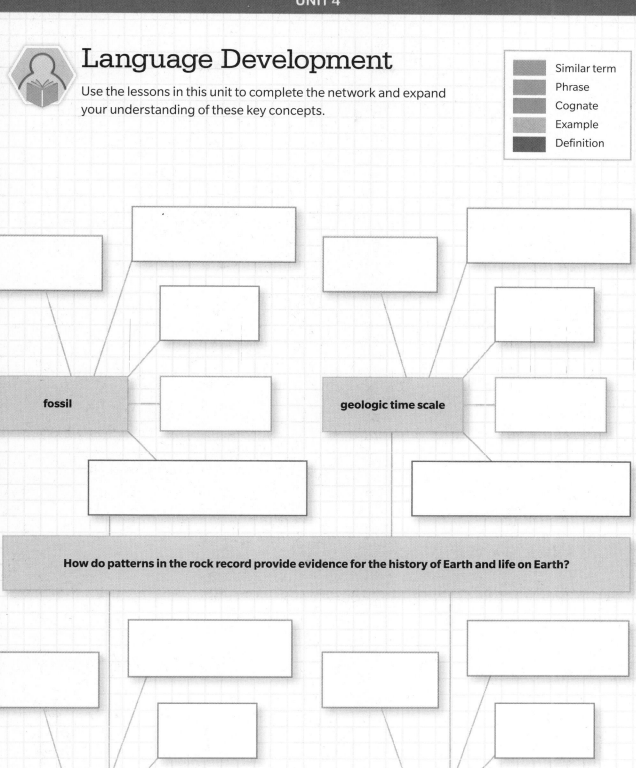

fossil

geologic time scale

How do patterns in the rock record provide evidence for the history of Earth and life on Earth?

relative dating

evolution

Rocks and Fossils Are Evidence of Earth's History

The colorful rock layers that make up these hills in Oregon contain clues about the history of the area.

Explore First

Inferring Sequence of Events Examine photos of curious situations to determine how they could have come about. In groups, list each step in order that it would have occurred to lead to the situation in the photo.

Go online to view the digital version of the Hands-On Lab for this lesson and to download additional lab resources.

CAN YOU EXPLAIN IT?

How can scientists determine when these ancient animals lived?

History of Dinosaur Provincial Park

About 76 million years ago, dinosaurs lived alongside turtles, crocodiles, and small mammals. The area consisted of swamps and lush vegetation, as well as many rivers that flowed into a nearby sea.

Around 75 million years ago, the sea rose and covered the area. In the sea lived shelled creatures such as ammonites and large marine reptiles such as this plesiosaur.

Today, sedimentary rock layers are exposed throughout the park. Fossils of the ancient plants and animals that once lived here are found within the sedimentary layers.

1. The rocks and fossils found today in Dinosaur Provincial Park tell us about the area's past environments, plants, and animals. How do you think scientists could determine the age of an ancient item such as a fossil or rock?

EVIDENCE NOTEBOOK As you explore this lesson, gather evidence to help explain how scientists can determine when these ancient animals lived.

Describing the Formation of Sedimentary Rocks and Fossils

Why would anyone want to study rocks? Rocks can tell us about Earth's past environments and organisms. Some rocks can tell us about events, such as meteorite impacts and volcanic eruptions, that happened in the distant past. It may seem like rocks are permanent, but they form and change over thousands or millions of years through processes such as erosion, deposition, melting, and burial. Different rocks form in different environments. For example, granite forms when magma cools under Earth's surface, while sandstone forms from grains of minerals or other rocks that settle in layers and harden over time.

2. **Discuss** With a classmate, look at the rock layers in the photo. Note any patterns in their ages. Which rock layer formed first?

This rock layer began forming about 145 million years ago. Patterns in the rock show that it formed in a desert environment with huge sand dunes, similar to today's Sahara Desert.

This rock layer formed about 200 million years ago. By studying this rock layer, scientists can tell that tropical lakes and streams once existed where it formed.

This layer formed about 250 million years ago. Fossils and patterns in the rocks suggest that the rock layer formed near a seashore.

Sedimentary Rock Formation

Sandstone is a type of sedimentary rock. Sedimentary rocks are made of tiny bits of material called *sediment*. Sedimentary rock can be made from smaller pieces of rock, or from the remains of plants and animals. For example, limestone can be made of the remains of microscopic organisms.

Sedimentary rock can form when erosion moves sediment to low-lying areas such as valleys and lake bottoms. The sediment settles in layers that become compressed as they are buried under the weight of layers above them. When water containing dissolved substances seeps through the sediment layers, the substances precipitate out of the solution and harden, acting as a cement.

Over time, shells and sediment pile up at the bottom of lakes and oceans and can eventually form sedimentary rock.

As sedimentary layers form, they stack up one by one. If undisturbed by Earth processes, sedimentary rocks stay in horizontal layers. The oldest layer is at the bottom and the youngest layer is at the top.

Fossil Formation

We know a lot about the history of life on Earth from studying fossils. **Fossils** are the remains or traces of once-living organisms. Fossils form when specific conditions occur that preserve an organism's remains. In most cases, an organism's remains are eaten, scattered, dissolved by water, or decomposed before they can be preserved.

The Making of a Fossil

Most fossils found today formed when the remains of dead animals were covered by sediment. Usually only the hard parts of the animal fossilized, but sometimes the soft parts fossilized too.

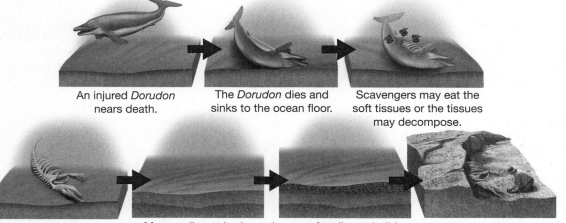

An injured *Dorudon* nears death.

The *Dorudon* dies and sinks to the ocean floor.

Scavengers may eat the soft tissues or the tissues may decompose.

The skeleton gets covered by sediments.

More sediment buries the entire skeleton.

Layers of sediment build up. They turn to rock. The ocean floor becomes dry land due to tectonic changes.

Erosion exposes the rock layer containing the *Dorudon* bones.

It is rare for an organism's remains to form a fossil. A very small percentage of species that have ever lived left behind fossils. Many processes can prevent fossil formation. Fossils form most often when an organism's remains are quickly buried by sediments. That is why most fossils are found in sedimentary rock. Because quick burial by sediments occurs more often in rivers, lakes, and oceans than it does on land, water-dwelling organisms are more likely to be fossilized than land animals.

Fossils may form from bones, teeth, or shells. They may also form from activity, as is the case with fossilized footprints. Fossils of soft-bodied animals such as jellyfish are rare, but they do exist. Proteins and genetic material may also fossilize, and cell structures in fossilized feathers have helped scientists determine the feathers' color.

3. Engineer It You want to explore rock layers in a region to find fossils and clues about the past. There is one problem: there are no exposed cliffs or areas where you can see the rock layers. They are all below the ground. Propose a solution to this problem. Can you think of any helpful tools or technology?

Case Study: The Morrison Formation

The Morrison Formation is a large area of sedimentary rock and is the most concentrated source of fossils in the United States. About 150 million years ago (mya), the area shown on the map was a large floodplain with many rivers. The conditions in this ancient floodplain environment were favorable for the quick burial of organisms that died there.

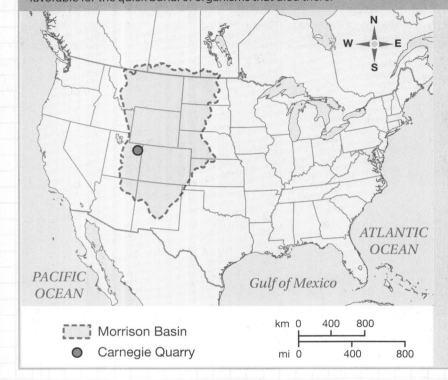

ATLANTIC OCEAN

PACIFIC OCEAN

Gulf of Mexico

⌐ ⌐ ⌐ ⌐ Morrison Basin
● Carnegie Quarry

km 0   400   800

mi 0   400   800

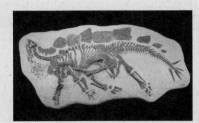

This is a reproduction of a nearly complete *Stegosaurus* skeleton found in the Morrison Basin.

Fossil remains are often scattered and mixed together, like these from the Carnegie Quarry.

4. Does the high concentration of fossils in the Morrison Formation mean that more organisms lived here 150 mya compared to other parts of the country? Explain your reasoning.

Analyze Fossils to Describe Earth's Past

Fossils provide evidence about past life and environments. For example, a fossilized fern like the one below looks similar to ferns found in tropical areas today.

WORD BANK
- a tropical forest
- a lake
- a grassland

5. Look at each image. Use the words from the word bank to label each fossil with the name of the environment in which it likely formed.

A. _____

B. _____

C. _____

Studying the Ages of Fossils

No one was around millions of years ago to observe fossils forming or to observe other natural processes that occur over very long time spans. Yet we can infer what happened in the past based on what we know about the natural processes that occur today. Scientists assume that the geologic events and phenomena that happen today also happened in the past and that they apply everywhere in nature. This scientific principle is called *uniformitarianism*. We can use these assumptions to interpret fossil data.

sedimentation

This satellite photo shows rivers that carry water and sediment out to sea. Soil and rock particles are eroded from the riverbanks by water, carried down the rivers, and deposited in the sea, which causes sediment to build up.

For example, scientists know that today, sedimentary rock forms when sediments carried by air, ice, water, or gravity are deposited in layers in a new location. Over time, the weight of new sediment layers puts pressure on the layers below, and rock forms. So we can assume that sedimentation and sedimentary rock formation in ancient seas occurred in a similar way.

6. How does knowledge of sedimentary rock formation help us to understand fossils?

Relative Ages of Rock Layers

How can we use rocks to learn about the past? One way is through their relative age. *Relative age* is how old something is compared to something else. You can determine relative age without knowing actual age. For example, you know that an adult is older than a baby, even if you don't know the exact age of either person.

When sedimentary rock forms, the layers on the bottom are deposited first. That means that, unless something happens to disturb the layers, the oldest layer is on the bottom, and the youngest is on the top. This idea is called the *law of superposition*. Scientists use it to find the relative ages of rock layers.

7. The rock layer on the top of the Grand Canyon is the *youngest / oldest* because it was deposited *most recently / in the distant past*. Layers in the middle are *younger / older* than the surface layer. The layer farthest down is the *youngest / oldest* because it was deposited *most recently / the earliest*.

Grand Canyon

Hands-On Lab
Model Rock Layers to Determine Relative Age

Build a physical model to help you determine the order in which rocks form and make observations about the rocks' relative ages.

In the real world, rock sequences can span large areas. Often, rocks are not visible because they are beneath Earth's surface, but sometimes they are exposed along cliffs or where a hill was cut through for road construction. A physical model can help you see how a sequence of rocks can form over time.

MATERIALS

- items such as beads or shells to represent fossils
- modeling clay (at least five different colors)
- plastic knife
- tray or container to hold the model

Procedure

STEP 1 **Discuss** Gather your materials. Discuss with a group or partner how you can use your materials to make a model of four sedimentary rock layers.

STEP 2 Choose four rocks from the list. Note the environment in which each type of rock formed. This is also known as a rock's depositional environment.

- **Sandstone with fossils** formed in a sandy ocean bottom (yellow clay with fossil materials)
- **Shale** formed in a deep, muddy lake (brown clay)
- **Siltstone** formed in a river floodplain (red clay)
- **Sandstone** formed in a sandy desert (yellow clay)
- **Coal** formed where a tropical swamp once existed (black clay)
- **Limestone** formed in a shallow sea (white clay)

STEP 3 Build your model. Starting at the bottom of the table, fill in Rows 1–4 with the information listed above for each rock you chose. (Leave Row 5 blank for now.)

Order of Events	Rock type or event	Depositional environment	Material used
5. Fifth			
4. Fourth			
3. Third			
2. Second			
1. First			

STEP 4 Choose one of these events to model in your set of rock layers. Be sure to add the event to the table in the top row. Use the plastic knife or another color of clay to represent the chosen event.

- **Igneous intrusion:** Magma rose and intruded through some of the rock layers. When it cooled it formed a type of rock called *igneous rock*.

- **Lava flow:** Magma intruded through all rock layers making its way to the surface (where it is then called lava). The lava flowed over the top of the existing rock layers and cooled into a new layer of igneous rock.

- **Fault:** Tectonic plate movements can cause rock to break and move along planes called faults. Rock layers can shift up, down, sideways, or at an angle along *faults*.

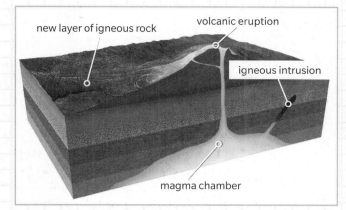

This diagram shows both an igneous intrusion below Earth's surface and a lava flow on Earth's surface.

Analysis

STEP 5 **Language SmArts** Use your table and knowledge of relative age to write a short, informative paragraph that explains how your model represents environmental changes in an area over time.

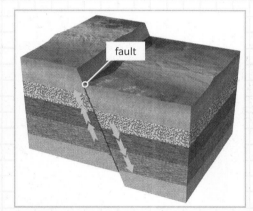

Forces deep within Earth can form a fault where rocks shift up or down.

STEP 6 **Draw** Exchange models with another group. Analyze the other group's model to identify the event and determine the order in which the layers formed. Make a sketch of the model and label it to show the relative ages of the rocks and the event. When you are done, exchange information with the other group to check if you identified the event and sequenced the layers correctly.

Relative Dating

Think about a stack of pancakes on a plate. Even if you don't know exactly what time each pancake was made, you know that the pancake at the bottom of the stack was probably made first, and the pancake on top was probably made last. In other words, you can determine the relative age of each pancake. This is an example of relative dating. **Relative dating** is any method of determining whether something is older or younger than something else.

Relative dating can also be applied to events or processes. In the pancake example, imagine that the stack is sliced in half with a knife. The slicing occurs after the pancakes are stacked on the plate, so it is "younger" than the pancakes themselves. The same logic can be used for sedimentary rock sequences that are disturbed by geologic processes. For example, if a fault or an igneous intrusion cuts across rock layers, scientists assume that the feature is younger than the rocks it cuts across.

Scientists use the relative ages of rocks to compile the rock record. The *rock record* is all of Earth's known rocks and the information they contain. The rock record allows scientists to piece together some of Earth's past environments and events.

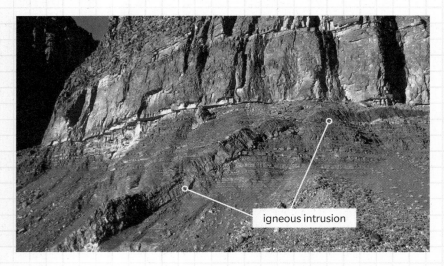

igneous intrusion

8. Magma intruded into these sedimentary rocks, cooled, and formed a diagonal band of igneous rock. The intrusion is older / younger than the sedimentary rocks it cuts through.

Index Fossils

In most cases, fossils are the same age as the rock in which they are found. An *index fossil* is the remains of an organism that was common and widespread but existed for only about 1 million years (or less). Index fossils can help scientists establish the ages of rocks and other fossils. For example, specific ammonite fossils found in Dinosaur Provincial Park serve as index fossils. They are about 75 million years old, which means that the rocks in which they are found, and any other fossils in those rocks, are also likely about 75 million years old.

Organizing all of Earth's known fossils from oldest to youngest shows how life on Earth has changed over time. All of Earth's known fossils and the information they provide are known as the *fossil record*. The fossil record grows as more fossils are discovered.

EVIDENCE NOTEBOOK

9. How can undisturbed sedimentary rock layers and index fossils in Dinosaur Provincial Park provide information about the ages of the park's ancient animals? Record your evidence.

10. This type of trilobite is an index fossil that lived about 440 million years ago. Fossils of the trilobite and the brittle star were found in the same rock layer. What can you infer about these two organisms?

   A. They likely lived at the same time.

   B. They are likely closely related.

   C. They likely lived in different habitats.

   D. They are likely younger than the rock layer.

Unconformities

Some rock layers are missing, forming gaps in the rock record. Such a gap is called an *unconformity*. These gaps can occur when rock layers are eroded or when sediment is not deposited for a period of time. In this way, rock layers are like pages in a book of Earth's history—only some pages were torn out or never written in the first place!

Explore Online

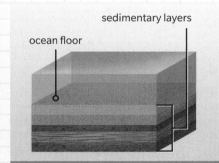

Over millions of years, sediment settles on the sea floor, forming layers.

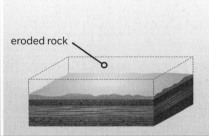

Sea level drops and exposes the sediment. Some layers are eroded.

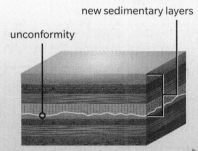

New layers form over the old set of layers—an unconformity now exists.

Determine Relative Age

The positions of rock layers, fossils, faults, and intrusions can be used to determine their relative ages. Scientists use relative dating to piece together Earth's history. Look at the rock layers and features in the diagram.

11. Number the diagram to show the relative ages of the rocks and features. Use the number 1 for the first (oldest) rock layer or feature. Use the number 7 for the most recent (youngest) rock layer or feature.

 Sandstone   Limestone   Igneous intrusion

Shale with fossils   Limestone with fossils   Andesite

Using Absolute and Relative Age

Relative age is described in terms of whether an object is older or younger than other objects. *Absolute age* identifies how old an object is, expressed in units of time. In other words, absolute age is the actual age of something.

12. Discuss How do you think scientists figured out the absolute age of the zircon crystal in the photo?

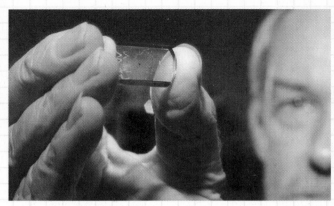

This tiny black speck is a zircon crystal. At about 4.2 billion years old, it is one of the oldest known crystals on Earth. The person holding it is Simon Wilde, who discovered it in Australia in 1984.

13. Write an A next to statements that describe absolute age.
Write an R next to those that describe relative age.

R	I am younger than my cousin.
	I am 14 years old.
	That is the oldest bicycle I've ever seen.

	My cat lived to be 15 years old.
	This coin is the newest in my collection.
	This is the last book in the series.

Absolute Dating

Observing rock layers can tell us about relative age but not absolute age. In the 1950s, technology made it possible to find the absolute ages of some rocks. **Absolute dating** is any method of measuring the actual age of something in years. Absolute dating can be used to find the ages of igneous rocks, which form when molten rock cools and forms crystals. These crystals contain unstable particles that begin to break down, or *decay*, as soon as the crystal forms. Scientists can measure and compare the amounts of unstable and stable particles in the rock, then use the data to calculate when the unstable particles began to decay. This will also tell them when the rock formed.

Rocks contain different types of unstable particles. Each type decays at a specific rate called a *half-life*. For example, unstable potassium decays into argon and has a half-life of 1.3 billion years. This means that it takes 1.3 billion years for half of the potassium to decay into argon. It takes another 1.3 billion years for half of the remaining potassium to decay. This pattern repeats as long as some of the unstable particles remain.

Absolute dating and relative dating are used together to provide a more complete understanding of Earth's history. For example, some of the rock in Dinosaur Provincial Park contains weathered volcanic ash. Absolute dating of the ash indicates that some of the rock layers in the park formed 76 million years ago. Fossils found in the same rock layers must also be 76 million years old.

Geologic Time Scale

Evidence from absolute dating indicates that Earth is nearly 4.6 billion years old. To help make sense of this vast amount of time, scientists use the geologic time scale to organize Earth's history. The geologic time scale divides Earth's history into intervals of time defined by major events or changes on Earth. The largest category of time is the eon, which is further divided into eras, periods, epochs, and ages. Dividing that long period of time into smaller parts makes it easier for scientists to communicate their findings about rocks and fossils.

The Geologic Time Scale

Unlike divisions of time such as days or minutes, the divisions of the geologic time scale are based on events in Earth's geologic history. Some divisions are based on the fossil record.

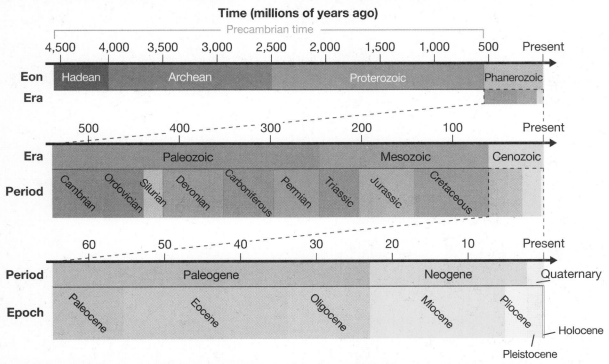

Source: International Commission on Stratigraphy, International Chronostratigraphic Chart, v2016

 Do the Math | Using Models Earth formed about 4.6 billion years ago. Use a football field, which is 100 yards long, to model the 4,600,000,000 years since Earth formed.

14. Using these data, how many years of Earth's history would each yard line on the football field represent?

15. The first modern humans appeared on Earth about 200,000 years ago. Would it be possible to represent that time frame by marking feet on a football field? Explain your answer.

16. Land animal fossils were found in the same layer as the volcanic ash in the park. What does this tell you about the age of these fossils? Record your evidence.

The Absolute Age of Earth

Absolute dating can be used to find the age of Earth, but not by using rocks from Earth. This is because the first rocks that formed on Earth had been eroded, melted, or buried under younger rocks long ago. Therefore, most rocks on Earth are younger than Earth itself—with one exception: meteorites.

Meteorites are small, rocky bodies that have traveled through space and fallen to Earth's surface. The absolute ages of meteorites can be determined. Because Earth formed at the same time as other bodies in our solar system, meteorites should be the same age as Earth. Absolute dating of meteorites and moon rocks suggests that, like these other bodies, Earth is about 4.6 billion years old.

17. Recall the zircon crystal found in Australia. The zircon formed long before the sandstone it was found in. It was part of an igneous rock before it became part of the sandstone. Complete each statement to make it true.

_____ dating was used to determine the age of the sandstone rock compared to the ages of the rocks around it. _____ dating was used to calculate the actual age of the zircon mineral.

Use Relative and Absolute Dating Together

Scientists use both relative and absolute dating to find the ages of rocks and fossils. A field geologist modeled a sequence of rocks to help determine their ages.

18. What can you conclude based on the absolute ages of the igneous rocks given? Check the statement(s) that are true:

_____ The shale with fossils is 175 million years old.

_____ The limestone is between 200 and 175 million years old.

_____ The sandstone must be less than 200 million years old.

_____ The rocks shifted along the fault less than 175 million years ago.

175 million years old

200 million years old

Sandstone	Limestone	Igneous intrusion
Shale with fossils	Limestone with fossils	Andesite

Continue Your Exploration

Name: _____ Date: _____

Check out the path below or go online to choose one of the other paths shown.

Exploring the Ashfall Fossil Beds

- **Exploring Local Geology**
- **Hands-On Labs**
- **Propose Your Own Path**

Go online to choose one of these other paths.

Although most fossils are preserved by sedimentary rock, some are preserved by igneous rock. Look at these fossils of ancient animals from the Ashfall Fossil Beds in Nebraska. The animals were killed after a supervolcano erupted nearly 1,000 miles away, in what is now Idaho. Volcanic ash covered the area, and the animals died from inhaling it. As the ash settled into thick layers around the animals, it cooled and hardened into rock, creating detailed three-dimensional fossils.

These rocks contain fossils of rhinos and horses that died in a volcanic ash flow.

 young adult male rhino "Tusker"

 large three-toed horse "Cormo"

 adult female rhino "Sandy" with baby "Justin"

 rhino calf

rhino calves (possibly twins) "T.L." and "R.G.C."

Continue Your Exploration

The following field notes were recorded in the area:

Date: October 9
Location: Ashfall Fossil Beds State Historical Park, Nebraska
Observations and Notes:

- The fossils in the photo were uncovered in the ash layer.
- Layers above and below the ash layer also contain fossils, as shown in the table.
- The ash layer is as thick as 3 meters (9.8 feet) in some places.
- Absolute dating shows that the ash layer formed 12 million years ago.

Rocks and Fossils from the Ashfall Fossil Beds State Historical Park		
Rock Layers	**Fossils Found**	**Position**
loose sand and gravel	zebras, lemmings, giant camels, muskrats, giant beavers	Top
sandstone	barrel-bodied rhinos, giant land tortoises, camels, rodents, horses	Middle
ash layer		
sandstone		
sandy and silty sedimentary rock	alligators, fish, hornless rhinos, giant salamanders	Bottom

Source: The University of Nebraska State Museum and Nebraska Game and Parks Commission, "Geologic Setting of Ashfall Fossil Beds and Vicinity," 2015

1. The ash layer is igneous rock. Absolute dating shows the ash layer is 12 million years old. What can you infer about the animals found in the ash layer?

2. Use the observations and notes to explain what happened in the area over time.

3. Based on the fossils found in each layer, what changes do you think happened in the area before the ash flow that formed the fossil beds?

4. **Collaborate** Many articles about the Ashfall Fossil Beds are available in magazines and on the Internet. Find several articles. In a group discussion, cite specific evidence that could help you identify the article that provides the most accurate and thorough information. Discuss the evidence with the group.

Can You Explain It?

Name: _____   Date: _____

How can scientists determine when these ancient animals lived?

76 million years ago   75 million years ago   Present day

EVIDENCE NOTEBOOK

Refer to the notes in your Evidence Notebook to help you construct an explanation for how we can determine when these ancient animals lived.

1. State your claim. Make sure your claim fully explains how the ages of the animals shown above were determined.

2. Summarize the evidence you have gathered to support your claim and explain your reasoning.

Checkpoints

Answer the following questions to check your understanding of the lesson.

Use the photo to answer Questions 3 and 4.

3. Which rock layer or feature of the cliff formed most recently?

   A. the thick black rock layer at the top

   B. the fault running through the center

   C. the white rock layer near the bottom

   D. the gray rock layer at the very bottom

4. Which of the following questions could be answered from the information in the photo? Choose all that apply.

   A. Which is the oldest rock layer?

   B. When did the oldest rock layer form?

   C. What are the relative ages of the rocks?

   D. What is the absolute age of the most recent layer?

   E. What year did the fault form?

Use the diagram of undisturbed rock layers and features to answer Questions 5 and 6.

5. Which of the following statements are true? Choose all that apply.

   A. All the fossils are over 175 million years old.

   B. The fault is over 175 million years old.

   C. All the fossils are less than 200 million years old.

   D. The sandstone is over 200 million years old.

   E. The sandstone is 201 million years old.

6. Circle the correct term to complete each statement.

   The igneous intrusion is *younger / older* than the fault.

   The fossils in the shale are from animals that lived *before / after* the animals that formed fossils in the limestone.

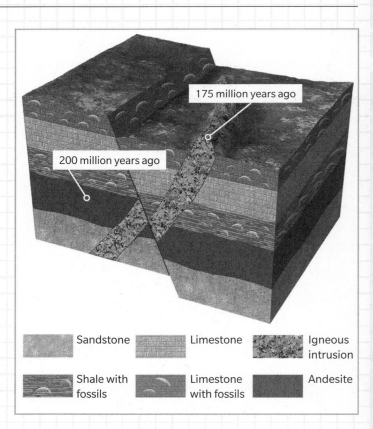

Sandstone

Limestone

Igneous intrusion

Shale with fossils

Limestone with fossils

Andesite

Interactive Review

Complete this interactive study guide to review the lesson.

Layers of sedimentary rock and the fossils they contain help us to understand Earth's history.

A. Summarize how sedimentary rock and fossils form.

Geologists use relative dating to compare the ages of different rock layers and the fossils in those layers.

B. A student makes a sandwich with several layers of bread and cheese. Then the student cuts the sandwich and says it models how a fault cut through rock layers after the rock layers formed. Explain how the example of the sandwich relates to relative dating.

The combination of absolute and relative dating allows scientists to determine the ages of rocks and fossils. Absolute dating provides evidence that helps us estimate the age of Earth.

C. How can scientists find the absolute ages of igneous rocks?

The Geologic Time Scale Organizes Earth's History

This fossil of a tyrannosaur skeleton was found buried in a layer of sandstone, a sedimentary rock.

Explore First

Modeling Earth's History Suppose the entire history of Earth is represented by a 12-month calendar. On what date do you think the first modern humans would appear? What about dinosaurs? Discuss your answers with your classmates.

CAN YOU EXPLAIN IT?

What evidence is used to construct this geologic timeline of Earth's history?

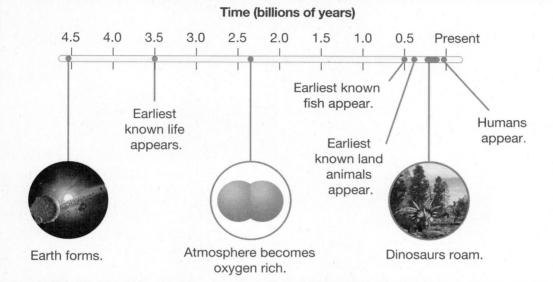

Time (billions of years)

4.5   4.0   3.5   3.0   2.5   2.0   1.5   1.0   0.5   Present

Earliest known fish appear.

Humans appear.

Earliest known life appears.

Earliest known land animals appear.

Earth forms.

Atmosphere becomes oxygen rich.

Dinosaurs roam.

A growing body of evidence shows that the first known life forms appeared at least 3.5 billion years ago. Complex life did not evolve until more than 1 billion years later, and the first humans showed up only 200,000 years ago.

1. Review this geologic timeline of events in Earth's history. What kinds of evidence are used to make timelines like this one?

EVIDENCE NOTEBOOK As you explore the lesson, gather evidence to help you explain what kinds of evidence are used to construct a geologic timeline.

Describing Geologic Change

You have likely changed a lot since you were born. Just imagine all the changes Earth has been through since it formed about 4.6 billion years ago! Geologic processes such as weathering, erosion, and tectonic plate motion constantly reshape Earth. Many landforms you see today—such as rugged mountains and steep canyons—formed from geologic processes over millions of years.

To learn about changes in Earth's past, we can look to the present. Many geologic processes that shape Earth today also shaped Earth in the past. For example, volcanoes erupted, glaciers carved valleys, and sediment was deposited to form sedimentary rock. These processes will continue to shape Earth in the future as well.

2. **Discuss** Analyze the two photos. How long do you think it took the U-shaped valley to form? Explain.

Glaciers are like slow-moving rivers of ice that scrape over land, picking up and moving rock. This glacier has been inching its way down this valley for thousands of years.

This U-shaped valley was shaped by a glacier that flowed through the area in the past.

The Rate of Geologic Change

Most geologic processes change Earth's surface so slowly that you would not notice a difference in your lifetime. But over thousands to millions of years, geologic processes cause major changes to landscapes. For example, weathering and erosion are wearing down the Appalachian Mountains by about six meters (6 m) every million years. Over time, the rugged peaks have become rolling hills. The movement of tectonic plates is another example—they move at a rate of a few centimeters (cm) each year. Yet over millions of years, this motion builds tall mountain ranges and forms entire ocean basins.

Not all geologic change is slow. Some processes can alter large areas or the whole planet within a short period. An example is the meteorite that struck the Yucatan Peninsula in Mexico about 65 million years ago. It sent debris into the atmosphere that blocked sunlight for years and likely contributed to a mass extinction.

The frequency of meteorite impacts, volcanic eruptions, and glacier coverage have varied during different periods of Earth's history. Scientists take this information into account when they reconstruct Earth's geologic past.

3. Geologic change is shown in each photo. Read each description, and then label the images to tell whether you think the change is relatively fast or slow.

For millions of years, two tectonic plates have been pushing up the Himalayan Mountains. The mountains are still growing today at about 1 cm per year.

The Colorado River has been carving a path through the Grand Canyon for at least 5 million years. In some spots, the canyon is over 1,800 m (1.1 miles) deep and continues to get deeper today.

This landslide happened when rocks and soil suddenly slid down the side of this mountain as a result of the force of gravity.

Do the Math
Describe Scales of Time

How long is 1 million years? It helps to think about this in terms of numbers that are more familiar to us. For example, how many human lifetimes are in 1 million years?

STEP 1 Assume the average human lifetime is 80 years. The question asks how many human lifetimes are in 1 million years, so we need to find out how many times 80 divides into 1,000,000. Let h represent the number of human lifetimes.

STEP 2 $h = \dfrac{1,000,000}{80} = 12,500$. There are 12,500 human lifetimes in 1 million years.

---

4. The Himalayan Mountains have been growing slowly for about 50 million years. Using the same method, find out how many human lifetimes have passed since the Himalayan Mountains began to grow.

STEP 1 I need to find out how many times _____ divides into _____.

STEP 2 $h =$

Compiling Evidence of Earth's Past

Scientists analyze Earth's rocks and fossils to piece together Earth's past. Rocks and fossils contain clues about how they formed. They also can tell us about the past conditions or environments in which they formed. Comparing rocks from around a region or around the world allows scientists to organize the timing of events in Earth's history.

These layers of volcanic tuff in California formed as volcanic ash settled and cooled. A section of this volcanic tuff came all the way from an eruption that occurred in Wyoming. The eruption was a supervolcano eruption that spread ash over a large part of the United States.

5. If you wanted to know how the supervolcano eruption 640,000 years ago affected living things and the environment, which layers of rock would you look at?

Rocks Give Clues about Earth's Past

Around the world, geologists collaborate and share information about rocks. The *rock record* is a compilation of all of Earth's known rocks. Major geologic events—such as a supervolcano eruption, an asteroid impact, or tectonic plate movements that form or break up continents—are recorded in the rock record. These events can be used as benchmarks to mark the beginning or ending of specific periods of time. Rocks and fossils can be identified as having existed before or after these events occurred. If the event can be given an absolute date, it can provide evidence for the ages of the rocks and fossils that surround it in the rock record.

Long ago, a supervolcano eruption happened in what is now Yellowstone National Park in Wyoming. The cooling ash formed deposits of rock, called volcanic tuff, of varying thicknesses over much of North America. Absolute dating indicates that the tuff is 640,000 years old. The information from all of the known tuff deposits, along with the rocks above and below it, can be compiled to give a big-picture view of what North America was like before, during, and after the eruption.

6. The rocks in the first row of photos give clues about how they formed. The photos in the second row show different environments. Match the rocks in the first row to the type of environment they likely formed in by writing A, B, or C in the correct box.

This dark layer of rock is called *coal*. Coal formation begins in swamp environments, and the entire process takes millions of years.

Rocks are worn down as they are tumbled along river bottoms. Over time, they can be cemented together to form a new rock called *conglomerate*.

This landscape is covered by an igneous rock called *basalt*. The basalt formed as lava flowed over the land and cooled into rock.

A

B

C

Fossils Give Clues about Earth's Past

Like the rocks they are found in, fossils also give clues about Earth's past environments. For example, the teeth of a 10-meter-long shark were found in a rock layer in Kansas and determined to be about 89 million years old. This indicates that a sea covered this part of Kansas about 89 million years ago.

Like major geologic events, fossils can be used to determine relative ages of surrounding rocks and as benchmarks to organize Earth's history. The *fossil record* is a compilation of all of Earth's known fossils and the information they provide about Earth's history. To get an idea of how the fossil record was compiled, imagine a sequence of rock layers, each containing distinctly different fossils. In a different location, researchers find another sequence of fossils that is identical to all or part of the first sequence. As sequences of matching fossils are correlated from around the world, scientists can apply the principles of relative dating to determine how life has changed over time. For example, rock layers that contain only extinct organisms are generally older than rock layers that contain fossils of organisms that still exist today. Appearances of new organisms or disappearances of previously existing organisms in the fossil record can also be related to geologic or environmental changes on Earth.

 EVIDENCE NOTEBOOK

7. What types of evidence can major geologic events and changes in organisms provide to help construct a timeline of Earth's history? Record your evidence.

Analysis of Rock Layers

A field geologist conducted a study of an undisturbed sequence of rocks. Explore her sketch, photos, and research notes.

8. Help the geologist complete her analysis to describe the geologic history of this location.

The oldest rock is shale and the youngest is the igneous rock. Evidence: _____

_____

_____

This igneous rock formed as ongoing eruptions covered the area with lava. Absolute dating shows this igneous rock ranges from 50–47 million years old.

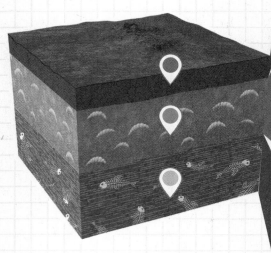

This fossilized sea turtle is found in sandstone along with other fossils of organisms that lived in a shallow sea. This fossil shows similarities to some living sea turtles. The oldest known sea turtle fossil is about 120 million years old.

From 450 to 120 million years ago, no rock was deposited, erosion removed rocks that were deposited, or both. Evidence: _____

_____

The area was covered by a shallow sea some time between 120 and 50 million years ago. Evidence: _____

_____

_____

The brittle stars lived long before the sea turtle lived. Evidence: _____

_____

_____

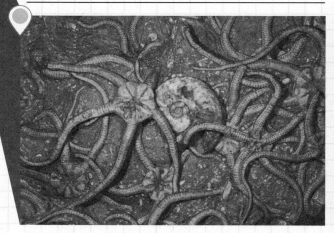

This shale formed in a deep sea and contains fossils of extinct brittle stars. Information from the fossil record indicates that they are between 451 and 443 million years old.

Correlate Rock Sequences

A team of geologists sketched these three different undisturbed rock sequences in a region. They worked together to build this diagram that correlates the fossils from each sequence.

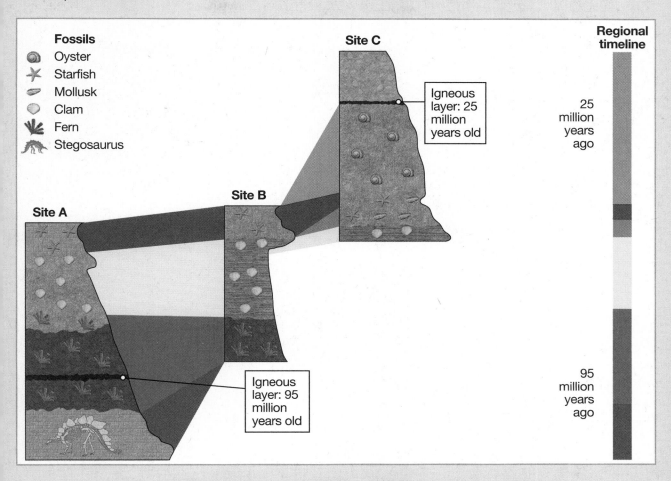

9. Fossils of extinct organisms, such as this *Stegosaurus*, are generally _younger / older_ than fossils that resemble living organisms. Assuming that the fossils formed at the same time as the rocks they are found in, the _oyster / Stegosaurus_ fossils are the oldest fossils shown here. The igneous layer indicates that *Stegosaurus* lived _before / after_ 95 million years ago.

10. Use the information about fossils, igneous layers, and rock types to divide the regional timeline into different sections of your choosing. Make up a name for each section and write it next to the timeline. Use your updated timeline to describe a brief history of life in the area.

_____

_____

_____

_____

_____

_____

Organizing Earth's History

How do the rock and fossil records provide evidence of change over time? Using these records, scientists can construct timelines that describe Earth's history. A geologic timeline can be detailed or general. Some timelines show geologic events, such as ice ages and periods of volcanic activity. Others focus on how life has changed throughout Earth's history.

This insect trapped in 45-million-year-old amber is part of the fossil record.

11. **Draw** A lot has happened on Earth over the course of 4.6 billion years. Create a timeline that shows at least four events or items from Earth's past. Can you make your timeline to scale? Add your own events, or choose from the list.

   • Oldest mineral—4 billion years old

   • First flowering plants appear—145 million years ago

   • Dinosaurs become extinct—65 million years ago

   • Breakup of the super-continent Pangaea—220 million years ago

Earth has existed for about 4.6 billion years. The **geologic time scale** is used to organize Earth's long history into manageable parts. The geologic time scale is continually updated as new rock and fossil evidence is discovered.

The further we go back in time, the less rock and fossil information we have. This is because Earth's oldest rocks have undergone great changes over the past few billion years. Many of the oldest rocks have either been eroded, buried deep below the surface, or melted in Earth's hot interior.

Construct a Timeline

Use absolute and relative dating to construct a timeline of different events from your life and the lives of others in a group.

MATERIALS
- markers
- masking tape
- personal items (optional)
- sticky notes

Procedure and Analysis

STEP 1 Gather two objects that represent two events in your life. Label one object with an absolute date. For example, you may have a painting you did when you were younger labeled "Painting of tree, March 2017." Label the second object with a relative date that is based on the absolute date of the first object. For example, your second object might be a book recently given to you, labeled "Book from friend, after March 2017."

STEP 2 In your group, display your labeled objects in a central area. Collaborate with your classmates to try to arrange everything from oldest to most recent. You may want to make a chart to help you organize the events.

STEP 3 Identify any gaps or difficulties you have in your timeline, particularly with events that have relative dates. Ask questions about one another's events and use the answers to finalize the timeline.

STEP 4 What methods did you use to sequence the events? Were you able to arrange all the events in correct chronological order? Why or why not?

STEP 5 How is this activity related to construction of the geologic time scale?

STEP 6 **Engineer It** Think about very slow geologic events that occur over time, such as glacial periods and mountain building. To study these events, scientists need to model them at observable time scales. Explain steps that scientists should take to make a scale model of such an event.

The Geologic Time Scale

Earth's entire history is divided into four major eons, shown in the top row of the diagram. In the second row, the three eras within the Phanerozoic Eon are shown. Within each era are several periods, and within each period are even smaller divisions of time called epochs. Currently, we live in the Holocene Epoch of the Quaternary Period, which is part of the Cenozoic Era and the Phanerozoic Eon.

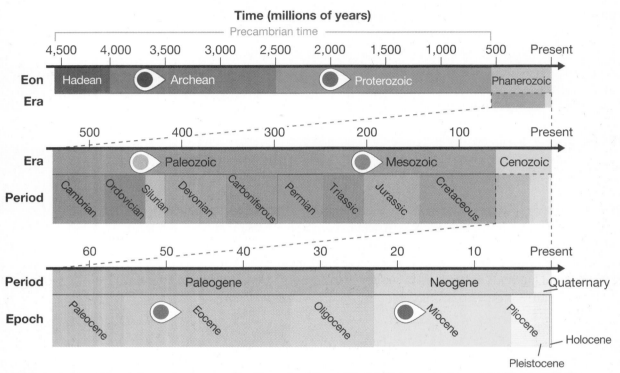

Source: International Commission on Stratigraphy, International Chronostratigraphic Chart, v2016

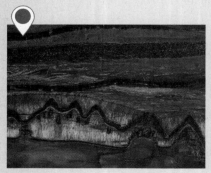

Over 3 billion years ago, photosynthetic organisms released oxygen into Earth's shallow iron-rich seas. Scientists think that oxygen combined with iron to form the red bands in this rock.

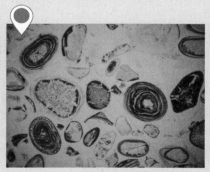

These photosynthetic sea creatures are about 2 billion years old. After all the iron in the seas was used up to form rock, oxygen released by these organisms was added to the air.

Crinoids are animals that flourished during the Paleozoic Era. These creatures lived anchored to the ocean floor. There are some species of crinoids that still exist today.

Divisions in Geologic Time

The geologic time scale is broken up into the following divisions of time: eons, eras, periods, and epochs. Divisions in the geologic time scale are not equal. This is because the divisions are based on major events and changes in Earth's history, such as extinctions.

Look at the clock-shaped diagram of geologic time. If Earth's history were squeezed into 12 hours, Precambrian time would take up most of that time. Precambrian time began around the time Earth formed and lasted for about 4 billion years. That is almost 90 percent of Earth's 4.6-billion-year history!

 12. Language SmArts How do divisions in the geologic time scale differ from the way we organize time using a clock? What are the reasons for these differences?

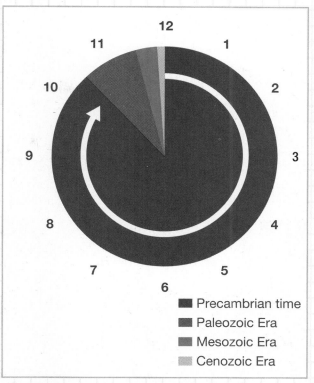

- ■ Precambrian time
- ■ Paleozoic Era
- ■ Mesozoic Era
- ■ Cenozoic Era

If all of Earth's history were squeezed into one 12-hour period, Precambrian time would end at about 10:30.

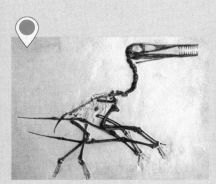

Pterodactylus was a flying meat-eating reptile. It lived during the Jurassic Period alongside dinosaurs. The fossil record shows that these animals went extinct at the end of the Cretaceous Period.

This fossil is of a horse-like mammal from the Paleogene Period. During this time, mammals diversified, leading scientists to call this the "Age of Mammals." The first marine mammals also appeared during this time.

This skull is from one of the earliest members of the genus *Homo*. Modern humans, or *Homo sapiens*, evolved about 200,000 years ago.

13. How can scientists use the rock and fossil records to organize Earth's history into a single timeline? Record your evidence.

Language SmArts
Explain Evidence

Fossils and rocks provide evidence of what Earth was like in the past.

A fossilized trilobite, an organism that once roamed Earth's oceans. Trilobites went extinct about 250 million years ago.

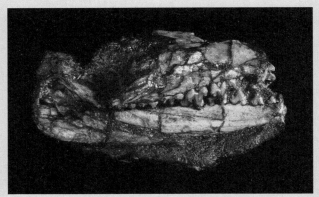

The skull of *Megazostrodon*, one of the first mammals to appear in the fossil record, about 200 million years ago.

Putorana Plateau in Siberia is made up of several layers of igneous rock deposited by volcanic eruptions in the area about 250 million years ago. Scientists think this may have contributed to the extinction of most life on Earth.

14. In your own words, describe how these fossils and rocks could be used as evidence to construct an explanation for an event that changed life on Earth.

_____
_____
_____
_____
_____
_____

Continue Your Exploration

Name: _____ Date: _____

Check out the path below or go online to choose one of the other paths shown.

Careers in Science

- **Exploring the Great Dying**
- **Hands-On Labs** 🖐
- **Propose Your Own Path**

Go online to choose one of these other paths.

Paleoartist

If you have ever seen a reconstruction of a dinosaur skeleton at a museum, you know how impressive these ancient creatures were. From rocks, fossils, and reconstructed skeletons, scientists can tell certain things about an extinct animal's appearance, how it moved, and where it lived. For example, fossil footprints can show how an animal walked. The rock that a fossil is found in gives clues about the past environment.

Paleoart is a profession that combines art and science. Paleoartists help us visualize extinct animals and their environments by creating art, including drawings, three-dimensional models, and digital images. Paleoartists work closely with scientists to make their art as accurate as possible—some paleoartists are even scientists themselves.

This is paleoart of a *Gigantoraptor* on its nest by artist Mohamad Haghani. This dinosaur lived during the Cretaceous Period.

Continue Your Exploration

A scientist exploring in the desert found fossil bones of a sheep-sized dinosaur. The bones were reconstructed as shown in this photo. Analysis of the fossil confirmed that the dinosaur was a land reptile that walked on four legs. The shape of its beak and jaw suggests that it was a plant eater. The fossil was found in a sandstone layer that was deposited along the shoreline of a shallow sea. The same sandstone rock in the area contained fossils of ferns and trees.

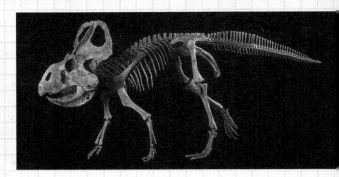

1. What evidence describes this dinosaur and its past environment?

2. **Draw** Use the evidence and the photo to help you draw the dinosaur in its past environment.

3. Fossil evidence does not tell paleoartists everything. For example, the color and skin texture of ancient animals are often unknown. However, paleoartists read scientific papers and study animals alive today to make inferences about these things. What aspects of your drawing are based on inferences (are not based on direct evidence)?

4. **Collaborate** Compare your paleoart with a classmate's. Discuss why there might be differences between your paleoart and your classmate's paleoart.

Can You Explain It?

Name: _____ **Date:** _____

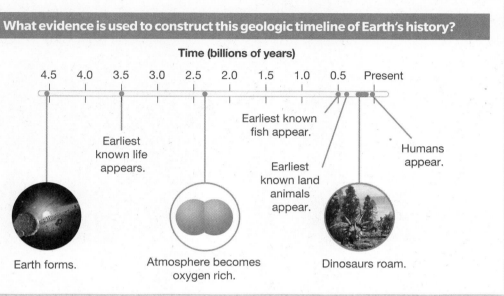

What evidence is used to construct this geologic timeline of Earth's history?

Time (billions of years)

4.5 4.0 3.5 3.0 2.5 2.0 1.5 1.0 0.5 Present

Earliest known
fish appear.

Earliest
known life
appears.

Humans
appear.

Earliest
known land
animals
appear.

Earth forms.

Atmosphere becomes
oxygen rich.

Dinosaurs roam.

EVIDENCE NOTEBOOK

Refer to the notes in your Evidence Notebook to help you explain what kinds of evidence are used to construct a geologic timeline.

1. State your claim. Make sure your claim fully explains what evidence is used to construct timelines of Earth's history.

2. Summarize the evidence you have gathered to support your claim and explain your reasoning.

Checkpoints

Answer the following questions to check your understanding of the lesson.

Use the diagram to answer Question 3.

3. What does this diagram tell you about these different time periods? Choose all that apply.

   A. the actual length of time for each one

   B. the order in which they occurred

   C. the length of time they lasted in relation to each other

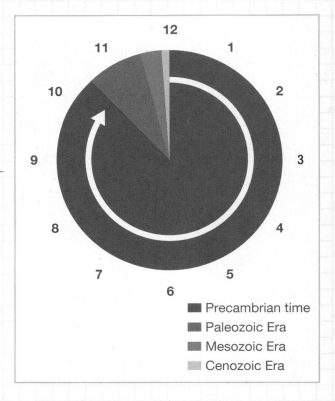

Precambrian time
Paleozoic Era
Mesozoic Era
Cenozoic Era

4. Which statements correctly describe the geologic time scale? Choose all that apply.

   A. It is divided into equal periods of time.

   B. It is divided based on evidence in the fossil record.

   C. Some events are arranged according to relative dates.

   D. It is divided based on evidence in the rock record.

Use the photo to answer Questions 5 and 6.

5. The rock layers in this photo were laid down horizontally and are undisturbed. Therefore, you can conclude that the white layer is older / younger than the red layer, and that the thick brown layer is the oldest / youngest of the layers shown here.

6. An extremely thin layer of volcanic ash is found between the white layer on top and the thin red layer in the middle. Absolute dating showed that the ash is about 43 million years old. What can you conclude based on this information? Choose all that apply.

   A. The top layer is also volcanic.

   B. The middle layer is also about 43 million years old.

   C. The top layer is younger than 43 million years old.

   D. The bottom layer is older than 43 million years old.

Interactive Review

Complete this section to review the main concepts of the lesson.

Scientists study current geologic processes to learn about past processes such as tectonic plate motion, weathering, erosion, and deposition.

A. How is it possible to look at geologic processes that shape Earth today to learn about the past?

Scientists use the rock record and the fossil record as evidence for events and conditions in Earth's past.

B. What can you infer from the rock record and the fossil record? Give two specific examples of evidence and how that evidence helps scientists organize geologic time.

The geologic time scale is used to organize Earth's long history.

C. Why do you think scientists need to organize Earth's history into a time scale?

Fossils Are Evidence of Changes in Life Over Time

Titanis walleri, or Waller's terror bird, was flightless. It could grow up to 1.8 m (5.9 feet) tall, about the same height as an adult human. It lived from about 5 to 2 million years ago.

Explore First

Modeling Fossil Formation   Use clay and a few common objects to model fossil formation. Press each item into a thick piece of clay to make a detailed impression. Remove the objects and exchange impressions with another group. What can you learn about the objects by studying their impressions?

Go online to view the digital version of the Hands-On Lab for this lesson and to download additional lab resources.

CAN YOU EXPLAIN IT?

What can explain the presence of a rock layer with no fossils between rock layers with different types of fossils?

fossils found

no fossils found

fossils found

Major changes to populations of organisms and environments happened in the past. Such events are recorded in rock layers as part of the fossil record.

1. What is needed for a fossil to form? Select all that apply.

A. The organism must first get stuck in rock.

B. The soft tissue of the dead organism must be eaten by scavengers before the bones can be preserved.

C. The tracks or burrows of an organism must be filled with sediments before they are disturbed.

D. The organism's body must be covered by sediment or another substance before its body decays.

2. What are some reasons that fossils may not form?

EVIDENCE NOTEBOOK As you explore the lesson, gather evidence to help explain why fossils might be absent from one layer but not surrounding layers.

Analyzing Evidence about the History of Life

Only a small percentage of the organisms that ever lived fossilized. Yet, these fossils help scientists learn about how life on Earth changed over time. Fossils show where and when certain extinct organisms lived. They also show patterns in how the body plans of organisms changed over time. Fossils can provide information about past environments. They can even give clues to how extinct species interacted. The fossil record also shows patterns in how species appeared and disappeared throughout Earth's history.

Glyptodonts were about the size of a small car. They ate plants and lived among early humans before the Ice Age.

The insect-eating armadillo shares many features with its extinct relative, the glyptodont. However, it is much smaller.

3. Compare the armadillo to the glyptodont (GLIP•tuh•dahnt). What similarities provide evidence that they might be related?

Evidence of Earliest Life Forms

Charles Walcott was an American paleontologist who, in 1909, discovered many well-preserved fossils of ancient sea organisms near Mount Burgess, Canada. The fossils were preserved in layers of shale left by an ancient ocean. The soft tissues of many of the fossilized organisms in the Burgess Shale were preserved in great detail.

Scientists used a method called radiometric dating to find the absolute age of nearby igneous rock layers. These layers contain a type of potassium that changes into argon at a constant rate. Scientists measure how much potassium in the rock has changed to argon. From this measurement, they can determine when the igneous rock formed. After finding the age of the igneous rock, they used relative dating to determine that the Burgess Shale fossils are over 500 million years old. This seems quite old. But, the earliest evidence for life dates back about 3.8 *billion* years! The earliest organisms were single cells, which rarely formed fossils. Evidence of these early cells was found in rock samples with high levels of a type of carbon found only in living things.

Traces of Carbon from Cells

There are different types of carbon atoms, but living organisms use only one of these types. Scientists detected high levels of this type of carbon in ancient rock. Fossilized cells were not found in this rock, but based on this chemical evidence of life, the scientists concluded that there was life on Earth at the time this ancient rock formed, 3.8 billion years ago. The scientists' reasoning is an example of an *inference*, or the use of evidence to draw conclusions when direct observation of a process or event is not possible. These rocks contain the earliest known evidence of life on Earth.

Many types of scientists work together to collect evidence of ancient life. Chemists isolate certain chemicals from rock samples to analyze them. Biologists study how living things use chemicals in their bodies. Geologists determine the age of rocks and what Earth conditions may have caused them to form. Paleontologists find and study fossils.

The ratio of different types of carbon in these 3.8-billion-year-old rocks in Greenland is interpreted as evidence of life on Earth at the time the rocks formed.

Fossil Evidence

The earliest fossilized cells scientists have found are about 3.5 billion years old. The fossils are of a type of *cyanobacteria*, a single-celled life form that makes its own food by photosynthesis. In Greek, *cyano-* means "blue." The bacteria left traces of the blue-green pigment protein that gives them their name. The cyanobacteria also left behind stromatolite formations. *Stromatolites* are layered mounds, columns, or sheets of calcium-rich sedimentary rock. They are made of layers of bacteria and sediment.

Evidence of Ancient Cellular Life

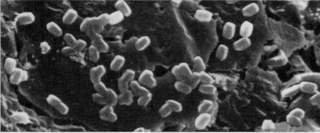

Ancient Cyanobacteria Fossils of bacteria similar to these were found in ancient stromatolites from western Australia. The stromatolites were about 3.5 billion years old. Cyanobacteria are a type of bacteria that capture the energy of sunlight and release oxygen during photosynthesis. They helped create an oxygen-rich atmosphere on ancient Earth.

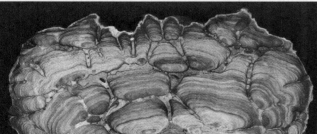

Stromatolite Growth Patterns Notice the light and dark layers of this stromatolite. They are caused by the growth patterns of cyanobacteria that were on Earth when each layer was formed. The bacteria release white-colored calcium compounds that mix with soil or sand deposits. Over time, the layers harden into rock.

Modern Stromatolites These stromatolites line the sea floor of Shark Bay in Western Australia. They are usually columns or domes because the cyanobacteria that form them group together in mat-like sheets. New groups form mats on top of the sediment deposits trapped by older groups.

4. Do the Math Scientists estimate that Earth is about 4.6 billion years old. The fossil record shows the first chemical evidence of life around 3.8 billion years ago. What percentage of Earth's history was without life? Write a formula for the calculation using variables you define. Then use your formula to find the answer.

5. Think about the process of identifying the age of the earliest fossils. How does it show how scientists use evidence and logic to answer scientific questions?

Evidence of Change Over Time

For more than 2 billion years, only single-celled life existed on Earth. That changed about 540 million years ago, during the Cambrian Period. Scientists found a large increase in the number and types of fossils in rock layers that formed during this time. Because of this increase, that time period is often called the *Cambrian explosion*. Cambrian organisms looked very different from living things today. Many Cambrian species, such as *Marrella*, were arthropods. *Arthropods* are a group of invertebrate animals that have segmented bodies. Cambrian arthropods are now extinct, but other arthropods, such as ants and lobsters, exist today.

Marrella is the most common fossil found in the Burgess Shale.

Many scientists think the Cambrian explosion happened in part because of an increase in oxygen levels in the air from cyanobacteria and new interactions among organisms. Scientists also infer that a rise of predators on Earth may have led to a greater diversity of life forms. The fossil record shows that many Cambrian animals had hard outer shells or spiny structures, which could protect the animals from predators. Over many generations, populations may have developed these and other characteristics in response to the activity of predators. The fossil record of the Cambrian explosion gives scientists a way to investigate how life changes over time.

6. What evidence from the fossil record supports the observation that life changes over time? Select all that apply.
   A. more fossils of the same species found in several rock layers
   B. increased numbers of fossils of different species found in younger rock layers
   C. several rock layers that do not contain fossils
   D. fossils of distant relatives of a modern species found in ancient rock layers

EVIDENCE NOTEBOOK

7. What does a rock layer with very few fossils suggest about conditions in that region when the rock layer formed? Record your evidence.

Increases in the Complexity of Fossils

Scientists find that more recent rock layers contain fossils that have more complex bodies and physical features than earlier fossils. Multicellular organisms first appeared in the fossil record more than 600 million years ago (mya). Jawless fish appeared in the fossil record about 500 mya. Fish with jaws appeared nearly 400 mya. Later rock layers include fossils of amphibians and then reptiles and mammals. Birds appeared more recently. This evidence suggests that new physical features such as feet and lungs enabled organisms to survive in more diverse habitats. Populations in different habitats became more different from each other over many generations.

Fossils from organisms with simpler body plans are found alongside more complex fossils in younger rock layers. This suggests that while life changes over time on Earth, not all populations change in the same ways or at the same rate. For example, modern bacteria do not appear to be more complex than bacteria found in ancient rock layers.

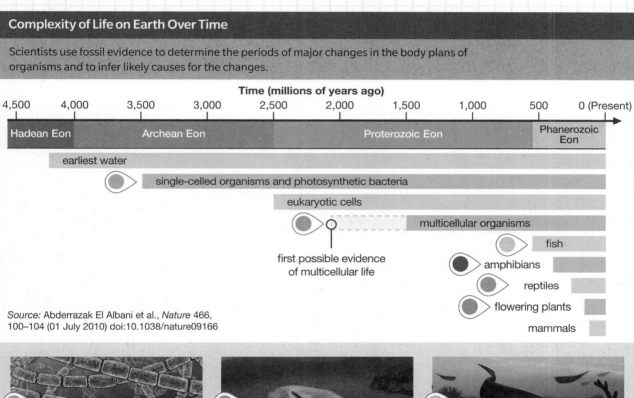

Complexity of Life on Earth Over Time

Scientists use fossil evidence to determine the periods of major changes in the body plans of organisms and to infer likely causes for the changes.

Time (millions of years ago)

4,500 4,000 3,500 3,000 2,500 2,000 1,500 1,000 500 0 (Present)

Hadean Eon | Archean Eon | Proterozoic Eon | Phanerozoic Eon

earliest water

single-celled organisms and photosynthetic bacteria

eukaryotic cells

first possible evidence of multicellular life

multicellular organisms

fish

amphibians

reptiles

flowering plants

mammals

Source: Abderrazak El Albani et al., *Nature* 466, 100–104 (01 July 2010) doi:10.1038/nature09166

The earliest life forms were single cells. These cells could perform only the most basic life functions.

The *Dickinsonia* genus included some of the first complex multicellular organisms, which lived about 600 mya.

Metaspriggina, a genus of the earliest fish, lived about 505 mya. They had gills, worm-like bodies, and large eyes.

Members of the *Cacops* genus lived about 280 mya. They evolved from fish with bony fins and lung-like organs.

The *Captorhinus* genus, the first reptiles to live on land, date back to 300 mya. They were similar to lizards.

Seed plants of the *Archaeosperma* genus lived about 375 mya. They gave rise to flowering plants 160 mya.

Transitional Fossils

Based on evidence from the fossil record, scientists conclude that life began in the oceans. Early fish-like organisms gave rise to fish, which gave rise to the ancestor common to amphibians. To determine how changes like these occur in nature, scientists look for *transitional fossils*. These are fossils of organisms that have body structures that are found both in an ancestral species and in its descendants. For example, when scientists investigated the origins of amphibians, they hypothesized that there might have been an organism that had traits of both fish and amphibians. This hypothesis was supported with the discovery of a fossil called *Tiktaalik*. *Tiktaalik* lived in the water. It had bones in its fins that were very similar to the wrist and foot bones of amphibians.

Fossil Evidence of the Transition from Water to Land

Tiktaalik is a transitional fossil in the evolutionary progression from fish to amphibians. It has characteristics of both fish and amphibians.

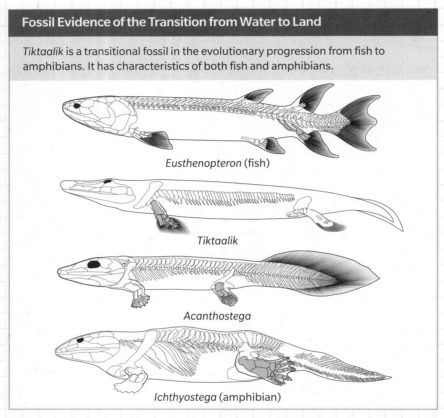

Eusthenopteron (fish)

Tiktaalik

Acanthostega

Ichthyostega (amphibian)

8. Over a period of time in the past, the bones in the fins of a population of fish became larger and longer. The bones became able to support the weight of the organisms when they were out of water. This change happened over many generations. What other changes over time would be needed for fish to live out of the water?

9. The shape (form) of an anatomical structure often enables an organism to perform particular a task (function). What do the forms of the highlighted limbs in the illustration tell you about their functions in each animal?

Infer How Features Changed Over Time

Whales swim and live in the ocean. Yet, they are mammals. They have traits similar to those of mammals that live on land. They give birth to live young, feed their young with milk, and have hair. Evidence from the fossil record supports the theory that the ancestors of whales lived on land before they lived in water. Over time, several body structures, such as the skull, hips, and legs, changed. These changes made the structures better adapted to swimming than walking.

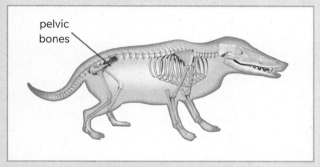

pelvic bones

Pakicetus inachus lived around 50 million years ago.

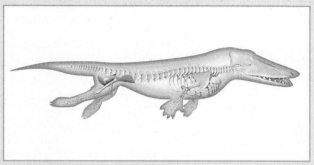

Ambulocetus natans lived 50–45 million years ago.

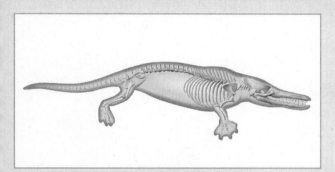

Kutchicetus minimus lived 46–43 million years ago.

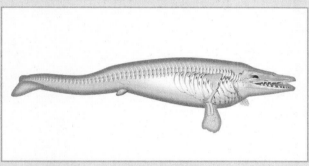

Dorudon atrox lived 40–34 million years ago.

10. Hind legs are connected to pelvic bones, which are important for walking. Modern whales have relatively small pelvic bones. How did the pelvic bones of whales' ancestors change over time?

_____

_____

_____

_____

_____

_____

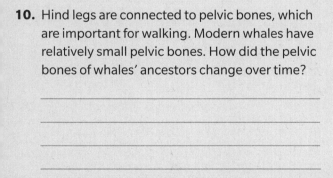

pelvic bones

The modern bowhead whale is a living species that has been on Earth for 35 million years.

11. The form of a body structure is related to its function. Given this, how can you tell that *Pakicetus inachus* most likely lived on land and that *Dorudon atrox* lived in water?

_____

_____

_____

Analyzing Patterns in the Numbers of Life Forms Over Time

The fossil record shows changes in species over time. It also documents **extinctions**, in which all members of a species die out. When a species becomes extinct, its fossils no longer occur in the fossil record. Scientists observe that the loss of species from the fossil record seems to happen at a regular rate, often called the *background rate* of extinction. But there have been periods in Earth's history when the rate of extinction was very high.

Identifying Extinction Events in the Fossil Record

Geologic time periods are identified by major changes in the fossil record. The side of this cliff in Palo Duro Canyon State Park in Texas includes the Permian-Triassic (P-T) extinction boundary. The P-T mass extinction happened about 248 million years ago.

Coelophysis fossils appear after the P-T extinction. They were a genus of small, meat-eating dinosaurs.

Trilobite fossils are found in the fossil record before the P-T extinction. They are not found afterward.

12. Study the rock and fossil images. What is one inference you can make about when the organisms shown lived? Explain your reasoning.

Extinction

The fossil record shows an extinction when a species is no longer found in sedimentary rock layers. For example, trilobites were once very common marine arthropods. They are not present in the fossil record after the Permian-Triassic extinction, which indicates that trilobites became extinct.

A *mass extinction* happens when whole groups of related species die out at about the same time. Mass extinctions appear to be caused by large changes to the environment. Some of these changes, such as volcanic eruptions or asteroid impacts with Earth, are natural, while others, such as climate change or habitat destruction, may be related to human activity. After a mass extinction, surviving species have many new opportunities to use ecosystem resources. They then thrive and change over time. The numbers of new species in the fossil record after a mass extinction increase over time.

The Five Mass Extinction Events on Earth

Extinction event	Proposed cause(s)	Organisms affected	A type of animal that went extinct
Ordovician-Silurian, 443 million years ago	Sea-level drop and climate change caused by formation of glaciers after rapid shifts in tectonic plates	Up to 85% of all species; 45%–60% of families of marine organisms died out	*Orthoceras*
Late Devonian, 354 million years ago	Possibly a large comet strike; possible decrease in global temperatures due to dust and debris from comet strike; drop in sea levels	70%–80% of all species; marine life affected more than freshwater and land organisms	*Dunkleosteus*
Permian-Triassic, 248 million years ago	Volcanic eruptions, release of methane from the sea floor; low oxygen levels in oceans; drop in sea levels	Largest extinction; over 95% of marine species and 70% of land species died out, including all trilobites and many insect species	*Dimetrodon*
Triassic-Jurassic, 200 million years ago	Poorly understood; possibly an extreme decrease in sea level and lower oxygen levels in oceans	About 76% of all species disappeared; end of mammal-like reptiles, leaving mainly dinosaurs	*Typothorax*
Cretaceous-Tertiary, 65 million years ago	Volcanic eruptions and climate cooling; drop in sea levels; large asteroid or comet strike	About 70% of all species died, including non-avian dinosaurs; mainly turtles, small reptiles, birds, and mammals survived	*Quetzalcoatlus*

13. Mass extinctions are caused by global / regional environmental changes. During a mass extinction event, biodiversity in the fossil record increases / decreases.

Do the Math
Analyze Extinction Data

Scientists compare rock layers before and after a mass extinction to estimate the number of affected species. They make estimates from several rock layer samples. Then they compare the loss of species to the normal rate of extinction that happens as life changes over time. This allows scientists to estimate the percentage of species on Earth affected by a mass extinction. The number of extinctions over time can be graphed. These graphs show a relatively constant extinction rate, broken up by large changes in the number of families of organisms lost during mass extinction events.

14. Describe the trends you see in each graph. What is the relationship between mass extinctions and biodiversity over time?

15. Does the top graph provide evidence that extinctions are a normal part of Earth's history? Explain your reasoning.

16. Mass extinctions *do / do not* cause permanent reductions in biodiversity on Earth. After each extinction event, the number of families *increases / decreases* rapidly over time.

Extinction Rate Over Time

The fossil record shows five mass extinctions. During each one, more than half of Earth's species went extinct.

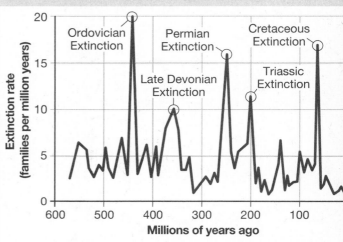

Credit: Adapted from www.biointeractive.org. Copyright © 2016 by Howard Hughes Medical Institute. Reprinted by permission of Howard Hughes Medical Institute. All rights reserved.

Diversity of Marine Organisms Over Time

Each mass extinction greatly reduced biodiversity. Yet, the species that remained expanded and diverged over time.

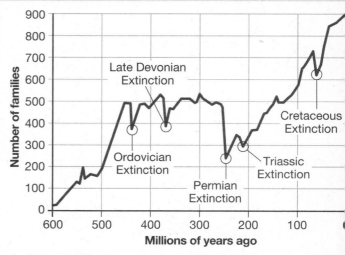

Credit: Adapted from "A kinetic model of Phanerozoic taxonomic diversity" by J. John Sepkoski, from *Paleobiology* 10(2), 246-267. Reproduced with permission.

Patterns in Extinction and Biodiversity Data

Scientists want to find the causes of mass extinctions. To do this, they analyze rock layers before, during, and after an extinction event. For example, when studying the Cretaceous-Paleogene, or K-Pg, mass extinction, scientists looked at the rock layers laid down at the beginning of this extinction. They discovered unusual amounts of a metal called *iridium* in one rock layer in many different places of Earth. Iridium is rare on Earth, but it is common in asteroids. They also discovered tiny glass formations

The *Alphadon* was a small mammal that survived the K-Pg extinction. It likely did so by burrowing underground to avoid the dangerous conditions.

that are often found near craters caused by meteorite impacts. The high temperature caused by the impact melts sand. Glass spheres and other shapes form from the melted sand. Scientists used this evidence to infer that a very large meteorite struck Earth and caused large-scale changes to Earth's environment. Large animal species were affected the most. Nearly all dinosaurs disappeared from the fossil record at this time. Fossil evidence shows that small mammals that could burrow to avoid the hot temperatures that resulted from the impact survived. It also shows that surviving species spread and diversified. Mass extinctions such as this are followed by periods of rapid growth in Earth's biodiversity.

17. Observe the patterns in plant diversity shown in the graph. How might species of flowering plants have survived the K-Pg extinction?

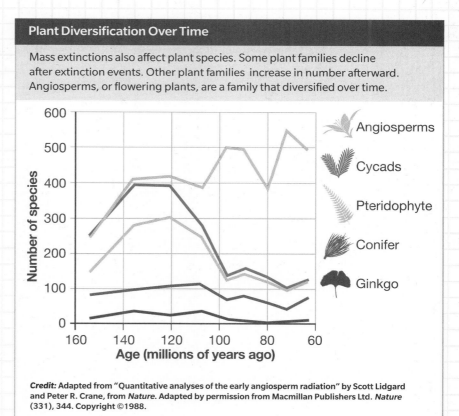

Plant Diversification Over Time

Mass extinctions also affect plant species. Some plant families decline after extinction events. Other plant families increase in number afterward. Angiosperms, or flowering plants, are a family that diversified over time.

Credit: Adapted from "Quantitative analyses of the early angiosperm radiation" by Scott Lidgard and Peter R. Crane, from *Nature*. Adapted by permission from Macmillan Publishers Ltd. *Nature* (331), 344. Copyright ©1988.

Hands-On Lab
Model Analysis of the Fossil Record

Analyze fossil data to identify evidence of extinction and the appearance of new species over time.

Scientists compare fossil evidence from different places on Earth. They observe certain fossil types in the same rock layers across multiple locations. In some layers, they observe the disappearance of certain fossil types. In some layers, they observe the appearance of new fossil types. By determining the relative age of rock layers that contain fossils, scientists can identify these patterns of appearance and disappearance in the fossil record.

MATERIALS
- colored pencils
- scissors

Procedure

STEP 1 On a separate sheet of paper, copy the *Sedimentary Rock Layers from Four Locations* shown on the next page. Be sure to include the symbols that represent different types of fossils. Cut out the rock sequence from each location. Then line them up so that rock layers with similar compositions are side by side.

STEP 2 Analyze the fossil types found in different layers. Identify the species that appear to have gone extinct based on these fossil data.

STEP 3 Complete the table by drawing the symbols of three different fossils.

Fossil from oldest layer	Fossil from youngest layer	Fossil species that goes extinct

Analysis

STEP 4 What patterns in the rock layer fossils helped you identify an extinction?

STEP 5 Why is it necessary to see a similar pattern of change in fossils from several places in order to conclude that an extinction happened?

STEP 6 Analyze the fossil types found in the youngest rock layer. Which of these fossil species appeared first in the fossil record? Which one appeared more recently? How do you know?

Sedimentary Rock Layers from Four Locations

The different colors represent different types of sedimentary rock. The symbols within the rock layers represent different types of fossils.

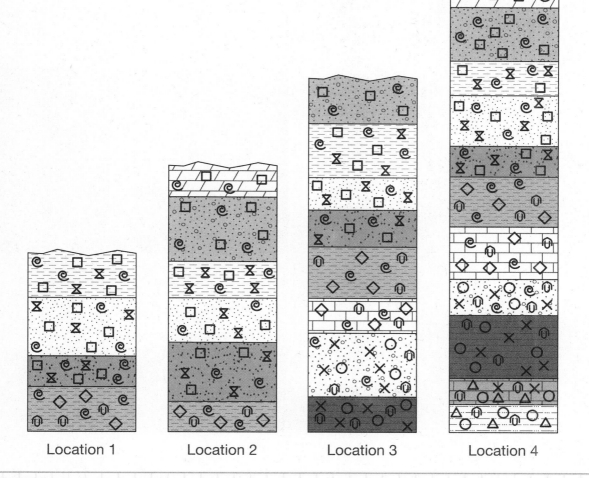

Location 1   Location 2   Location 3   Location 4

 EVIDENCE NOTEBOOK

18. Why might different types of fossils be found in rock layers that come before and after a rock layer that contains no fossils? Record your evidence.

19. Engineer It Computed tomography (CT) scanners are often used by doctors to gather information about the inside of something, such as a person's head, without cutting it. The scanners do this by collecting x-ray images that can be combined to form a 3D virtual model. These virtual models can then be used to make physical 3D models of the object that was scanned. Imagine you are a scientist studying a very delicate skull fossil from an early human ancestor. How could you use a CT scanner to learn more about this fossil without damaging it?

Language SmArts
Explain Inferences from Fossil Record Evidence

Ancient insects grew very large during the Carboniferous Period, about 320 million years ago. Scientists believe this was due in part to air that was high in oxygen. *Meganeura* was an ancestor of dragonflies, but it was more than four times bigger than the dragonflies we see today. It had a wingspan of over 70 centimeters (2 feet)!

Scientists have found thick coal deposits in Carboniferous rocks near *Meganeura* fossils. Coal deposits form from large amounts of decaying plant material. Such large amounts of plant material generally require warm and wet conditions.

Meganeura used its spiny legs to catch and eat other insects living near ponds. Scientists think that these *Meganeura* grew so large because of the high oxygen levels in the air.

20. What modern organisms have an ecological role around ponds today that is similar to the role of *Meganeura* during the Carboniferous Period? Explain your answer.

_____

_____

_____

21. Write a series of logical steps that you could use to infer the type of climate that existed during *Meganeura's* time.

_____

_____

_____

_____

Continue Your Exploration

Name: _____   Date: _____

Check out the path below or go online to choose one of the other paths shown.

Prediction of a Transitional Fossil

- **Reconstruct the Past from Physical Evidence**
- **Hands-On Labs**
- **Propose Your Own Path**

Go online to choose one of these other paths.

Transitional fossils are an important part of the fossil record. But how do scientists know how to spot a transitional fossil? They make hypotheses about the types of organisms that may have descended from earlier organisms and given rise to more recent organisms.

Scientists studied both ancient fish and amphibian fossils. They then predicted that an organism that shared some features in common with both fish and amphibian families likely lived in the past. They identified certain features that the hypothetical species—a "fishapod"—might have, such as a fish with feet. Their predictions were confirmed when fossils of the "fishapod" *Tiktaalik roseae* were found. The fossils showed that *Tiktaalik* had a skull and ribs like land animals. It also had several fish features, including fins and scales.

Tiktaalik roseae was found in the Canadian Arctic. Scientists found the front end of *Tiktaalik* 10 years before finding the hind end in different rock.

Continue Your Exploration

1. In order for *Tiktaalik* to be considered a transitional fossil, when does it need to have appeared in the fossil record?

    A. before fish and amphibians

    B. after amphibians

    C. at the same time as amphibians

    D. between fish and amphibians

2. It took more than 3 billion years for life to spread from the oceans onto land. All organisms that lived on land evolved during the 550 million years that followed. How might this relatively rapid diversification of land species be explained?

    A. The move to land environments led to more changes in species over time.

    B. The move to land environments led to fewer changes in species over time.

    C. Spreading to land did not affect the amount of change in species over time.

    D. The change in environments resulted in lower biodiversity.

3. Draw a simple sketch of a transitional fossil that might link feathered, tree-climbing reptiles to early birds. Label the features that connect the fossil to the reptile and to the bird.

4. **Collaborate** Work with a small group to research another transitional fossil discovery. What evidence did scientists provide to support the identification of the transitional fossil? Present your findings to the class.

Can You Explain It?

Name: _____   Date: _____

What can explain the presence of a rock layer with no fossils between rock layers with different types of fossils?

fossils found

no fossils found

fossils found

EVIDENCE NOTEBOOK

Refer to the notes in your Evidence Notebook to help you construct an explanation for how a rock layer with no fossils might have formed between rock layers with different types of fossils.

1. State your claim. Make sure your claim fully explains how a rock layer with no fossils might have formed between rock layers with different types of fossils.

2. Summarize the evidence you have gathered to support your claim and explain your reasoning.

Checkpoints

Answer the following questions to check your understanding of the lesson.

Use the diagram to answer Question 3.

3. How are the bones in the fin structure of the *Tiktaalik* evidence of a transition from fish to amphibian? Select all that apply.

   A. It has fins like a fish.

   B. It has limb bones like an amphibian.

   C. It is older than fish fossils.

   D. The limb bones do not look as developed as they do in the amphibian.

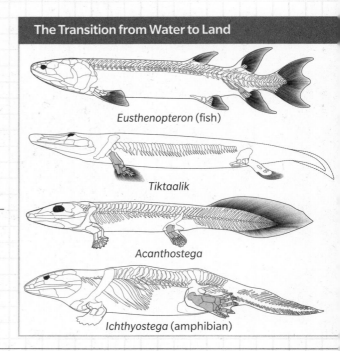

The Transition from Water to Land

Eusthenopteron (fish)

Tiktaalik

Acanthostega

Ichthyostega (amphibian)

4. Organisms with more complex body plans are more likely to be found in older / younger rock layers. This prediction is based on observed patterns of increasing / decreasing complexity of physical structures in organisms over time.

Use the graph to answer Question 5.

5. Based on the graph, biodiversity increases / decreases during a mass extinction event and then increases / decreases after the event. In general, biodiversity on Earth increases / stays the same over time.

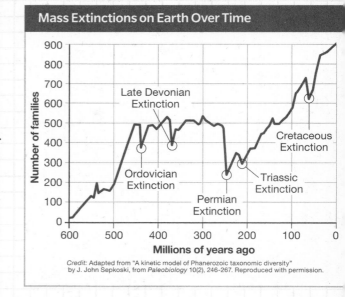

Mass Extinctions on Earth Over Time

Number of families

Late Devonian Extinction

Ordovician Extinction

Permian Extinction

Triassic Extinction

Cretaceous Extinction

Millions of years ago

Credit: Adapted from "A kinetic model of Phanerozoic taxonomic diversity" by J. John Sepkoski, from *Paleobiology* 10(2), 246-267. Reproduced with permission.

6. What types of evidence allow scientists to infer that single-celled life likely existed 3.8 billion years ago? Select all that apply.

   A. transitional fossils in ancient rocks

   B. certain forms of carbon in ancient rock

   C. fossil evidence, such as stromatolites

   D. evidence of extinction events

Interactive Review

Complete this page to review the main concepts of the lesson.

Scientists use the fossil record to identify patterns of change in life on Earth. They use evidence to infer possible causes of the changes they observe.

A. What types of changes are recorded in the fossil record?

The fossil record provides evidence of five mass extinctions. Scientists compare fossils found in rock layers to find evidence about how organisms were affected by extinction events.

B. Draw a sketch of rock layers that includes evidence of an extinction. Use symbols to represent species that existed before, during, and after the extinction event.

Fossils and Living Organisms Provide Evidence of Evolution

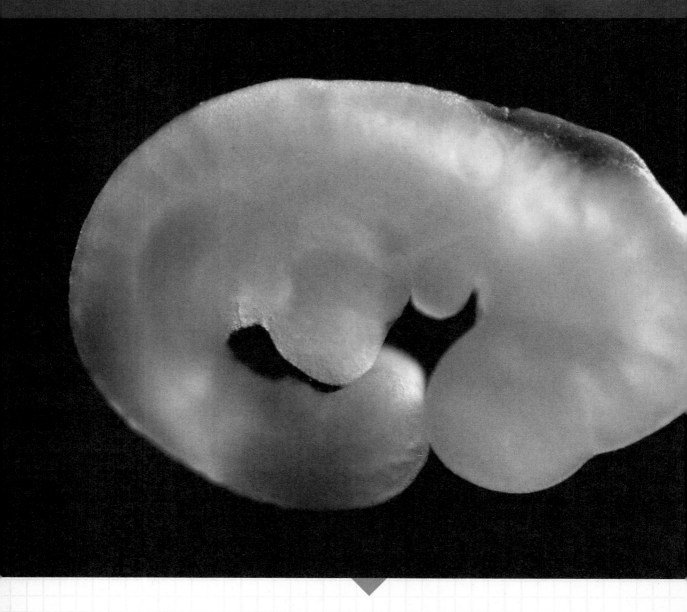

This is a 9.5-day-old mouse embryo. It has yet to grow organ systems, but it has a head, a tail, and tiny limb buds. Its heart is developing in the larger bulge below its head.

Explore First

Inferring Relationships Sort mixed-up images of organisms at different stages of development. What features helped you match the images? Were you surprised by any mismatches?

Go online to view the digital version of the Hands-On Lab for this lesson and to download additional lab resources.

CAN YOU EXPLAIN IT?

What evidence supports a relationship between *Confuciusornis* and modern birds?

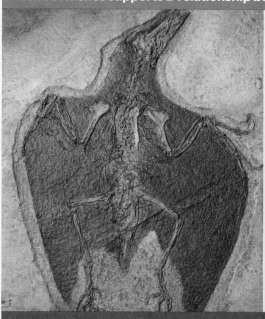 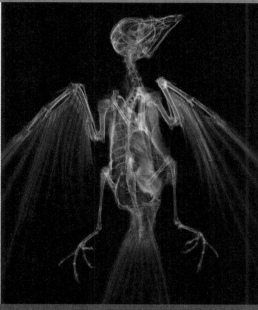

The fossil on the left is of an extinct animal called *Confuciusornis* that lived over 100 million years ago. The x-ray on the right shows the skeleton of a living crow species, *Corvus frugilegus*.

1. What similarities and differences can you observe from these photos?

2. Based on the fossil organism's body structures, how do you think it moved?

 EVIDENCE NOTEBOOK As you explore this lesson, gather evidence to help explain the relationship between *Confuciusornis* and modern birds.

Identifying Similarities among Organisms

What would you think if you planted a sunflower seed and it grew into an oak tree? You would probably be very surprised! Of course, that would never actually happen. You know that sunflower seeds grow into sunflower plants. Oak tree seeds, or acorns, grow into oak trees. This is an example of a consistent and observable pattern in nature: Offspring look similar to their parents. A key assumption of science is that natural systems have consistent, observable, and measurable patterns. These patterns and events happen in the same way today as they did in the past.

Explore Online

The baby elephant has a combination of genes from each parent. This is true of all offspring of living things that reproduce sexually. Because of this genetic recombination, the elephant will not be identical to either of its parents.

3. Would a baby elephant be more likely to look like its parent or to look like one of its great-great-great-grandparents? Explain your reasoning.

Living Organisms Reproduce and Pass on Traits

Organisms reproduce today just as they did in the past. In fact, organisms must reproduce or else life would no longer exist! We know that the offspring of sunflowers look similar to sunflowers, not oak trees. And the offspring of elephants look similar to elephants, not zebras. Offspring look similar to their parents because heritable traits are passed down from generation to generation. These heritable traits are encoded in genetic material called *DNA*. Genetic material is passed from generation to generation through the same processes today as it was in the past.

    Evolution is the process of biological change by which populations become different from their ancestors over many generations. Differences develop in populations due to changes in the genetic material of individuals and the genetic make-up of populations. These changes build up over time, so the more recently two species shared a common ancestor, the more closely related those species are. **Common ancestry** is the idea that two or more species evolved from a single ancestor.

Evolution of Populations Over Time

Whales and fish have similar body shapes. However, they are not closely related. Whales, dolphins, and porpoises share a more recent common ancestor with land animals than they do with fish. In fact, these water dwellers' closest living relatives are hippos! Whales are very different from fish. They have lungs, nourish developing young inside the female's body, and produce milk. These characteristics are different from those of fish, but they are shared with mammals such as hippos.

Scientists learn about evolutionary relationships in many ways. They use a variety of evidence, including fossil evidence. They also analyze body structures and genetic evidence. All of these types of evidence support the hypothesis that modern whales evolved from hoofed mammals called *Anthracotheres* that lived on land.

Most Recent Common Ancestor of Whales and Hippopotamuses

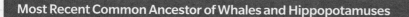

Anthracotheres lived around 50–60 million years ago. Over many millions of years, *Anthracotherium* populations evolved and developed into two main groups of organisms.

One group that is descended from anthracotheres lived entirely in water. This group includes all species of whales, dolphins, and porpoises.

The other group lived mostly on land. Today, there are two species of hippos. They are the only remaining members of that group of land animals.

Evolution of Whales

The extinct species shown here are all ancient relatives of whales. The fossils of these extinct species have skeletal features that are similar to whales. Some features, such as the ear structure of the *Pakicetus*, are very similar to modern whales but unlike any other known mammal.

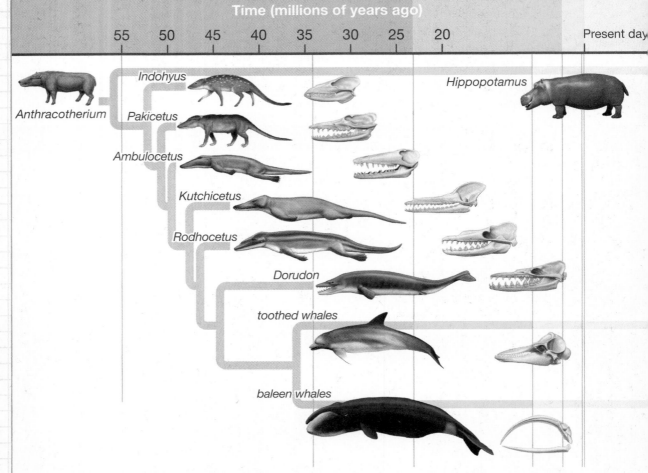

Time (millions of years ago)

55 50 45 40 35 30 25 20   Present day

Anthracotherium · Indohyus · Pakicetus · Ambulocetus · Kutchicetus · Rodhocetus · Dorudon · toothed whales · baleen whales · Hippopotamus

Credit: Adapted from *The Tangled Bank* by Carl Zimmer. Copyright © 2012 by Roberts and Company Publishers. Adapted and reprinted by permission of Macmillan Publishing Company.

4. Genetic information, in the form of DNA / fossils , gets passed from generation to generation. Because of this, offspring look similar to / very unlike their parents. Over time, genetic changes add up. Populations come to look more and more similar to / different from their ancestors. For whales, this explains why Pakicetus / Rodhocetus looks the most different from modern whales. It looks most different because it is a very ancient / recent relative of whales.

5. Which conclusion can be made from the diagram of whale evolution?

   A. All known whale ancestors had four legs.

   B. Whale ancestors transitioned from land to water habitats.

   C. Only skulls show evidence of relationships among whale ancestors.

   D. Whales always existed in their current form, along with many other relatives.

Engineer It
Apply the Use of 3D Printing to Model Fossils

Fossils can be both fragile and tiny, making them very difficult to study. One solution to this problem is using 3D printing technology. People can use 3D printers to make copies of fossils out of sturdy materials such as plastic. They can even make copies that are smaller or larger than the original fossil. Another advantage of 3D printing is that many copies of the fossil can be made.

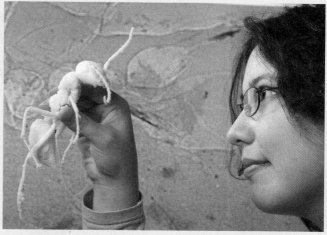

A 3D printer allows this scientist to create a large model of a tiny 100-million-year-old fossilized ant.

6. Propose at least two ways that 3D printing could help students who are interested in studying fossils but do not have access to actual fossils.

Evidence of Evolutionary Relationships

Evolutionary relationships are inferred based on evidence from the fossil record. They are also inferred from similarities in the bodies of living organisms, similarities between living and fossilized organisms, and similarities among the embryos of different types of organisms. Recently, evolutionary relationships have also been studied at the genetic and molecular level. Scientists infer that the more similar species are at any level, the more closely related they are to each other.

Similarities in Anatomy

The **anatomy** of an organism is its body structure and its structural traits. Related organisms have a similar anatomy. For example, the body structures of insects are more like those of other insects than those of birds. Consider a structural trait such as feathers. It was once accepted that only birds had feathers. Soft, fluffy feathers provide insulation. Longer, sleeker feathers enable flight, but recent fossil discoveries reveal short structures in certain dinosaur fossils that look similar to certain modern bird feathers. Scientists identified these structures as feathers. These feathers provide evidence that dinosaurs and birds are more closely related to each other than was once thought.

7. The front limbs of the bat, dolphin, horse, and cat look different from each other and are used in different ways. But the skeletal structure of the limbs is similar. Use the colors of the leg bones of the bat, dolphin, and horse to color the similar bones of the cat.

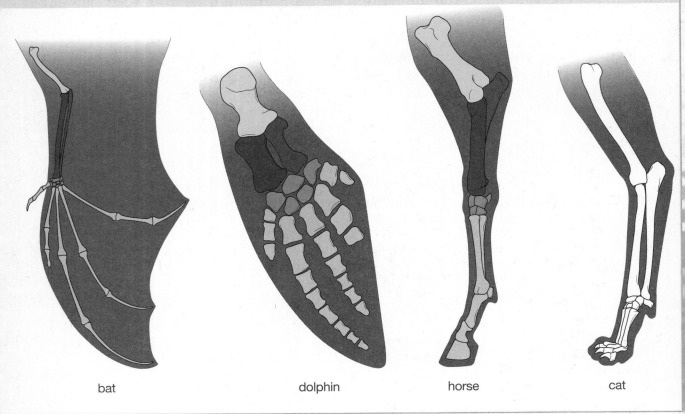

bat   dolphin   horse   cat

8. These limb bones have similar / different overall patterns of bones which can indicate a close / distant evolutionary relationship. However, the limb bones are different sizes and shapes. For example, the "finger" bones, shown in light blue and pink, are different in each animal. The form / color of the bones can help you identify the function / age of the limb.

Many four-legged organisms have similar leg structures that carry out similar functions. Similarities in anatomy can indicate evolutionary relationships. But they are not always the result of a close relationship. Some body structures evolved at different times. Some structures with similar functions also evolved in very different species. Think about the fins of whales and fish. The fins help both animals move in water. But they developed along very different evolutionary paths. So too did the wings in birds, bats, and insects. The presence and function of wings does not indicate a close evolutionary relationship between these groups of organisms because the anatomy of their wings differs so much.

 EVIDENCE NOTEBOOK

9. What anatomical structures do the *Confuciusornis* fossil and the *Corvus* (crow) share? Record your evidence.

Similarities in Embryo Development

The study of the development of organisms from fertilization until they are born or hatch is called **embryology**. Embryos undergo many changes as they grow and develop. Scientists compare the embryo development of different species to look for similar patterns and structures. Based on research and observation, scientists infer that such similarities come from an ancestor that the species have in common. For example, at some time during development, all animals with backbones have a tail. This observation suggests that all animals with a backbone have a common ancestor.

Pharyngeal arches are another example of a structure that is present in the early embryos of several animal species. For example, chicken embryos and human embryos both have a stage in which they have structures, called *pharyngeal arches*, that look similar to gill arches, the structures that form gills in fish. The tissues that make up these pharyngeal arches develop further to become parts of the jaw, ears, and neck. Based on this and other evidence, scientists infer that chickens and humans share a common ancestor with fish. Studies of embryo development are not limited to living species. Some fossilized embryos have been found. Scientists use observations from these embryos as evidence to explain the universal process of embryo development.

Early Stages of Embryo Development

A wide range of species go through the same stages of early embryo development. These similarities indicate that these species share a common ancestor.

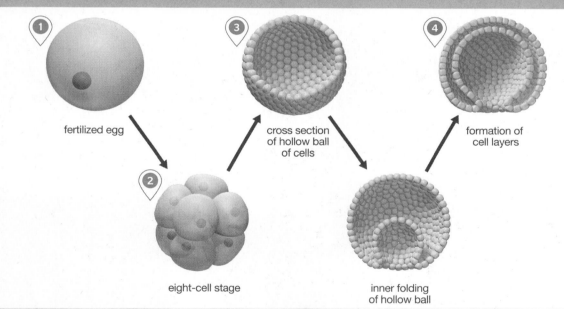

fertilized egg

eight-cell stage

cross section of hollow ball of cells

inner folding of hollow ball

formation of cell layers

1. A fertilized egg contains the correct amount of genetic material needed to develop further.

2. The fertilized egg soon divides into two cells. When the two cells each divide, four cells result, then eight cells. This pattern of cell division continues.

3. Eventually, a hollow ball of cells forms. At this time, genes are activated or turned off in cells, depending on where they are in the hollow ball.

4. Three distinct cell layers develop. These layers will give rise to all of the organism's tissues and structures.

10. Why might many different organisms have similar stages of early embryo development even when they have different traits at later stages? Explain your reasoning.

Different types of animals go through similar stages of embryo development.

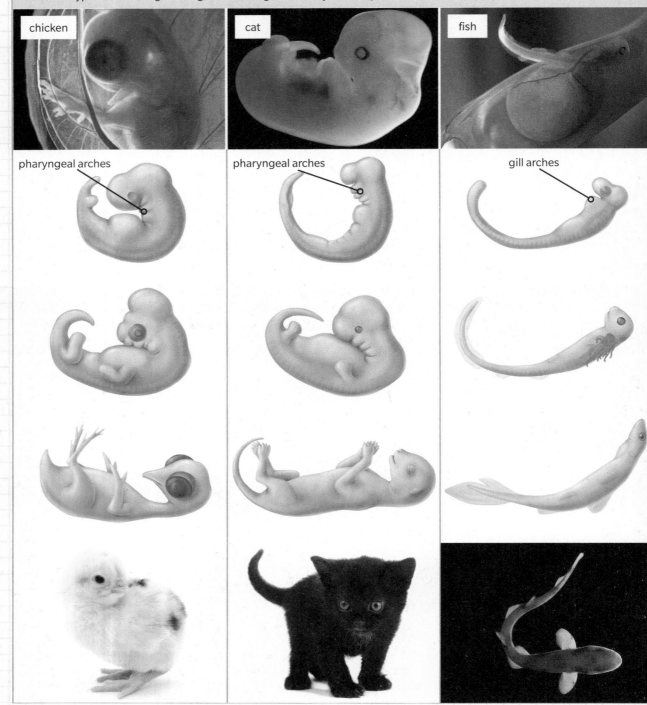

chicken   cat   fish

pharyngeal arches   pharyngeal arches   gill arches

11. Compare the structures of the cat and chicken embryos in the images above. Which characteristics do the species share as embryos that they do not share when they are fully developed? Select all that apply.

    A. Both animals have structures similar to gill arches as embryos.

    B. Both animals have feathers as embryos.

    C. Both animals have similar upper limb buds as embryos.

    D. Both animals have tails as embryos.

EVIDENCE NOTEBOOK

12. What types of similarities would you expect to find in the embryo development of extinct and modern birds? Record your evidence.

Do the Math
Interpret the Geometry of Body Plans

The symmetry of an organism's body is inherited. So similarities and differences in body plans can be used to infer relatedness. Different groups of animals have characteristic body plans. For example, most animals' bodies have *bilateral symmetry*. For these animals, you could draw an imaginary line down the center of their bodies and both sides would be more or less identical to each other. Other animals have *radial symmetry*. These animals have many lines of symmetry. Sponges are an example of an organism with an *asymmetrical* body plan, which means their bodies have no symmetry.

Body Symmetry of Animals

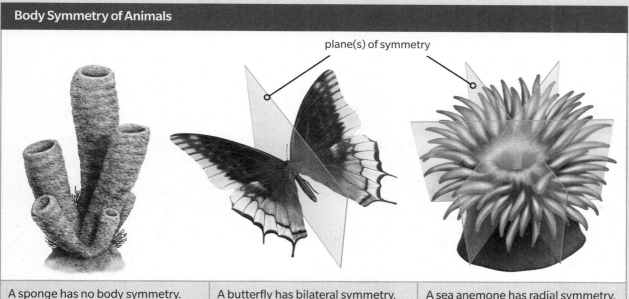

plane(s) of symmetry

A sponge has no body symmetry.	A butterfly has bilateral symmetry.	A sea anemone has radial symmetry.

13. The body plan of the sea slug shown in the photo has
   no / bilateral / radial symmetry.

14. Organisms that have similar body symmetry are considered to be more closely related to each other than to organisms with different body symmetry. Which organism in the diagram do you think this sea slug is more closely related to? Explain your answer.

_____

_____

_____

_____

EXPLORATION 2

Inferring Evolutionary Relationships among Organisms

Data from fossils help scientists to make inferences about extinct organisms. For example, data from fossils can be used to infer the sizes of living things, their life spans, what they ate, and how they moved. As new fossils are found, new observations are used to support, modify, or correct earlier ideas. Understanding how living things have changed over time is an ongoing process. New information adds to what scientists understand about evolutionary processes.

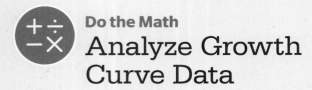

Do the Math

Analyze Growth Curve Data

Scientists have found fossils of the various growth stages of many extinct species, including *Tyrannosaurus rex* (*T. rex*). Observations from these fossils are used to infer how the extinct species grew. When the different ages of *T. rex* fossils were first found, it was thought that they were different species because they looked so different. The data used to plot the graph were collected from the fossils of seven *T. rex* individuals.

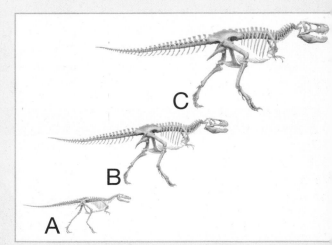

15. Imagine you are a scientist studying two different *T. rex* fossils.

- Observations from one fossil suggest it is from a *T. rex* with a body mass of about 2,000 kg.

- The other fossil is from a *T. rex* with a body mass of about 3,500 kg.

Based on the growth curve data, what is the age difference between these two fossilized dinosaurs? Why can you assume the larger *T. rex* is more mature, not just bigger? Defend your answer using evidence from the graph.

Growth Curve of *T. rex*

Points A, B, and C represent the sizes of the juvenile, adolescent, and adult *T. rex* shown in the illustration.

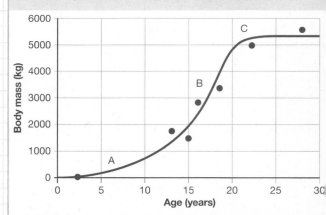

Credit: Adapted from "Gigantism and comparative life-history parameters of tyrannosaurid dinosaurs" by Gregory M. Erickson, et al, from *Nature*. Adapted by permission from Macmillan Publishers Ltd: *Nature* (430), 772–775. Copyright © 2004.

Hands-On Lab
Make Inferences from Evidence

Make inferences based on visual observations, then modify these inferences based on new information and data.

Scientists usually do not have all of the pieces of evidence for the topic they are studying. Instead, they work to understand the natural world by making connections, inferences, and predictions using the information they have.

MATERIALS
• picture, cut into strips

Procedure

STEP 1 Study the strips of an image provided by your teacher. Write down all observations and inferences that you can make about this picture.

STEP 2 Make a prediction about what is shown in the picture. Use your observations to support your prediction.

STEP 3 Record observations, inferences, and a prediction as you receive each remaining strip of "new information" from your teacher.

Analysis

STEP 4 Explain how you modified your prediction about what the picture shows as you gathered more information about the picture.

STEP 5 How is this process similar to how scientists make inferences from fossil evidence? How is it different?

Relationships among Fossil Organisms and Living Organisms

Body structures and other features of fossilized organisms may be similar to features present in modern organisms. In general, the more recently the fossilized organism lived, the more similar its body structures are to modern, living organisms.

Similarities and differences in anatomy are used to make inferences about evolutionary relationships among living and extinct organisms. Scientists revise and refine their understanding of evolutionary relationships as new evidence is found.

Case Study: Evolution of Elephants

Modern elephants belong to a group of mammals that includes extinct animals such as the mammoth and the mastodon. Until recently, it was thought that there were only two living elephant species: the African elephant and the Asian elephant. There were two types of African elephant that looked very different from each other. After analyzing DNA, scientists found larger differences between the two types of African elephants than they would expect from the same species. They concluded that there are two African elephant species: savanna elephants and forest elephants.

Scientists have also used anatomical data to make inferences about how modern elephants are related to extinct relatives. For example, scientists use tooth shape to study relatedness among elephants and their ancestors. Modern elephants have flat, ridged teeth to grind up the tough plants they eat. Like elephants, mammoths and mastodons were herbivores. The form of their teeth helped them chew their food.

Teeth of Modern Elephants and Extinct Ancestors

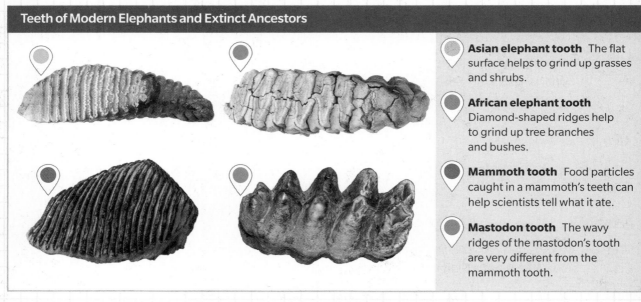

Asian elephant tooth The flat surface helps to grind up grasses and shrubs.

African elephant tooth Diamond-shaped ridges help to grind up tree branches and bushes.

Mammoth tooth Food particles caught in a mammoth's teeth can help scientists tell what it ate.

Mastodon tooth The wavy ridges of the mastodon's tooth are very different from the mammoth tooth.

16. Look at the teeth of the four different animals. Based on the structure of the teeth, which extinct animal do you think is most closely related to the Asian elephant? Support your answer with evidence.

Elephant Lineage

The relationships in this diagram were determined by examining the anatomy of modern animals and extinct animal fossils, as well as embryological and genetic data.

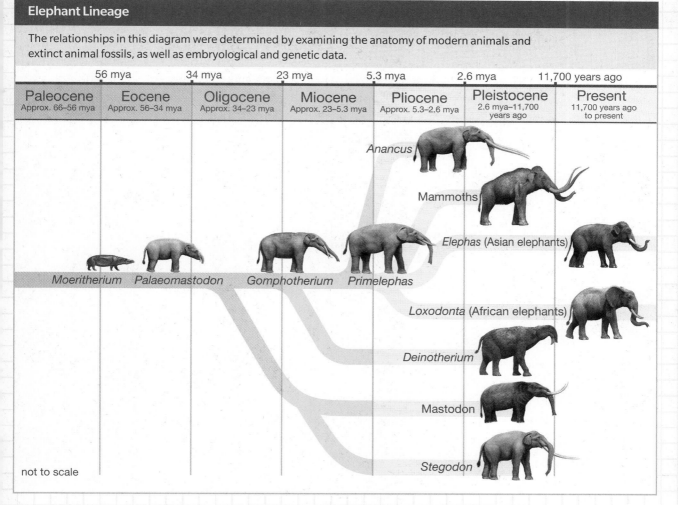

56 mya	34 mya	23 mya	5.3 mya	2.6 mya	11,700 years ago	
Paleocene Approx. 66–56 mya	**Eocene** Approx. 56–34 mya	**Oligocene** Approx. 34–23 mya	**Miocene** Approx. 23–5.3 mya	**Pliocene** Approx. 5.3–2.6 mya	**Pleistocene** 2.6 mya–11,700 years ago	**Present** 11,700 years ago to present

Anancus

Mammoths

Elephas (Asian elephants)

Loxodonta (African elephants)

Moeritherium   *Palaeomastodon*   *Gomphotherium*   *Primelephas*

Deinotherium

Mastodon

Stegodon

not to scale

17. Scientists work to understand the evolutionary history of elephants. They look at embryological / anatomical data, such as tooth structure. They infer that Asian / African elephants are most closely related to the mammoth because both animals have very similar / different tooth structures.

18. Based on the diagram, which animal—extinct or alive—would you expect to be most closely related to the mastodon? How long ago did this animal live? Explain your answer.

EVIDENCE NOTEBOOK

19. What evidence from the *Confuciusornis* fossil could help explain its evolutionary relationship with living birds? Record your evidence.

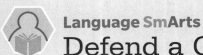
Defend a Claim with Evidence

The Ashfall Fossil Beds in northeast Nebraska contain many well-preserved fossils of ancient animals. The most common fossilized animal found there is the barrel-bodied rhinoceros (*Teleoceras major*). Fossils of five different species of horses are also found at the beds. About 12 million years ago, these animals all died and were buried in volcanic ash.

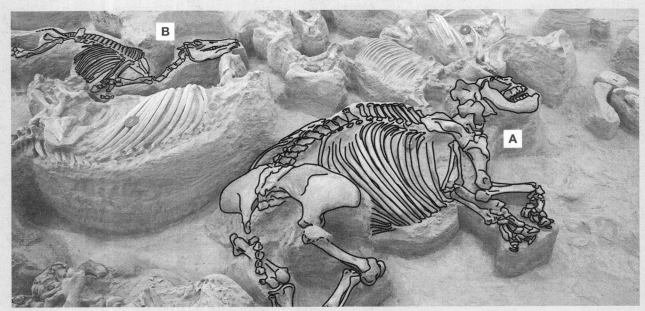

The lines on this photo outline the bone structures of an extinct rhino and a horse that are found in the Ashfall Fossil Beds. It is possible to see some of the anatomical similarities between the fossilized rhino and the living rhino and between the fossilized horse and the living horse.

Black rhinoceros (*Diceros bicornis*)

Przewalski's horse (*Equus ferus*)

20. Make a claim about which fossil, A or B, is the rhino and which fossil is the horse. Use anatomical evidence from the photos to defend your claim.

_____

_____

_____

_____

_____

Continue Your Exploration

Name: _____   Date: _____

Check out the path below or go online to choose one of the other paths shown.

Careers in Science	• **People in Science** • **Classification of Living Things** • **Hands-On Labs** 🖐 • **Propose Your Own Path**	*Go online to choose one of these other paths.*

Museum Exhibit Designer

Museum exhibit designers and educators help communicate scientific ideas to the general public through fun exhibits. Exhibit designers use creativity and innovation to share complex ideas in understandable, engaging, and interactive ways. They need a deep understanding of scientific ideas. They also need an understanding of how people learn about science and interact with museum exhibits. A successful exhibit connects with the people who go to the museum. Designers, educators, and others often collaborate to come up with new and exciting ways to share scientific ideas with learners of all ages. Today's science museums often have many opportunities for visitors to actively participate in science.

Interacting with a "living dinosaur" allows students to have fun while learning about the past.

Continue Your Exploration

1. Think of a topic that you would enjoy learning about through a museum exhibit. Describe the topic and why you chose it.

2. Imagine you are an exhibit designer. Using words and drawings, describe how you would set up an exhibit about the topic you chose in order to share it with visitors.

3. What are some limitations you may need to consider while designing your exhibit?

4. **Collaborate** Work with classmates to design an exhibit about a topic from this lesson.

   - Identify the likely visitors to your exhibit (for example, third- to fifth-graders).
   - Propose one or two key messages that you want to communicate in the exhibit.
   - Describe or produce at least one interactive experience for your exhibit.
   - Share your exhibit design with others.

Can You Explain It?

Name: _____   **Date:** _____

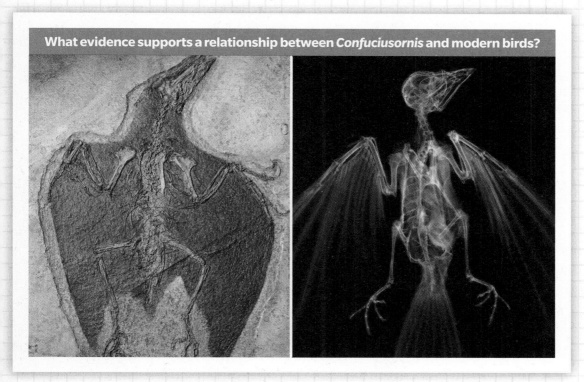

What evidence supports a relationship between *Confuciusornis* and modern birds?

 EVIDENCE NOTEBOOK

Refer to the notes in your Evidence Notebook to help you construct an explanation of how evidence indicates that *Confuciusornis* and modern birds are related.

1. State your claim. Make sure your claim fully explains how the extinct and modern organisms might be related.

2. Summarize the evidence you have gathered to support your claim and explain your reasoning.

Checkpoints

Answer the following questions to check your understanding of the lesson.

Use the image to answer Question 3.

3. Pharyngeal arches are structural features in cat embryos that *are / are not* found in a fully developed cat. The presence of pharyngeal arches is evidence that cats share a common ancestor with chickens and other organisms that have pharyngeal arches *as adults/ during embryo development.*

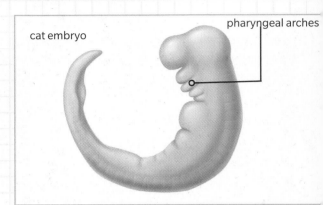

cat embryo

pharyngeal arches

4. Which of the following observations provide evidence of evolutionary relatedness among organisms? Select all that apply.

   A. similarities in body structures

   B. similarities in molecular structures

   C. similarities in embryological development

   D. similarities in the foods that organisms eat

Use the photos to answer Question 5.

5. Which statement is the most logical inference that can be made based on observations of the photos?

   A. The two organisms shown are likely related because they have similarities in leaf structure.

   B. The two organisms shown are likely related because the fossilized plant was green like the living plant.

   C. The two organisms shown are NOT likely related because one is a fossil and the other is living.

   D. The two organisms shown are NOT likely related because there is no evidence that they grow and develop in similar ways.

fossil fern

live fern

6. Which description best explains what scientists do if new evidence is found about evolutionary relationships that is different from evidence already gathered?

   A. Scientists discard earlier ideas about the evolutionary relationships.

   B. Scientists revise their understanding about evolutionary relationships.

   C. Scientists rarely change their ideas even if new evidence is found.

   D. Scientists change evidence to fit existing ideas of evolutionary relationships.

Interactive Review

Complete this section to review the main concepts of the lesson.

Offspring look similar to their parents because heritable traits are passed down from parent to offspring. Over time, genetic changes in populations build up.

A. How can anatomy be used to study relationships among different types of organisms?

Scientists use fossil, anatomical, embryological, and genetic evidence to make inferences about evolutionary relationships.

B. Explain how inferences about evolutionary relationships can change as new evidence is discovered.

Choose one of the activities below to explore how this unit connects to other topics.

☐ People in Science

Marie Curie, Chemist and Physicist

Marie Curie was the first woman to win a Nobel prize, and the first person to win two Nobel prizes. The second prize was for her discovery of the elements radium and polonium. Curie found that some forms of these elements break down into different elements by releasing particles. Until her discovery, scientists thought that atoms could not change.

Research social conditions for women during Marie Curie's life. How common was it for women to be scientists? Create a pamphlet from your findings.

☐ Computer Science Connection

Recreating Dinosaurs Using 3D Technology

Advancements in computer animated three-dimensional (3D) technology allow paleontologists to create replicas of dinosaur bones, or fill in missing bones of a partial skeleton fossil. This technology allows scientists to test hypotheses about how dinosaurs and other prehistoric animals moved and lived in their environment.

Using library or Internet resources, research how paleontologists use advancements in 3D scanners and printers to learn more from fossils. Present your findings to the class.

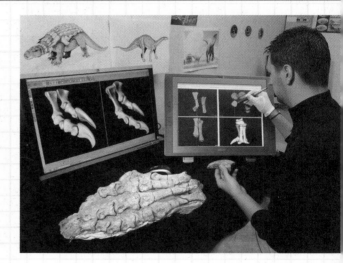

☐ Physical Science Connection

Rock Dating Radioactive isotopes are unstable particles that break down, or *decay*, into more stable particles at a precise rate. Different radioactive isotopes decay at different rates. Scientists compare the amount of a radioactive isotope to the amount of stable particles in a rock sample to find its age.

Research a radioactive isotope that scientists use to estimate the ages of rocks. Identify the *half-life* of this isotope and the stable particles that are formed. Present a graph that shows the decay rate of the isotope over time. Use the graph to help explain what a half-life is and how scientists use the decay rate to estimate the age of the rock sample in which the isotope is found.

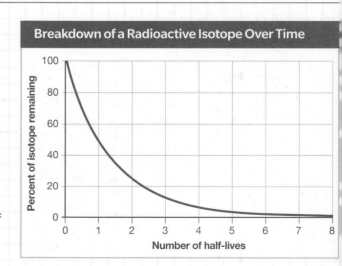

Breakdown of a Radioactive Isotope Over Time

Percent of isotope remaining vs. Number of half-lives

Name: _____   Date: _____

Use the images to answer Questions 1–3.

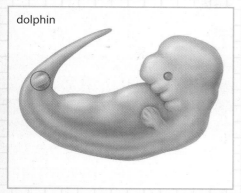

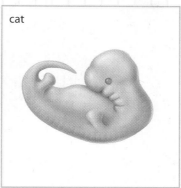

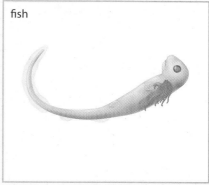

Shown are a dolphin, a cat, and a fish embryo. The red circle on the dolphin embryo indicates the beginning of a hind limb structure.

1. Compare the embryo images above. Describe any similarities you see.

2. Dolphins, whales, and porpoises belong to a group of marine animals that are related to hippos. What evidence of this relationship is present in the images above that is not present in the adult animals? Explain your answer.

3. Based on the images above, which two animals would you expect to have the most recent common ancestor? Explain your answer.

Use the chart to answer Questions 4–7.

4. Which group of organisms represented in this graphic appears earliest in the fossil record? Which group appears most recently?

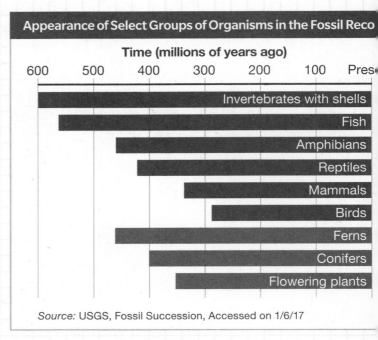

Appearance of Select Groups of Organisms in the Fossil Reco

Time (millions of years ago)

600   500   400   300   200   100   Pres

Invertebrates with shells

Fish

Amphibians

Reptiles

Mammals

Birds

Ferns

Conifers

Flowering plants

Source: USGS, Fossil Succession, Accessed on 1/6/17

5. Would you expect the earliest mammal fossils to be found in deeper or shallower layers of rock than the earliest fern fossils? Explain your reasoning.

6. Describe how this graphic provides evidence for the general pattern of increasing diversity of life over time.

7. Only multicellular organisms are represented in this graphic. Given that most fossils older than 500 million years are single-celled marine organisms, describe the changes in the level of complexity of organisms in the fossil record over time.

Name: Date:

How did marine fossils end up in the desert?

Imagine that you were hiking at the Grand Canyon in Arizona and you discovered a fossil of a cephalopod embedded within limestone rock. You asked the tour guide about the fossil and learned that a cephalopod was a marine organism that is closely related to a squid. You began to wonder how a marine fossil ended up in this dry, hot desert region. You decided to learn more about the age of this fossil and the environment in which this organism thrived. In order to do this, you need to research the Grand Canyon area and its geologic history. Construct an explanation of how the cephalopod fossil's age was determined and how it ended up in this region.

Cephalopod fossil

The Grand Canyon in Arizona

The steps below will help guide your research and help you construct your explanation.

1. **Define the Problem**   Investigate to learn more about cephalopods and other marine fossils found in the Arizona desert. Define the problem you are trying to solve.

2. **Conduct Research** Do research to identify the rock layers in the Grand Canyon and the types of fossils found in each layer.

3. **Analyze Data** What is the name of the rock layer in which cephalopod fossils are commonly found? What type of rock is this layer? Explain your answer.

4. **Interpret Data** Using the data you collected in Steps 1–3, what can you infer about the past environments of this area? Describe any events in Earth's history or geologic processes that may have contributed to the changing environment.

5. **Construct an Explanation** What is the age of the cephalopod fossil you found? What was the environment like in the area at that time? Provide evidence to support your claim.

✓ **Self-Check**

	I identified the rock layer and type of rock in which the fossil was found.
	I researched how geologic processes could have contributed to the Grand Canyon's past environments.
	I analyzed data to estimate an age of the cephalopod fossil.
	I provided evidence to identify the environment of the cephalopod.

Evolution and Biotechnology

How do biological processes explain life's unity and diversity?

The Galápagos prickly pear cactus is common on the Galápagos Islands, but they do not live anywhere else on Earth. Small finches build their nests between the prickly cactus pads.

You Solve It How Can You Engineer Fluorescent Algae?

Use a bioengineering simulation to produce microalgae that have fluorescent organelles.

Go online and complete the You Solve It to explore ways to solve a real-world problem.

391

Explore Biotechnology and Crops

The banana trees grown on this banana plantation are all almost genetically identical.

A. Look at the photo. On a separate sheet of paper, write down as many different questions as you can about the photo.

B. **Discuss** With your class or a partner, share your questions. Record any additional questions generated in your discussion. Then choose the most important questions from the list that are related to food or fiber crops that humans have influenced genetically. Write them below.

C. Choose a food or fiber crop that humans have influenced genetically through artificial selection, genetic modification, or a combination of both. Here's a list of crops you might consider:

bananas	cotton	wheat
corn	soybean	potatoes
jute	tomato	

D. Use the information above, along with your research, to create a timeline that explains the development of a crop over time and how this crop has affected society.

Discuss the next steps for your Unit Project with your teacher and go online to download the Unit Project Worksheet.

Language Development

Use the lessons in this unit to complete the network and expand your understanding of these key concepts.

- Similar term
- Phrase
- Cognate
- Example
- Definition

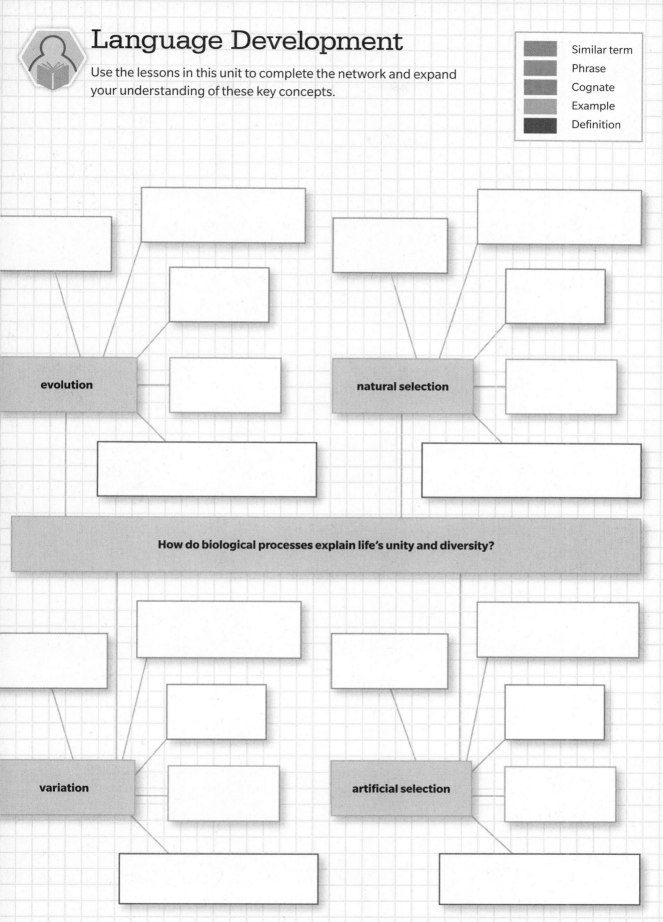

evolution

natural selection

How do biological processes explain life's unity and diversity?

variation

artificial selection

Natural Selection Explains How Populations Can Change

A manta ray uses long fins on each side of its head to funnel tiny organisms into its mouth. This adaptation helps manta rays gather enough food to support their huge size.

Explore First

Modeling Change Design an activity, model, or experiment that demonstrates how small changes over time can lead to large differences. What examples of change can you find in natural and human-made systems?

Go online to view the digital version of the Hands-On Lab for this lesson and to download additional lab resources.

CAN YOU EXPLAIN IT?

How has the smell of rotting flesh become an adaptation for the rafflesia flower?

Rafflesia flowers smell like rotting flesh. This attracts flies and other insect pollinators.

1. Flowers of many plants produce scents. A flower can smell sweet, fruity, musty, or spicy. How do you think having a specific flower scent benefits a plant?

EVIDENCE NOTEBOOK As you explore the lesson, gather evidence to help explain how the rotting flesh smell became an adaptation for the rafflesia flower.

Explaining the Diversity of Life

Life on Earth comes in many forms. The diversity of life includes tiny bacteria, giant redwood trees, and everything in between. There are millions of known species on Earth and new ones are discovered every day. Classifying the diversity of life is made easier by using a field of biology called *taxonomy*. This system groups organisms based on similarities and differences between them.

2. **Discuss** Pick three living things. Take turns asking a partner simple questions about his or her living things to help determine how they are similar and how they are different.

Change over Time

Ideas of how life changes over time started to come together in the early 1800's. Naturalists thought about how traits are inherited, or passed from parent to offspring. Acquired traits—traits that an organism develops during its lifetime—are not heritable. However, traits with a genetic basis can be passed from parent to offspring.

Around the same time, geologists were studying how Earth changes gradually over time. The processes that change Earth are the same now as they have been in the past, and will be in the future. If Earth can change slowly over time, maybe populations could also change over time.

Studies of human populations also helped scientists think about change over time. Human populations can grow exponentially, but food and other resources cannot be increased as quickly. This leads to competition over resources that drives changes in human populations.

Incorporating many of these ideas, Alfred Russel Wallace and Charles Darwin separately developed an explanation for how life changes over time. Darwin used evidence from living and fossil organisms to support his ideas. There is competition among organisms to survive. Organisms that are well suited to an environment are more likely to survive and reproduce than organisms that are less suited to the same environment. These organisms pass their traits to their offspring. Over time, beneficial traits may increase in frequency in a population.

These rock layers formed over millions of years.

Evidence of Change

It can be difficult to observe change in a population, especially for organisms that live a long time. However, there are many lines of evidence that support the claim that populations change over time. This evidence includes changes seen in the fossil record, patterns in biogeography (where organisms are located), DNA analysis of degree of relatedness, directed change through selective breeding, and comparative anatomy and embryology that show similarities and differences in how organisms develop.

The Galápagos Islands were visited by Darwin during an international sea voyage. Darwin studied populations and fossils on the islands and found evidence of populations changing over time. When organisms on the islands are compared to related organisms on the mainland, it is possible to determine when some organisms arrived on the islands and how the island populations have changed in response to their new environments.

3. **Collaborate** With a partner or group, select one line of evidence that can be supported by examples from the Galápagos Islands to explain how populations change over time. Combine examples into a class-wide case study about population change on the Galápagos Islands.

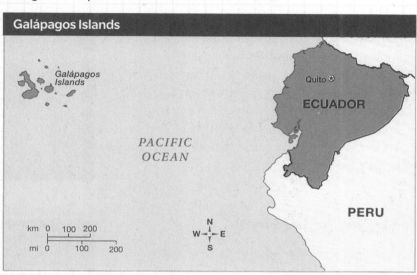

Linking Change over Time to the Diversity of Life

Populations naturally change over time as beneficial traits become more common in a population. Eventually, a population of organisms may change so much that a new species develops.

4. The beetles on the previous page are all different species. How can change over time account for the diversity of beetles?

_____

_____

_____

_____

_____

_____

_____

_____

_____

_____

_____

Modeling Natural Selection

The three-toed sloth and the nine-banded armadillo look very different from each other, but fossil evidence, DNA analysis, and comparative anatomy indicate that they share a common ancestor that lived millions of years ago. Genetic change over many generations resulted in these two species. Three-toed sloths have strong arms and sharp claws, adaptations that allow them to live in trees. Armor-like plates provide protection for armadillos, which live on the forest floor. How did these adaptations arise? **Evolution** is the change in the inherited traits of a population over many generations. On a small scale, evolution leads to the adaptation of a population to its environment. On a large scale, evolution leads to the amazing diversity of life on Earth. But in order for evolution to occur, a population must have genetic variation.

three-toed sloth

nine-banded armadillo

Natural Selection

Genetic variation determines the traits possible in a population. However, a population's current environment determines if any of those traits provide advantages or disadvantages. For example, the ability for the horned lizard to squirt toxic blood from its eyes helps the lizard avoid becoming a meal for a coyote. However, a coyote with very strong legs might be able to run fast enough to attack the lizard by surprise. **Natural selection** is a process by which a population's environment determines which traits are beneficial and which are not.

Evolution by natural selection occurs in populations, not individuals. Individuals with traits that are advantageous in an environment are better able to survive and reproduce. These traits get passed on more often to the next generation than less helpful traits. While evolution can occur by several different processes, natural selection is the only nonrandom cause of evolution in nature.

Explore Online

This horned lizard has poisonous, foul smelling blood that it squirts out of its eyes as a defense against predators.

Evolution by Natural Selection

Owls are birds of prey that hunt other animals for food. The great horned owl can be found in many habitats between the Arctic and South America. These owls are named for tufts of feathers on their heads that look like horns. A wide wingspan, powerful talons, and keen eyesight make these owls effective hunters. Evolution by natural selection over many millions of years resulted in these adaptations. In order for natural selection to occur, certain conditions must be present in a population.

Great horned owls can catch large prey, such as other birds. They also eat small rodents, frogs, and scorpions.

Variation in Traits

Through sexual reproduction, offspring get half of their genes from one parent and half from the other parent. There is also variation in which of each parent's genes are passed to each offspring. These owl chicks receive unique genetic combinations that result in genetic variation in the owl population. Random genetic mutations can also add new traits to the owl population. Adaptation is possible when genetic variation provides a variety of traits in the population. Some of these traits may increase a chick's chance of surviving and reproducing.

There are genetic differences between young owls in the same clutch.

5. **Discuss** Brainstorm a list of traits for which there might be genetic variation in this clutch of owls.

Inheritance of Variation

Great horned owl offspring inherit different traits from their parents. For example, some owl chicks may inherit traits that provide advantages in the environment, such as longer talons or sharper eyesight. Others may receive less beneficial traits, such as weaker wing muscles or low birth weight. Animals tend to overproduce, which means they have more offspring than will survive to maturity. The offspring that do survive can pass their traits to their own offspring.

Nearly 30 pounds of force is needed to open the talons of a great horned owl. Captured prey have little chance of escape.

6. Variation in great horned owl body size due to food supply *can / cannot* be acted on by natural selection. Variation in body size due to inherited traits *can / cannot* be acted on by natural selection.

Differential Survival

A population's environment determines which traits allow for a better chance of survival and reproductive success. Over many generations, traits that help an organism survive in the environment tend to add up in a population. Owls with sharper vision can hunt prey better and outcompete owls with poorer vision. These well-fed owls are more likely to survive and pass on their genes to the next generation. Competition is one contributor to natural selection. As the process of natural selection continues through each generation, more and more owls inherit helpful traits.

7. Most birds have feathers that make "whooshing" sounds when they fly. Owls have feathers that result in near-silent flight, allowing them to sneak up on prey. Explain how natural selection led to this adaptation for owls.

Hands-On Lab
Analyze Salamander Species Distribution

Use habitat comparisons and a map to analyze the distribution of a group of closely related California salamanders. Use your analysis to write an explanation about how these different salamanders may have arisen from a common ancestor.

MATERIALS
• colored pencils
• index cards

Procedure and Analysis

STEP 1 Read the information about each salamander and its habitat. These salamanders are subspecies of *Ensatina eschscholtzii*. A *subspecies* is a specific group within a species. Make your own salamander card for each subspecies.

STEP 2 On the next page, study the map that shows salamander distribution. Notice that the Central Valley forms a barrier between certain subspecies. Identify which salamanders live on each side of the valley.

STEP 3 Describe any patterns in physical appearance and habitat with the subspecies on each side of the Central Valley.

Habitats of *Ensatina* Salamanders in California

E.e. xanthoptica live in coastal mountain ranges, often hiding under moist logs within coastal forests. The region has a Mediterranean climate.

E.e. platensis live in the inland forests of the Sierra Nevada mountains. Patterned skin helps them hide from predators during the dry summers.

E.e. oregonensis live in coastal mountain ranges and northern forests. They find ample hiding places within the damp forests of the north.

E.e. eschscholtzii live in coastal mountain ranges. They forage for worms and centipedes within the moist soil of coastal forests.

E.e. klauberi live in inland forests of the southern coastal mountain range. Closest to the Mojave Desert, they seek shelter from hawks within lakeside forests.

E.e. croceater live in dry forests of the southern coastal mountain range. With few shrubs for cover, yellow patterning helps them hide on lichen-patched trees.

E.e. picta live in a small range along the Pacific coast in northwest California. Their coloring helps them blend in with logs and leaves they live in on the forest floor.

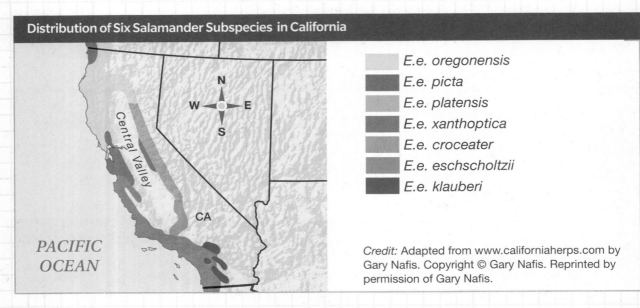

Distribution of Six Salamander Subspecies in California

- E.e. oregonensis
- E.e. picta
- E.e. platensis
- E.e. xanthoptica
- E.e. croceater
- E.e. eschscholtzii
- E.e. klauberi

Central Valley

N W E S

CA

PACIFIC OCEAN

Credit: Adapted from www.californiaherps.com by Gary Nafis. Copyright © Gary Nafis. Reprinted by permission of Gary Nafis.

STEP 4 Use the salamander cards to model how these subspecies may have arisen from a common ancestor as populations spread from the north around California's long Central Valley. Describe your model as a sequence of steps that account for how each subspecies could have formed.

STEP 5 Compare your sequence from Step 4 with the sequence of another classmate or group. Do you have similar evolution stories? Describe any differences.

8. When an environmental change is extreme and rapid, populations may be less / more likely to adapt because the process of natural selection occurs over one / many generation(s). In these cases, populations may be less / more likely to become extinct.

9. What environmental factors might make a strong odor an advantage for the rafflesia plant? Record your evidence.

Engineer It

Control Selection to Meet Human Needs

Scientists can use their understanding about how the natural world works to engineer solutions to problems. For example, understanding the process of natural selection allows scientists and farmers to work together to produce healthy, plentiful crops for the rapidly growing human population. They can identify beneficial plant traits and control reproduction, making it possible for these traits to be passed on to offspring. This is called *artificial selection* because people, not nature, are selecting desired traits.

10. One source of groundwater pollution is pesticide runoff from crop fields. How could artificial selection be used to address this problem?

Using artificial selection to improve plant resistance to pests can greatly increase crop yields.

   A. Farmers select plants that are most resistant to pests, which reduces the need for pesticides.

   B. Farmers select plants that are least resistant to pests, which increases the need for pesticides.

   C. The environment selects plants that are most resistant to pests, which reduces the need for pesticides.

   D. The environment selects plants that are least resistant to pests, which increases the need for pesticides.

11. What trait would make an individual likely to survive and reproduce in a pest population that feeds on pest-resistant plants? Use your answer to describe a trade-off to using artificial selection to reduce pesticide use.

_____

_____

_____

_____

Relating Genetic Variation to the Distribution of Traits

The distribution of traits in a population can change over time. Sometimes, a sudden change in the environment can affect the distribution of traits in a random way. For example, after a wildfire there might randomly be mostly blue flowers in a lupine population. Other distribution changes are not due to chance and may be predicted using evidence. For example, a newly arrived butterfly population prefers to pollinate white lupine. It is reasonable to predict that lupine color will shift toward white in future generations.

conehead katydid

12. The conehead katydid is an insect that can be either brown or green in color. They are eaten by many predators, including birds, bats, and lizards. What are some random and nonrandom factors that might change how many katydids of each color are found in an area?

Variation in Populations

All organisms of the same species that live in the same geographical area make up a *population*. **Variation** refers to differences between organisms in a population. This variation can be in physical features, behaviors, or any other characteristic that is measurable. *Genetic variation* refers to different types of genes in a population for an inherited characteristic, such as flower color or tail length. For evolution to occur, there must be genetic variation in some of the traits present in the population. Genetic variation can be introduced in a population through gene mutations and the movement of individuals between populations. It can also be introduced by new combinations of genes formed during the process of sexual reproduction.

Calculate Allele Frequencies

Different forms of the same gene are called *alleles*. Biologists study how populations evolve by measuring allele frequencies. An **allele frequency** is a measurement of how common a certain allele is in a population. Evolution can occur when an allele frequency changes in a population from one generation to the next.

Mongolian gerbils can be agouti (brown) or black, depending on the combination of alleles they inherit for fur color. The combination of inherited alleles is called a *genotype*. The genotype determines the organism's *phenotype*, or physical characteristics, such as fur color.

13. A population of 200 Mongolian gerbils living near Russia's Lake Baikal includes 80 brown gerbils with the *AA* genotype, 64 brown gerbils with the *Aa* genotype, and 56 black gerbils with the *aa* genotype. Use this information to complete the table.

Genotype	Number of individuals	Number of A alleles	Number of a alleles
AA			
Aa			
aa			
Total number of each allele			
Total number of alleles (A+a)			

The frequency of an allele can be found by first writing a ratio that compares the number of that allele in the population to the total number of alleles in the population. For example:

$$\text{Frequency of the } A \text{ allele} = \frac{\text{number of } A \text{ alleles in population}}{\text{total number of alleles in population}}$$

14. Calculate the frequency of the *A* (brown) allele and the *a* (black) allele.

15. The gerbils are prey for sharp-eyed hawks. How might the frequency of the black fur and brown fur alleles change in the population after a fire blackens the area? Will the frequencies vary proportionally (at the same rate)? Explain your answer.

Distribution of Traits

Genetic variation causes differences in traits. Some traits may have only one or two possible phenotypes. Other traits may have a wide range of possible phenotypes. For example, wild lupine flowers can be purple, white, blue, violet, or purple-pink. The frequency of each flower color in a lupine population can be shown in a graph. This type of graph shows the *distribution* of different phenotypes for the flower color trait.

lupines

16. Study the distribution graph for wild lupines. Which statement could be defended using data from the graph?

A. The population has only one allele for flower color.

B. Conditions in the environment favor purple lupines.

C. All flower color alleles have an equal chance of appearing in the next lupine generation.

D. There are fewer pink and white lupines due to drought.

Color Distribution of Lupine Flowers

This graph shows the distribution of flower color for a population of wild lupines. Biologists might compare this graph with one made in the past to study how flower color in the lupine population may be changing.

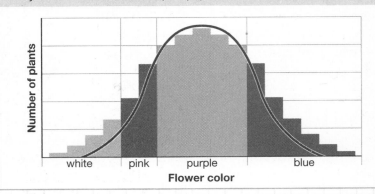

EVIDENCE NOTEBOOK

17. Think of odor strength as a range of phenotypes (weak to strong) in the rafflesia population. What might the distribution of traits look like on a graph? Record your evidence.

Describe Trait Distribution

Monkey flowers are found in a variety of colors ranging from white to pink to red. Animals, such as bees and hummingbirds, help these plants reproduce by transferring pollen as they travel from flower to flower. Hummingbirds prefer to visit red monkey flowers. Bumblebees prefer to visit pink flowers.

18. Predict what color of monkey flower has the highest likelihood of occurring in a habitat with a large population of bees and few hummingbirds. Graph the distribution of color in monkey flowers in this habitat to support your answer.

Analyzing Patterns of Natural Selection

Hammerhead sharks are predators that can often be found prowling reefs in shallow ocean waters. They eat a variety of prey including fish, octopus, and crabs. Scientists have made hypotheses about the unusual head shape of these sharks. Research suggests that the wide-spaced eyes improve the shark's vision. Improved vision may help the shark better track fast-moving prey. Researchers have also hypothesized that the head shape may help the shark dive and perform movements needed to catch its favorite meal—stingrays. The shark uses its wide, flat head to pin down stingrays that are hiding under the sand on the ocean floor.

Hammerhead sharks are named for their unusual head shape.

19. Discuss Choose one of the hypotheses about the function of the shark's head shape. Describe how a scientist might design an experiment to test the hypothesis.

20. Discuss Researchers have discovered that the wide-set eyes result in a large blind spot directly in front of the shark's head. How is it possible that this head shape evolved given this disadvantage?

Patterns of Natural Selection

Natural selection is a process that can be observed, measured, and tested. Data have been gathered from the field and the laboratory by thousands of scientists. These data document the evolution of populations in response to changes in their environment. For example, the increase in antibiotic-resistant bacteria, pesticide-resistant insects, and herbicide-resistant plants shows that these populations are changing by the process of natural selection. Scientists have also measured changes in the timing of animal migrations and flowering of plants in response to changes in climate. The patterns observed in these data can help scientists explain how populations may have changed in the past. They can also be used to predict how populations might change in the future.

Case Study: Body Size in Male Salmon

The graph below shows a pattern of selection in male coho salmon. The red-dotted line shows a normal distribution for the trait, where most males have a medium body size. The blue line shows the distribution after selection has occurred.

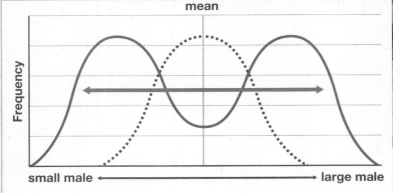

Male salmon, such as this coho salmon, defend territory.

21. Large male salmon defend territory and keep other males away from females. Small males can often sneak into a territory, unseen by the large male. How might this explain the pattern shown in the graph?

Case Study: Coat Color in Polar Bears

Genetic evidence reveals that polar bears are most closely related to a species of brown bear living on Alaska's ABC islands. Brown bears show a range of coat colors from solid brown to brown with light spots. The graph shows the selection pattern for coat color that occurred in polar bears.

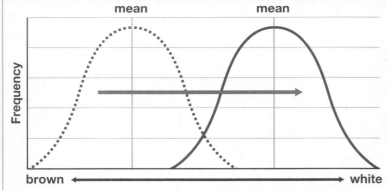

Polar bears spend much of their time on sea ice hunting for seals.

22. Polar bears have coats that help them survive in the cold Arctic where they live. The color of the coat helps them to blend in with their environment. The specialized hair cells that make up the coat keep the bear warm and dry. It is likely that *one/more than one* environmental factor caused the evolution of *one/more than one* trait in the polar bear.

Case Study: Spine Number in Cacti

A population of desert cacti shows variation in the number of spines on the cactus surface. Imagine that a new species migrates to the area. This species prefers to eat cacti with fewer spines. There is also a parasite in the area that prefers to lay its eggs on cacti with more spines.

Cactus spines are a limited defense against predators. Predator populations also evolve adaptive traits because of natural selection.

23. Draw Create a distribution graph of the spine-number trait for the cactus population based on the information provided.

24. Language SmArts Write an explanation of the selection pattern shown in your graph. Explain how changes in the cacti's environment resulted in changes in the spine number trait.

EVIDENCE NOTEBOOK

25. How would you expect the distribution of traits for odor strength in rafflesia to change over many generations? How might populations of pollinators be changing at the same time? Record your evidence.

Analyzing Natural Selection in Medium Ground Finches

In studies conducted on one of the Galápagos Islands, scientists observed the effect of natural events on the beak shape of a population of medium ground finches. These studies involved measuring the size and shape of the beaks of thousands of finches on the island.

Medium ground finches usually eat small, soft seeds that are plentiful on the island. During a drought in 1977, plants on the island did not produce many seeds. The soft seeds were quickly eaten up. Finches that could eat larger, harder seeds instead of small, soft seeds were able to survive. Finches that could not eat the larger seeds died of starvation. Researchers compared measurements of average beak size before and after the drought.

26. Create a bar graph that shows the average beak measurements before and after the drought.

Average Beak Size in Medium Ground Finches		
	1977 (before drought)	1978 (after drought)
beak length (mm)	10.68	11.07
beak depth (mm)	9.42	9.96
beak width (mm)	8.68	9.01

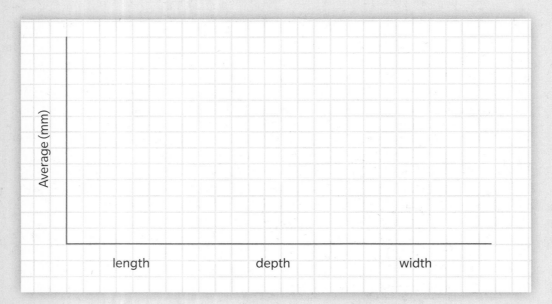

27. Use the graph and the text to summarize how the drought resulted in the selection pattern shown in the ground finches.

_____

_____

_____

_____

_____

Continue Your Exploration

Name: _____   Date: _____

Check out the path below or go online to choose one of the other paths shown.

People in Science

- **Endangered Species**
- **Hands-On Labs** 👋
- **Propose Your Own Path**

Go online to choose one of these other paths.

Dr. Nancy Knowlton, Marine Biologist

Nancy Knowlton fell in love with marine life while wandering the ocean shore as a child. Her work studying shrimp evolution began in Jamaica, where she learned that the native shrimp population that scientists thought to be a single species actually included four species. Her work with shrimp continued along the Isthmus of Panama—a narrow strip of land that separates the Atlantic and Pacific Oceans. There she studied how the formation of the isthmus contributed to the evolution of several shrimp species.

1. Imagine you were a member of Dr. Knowlton's team conducting research about shrimp species in the waters off Panama. What types of data would you need to collect to determine if the shrimp populations were separate species? What do you think a typical research day would be like?

Dr. Nancy Knowlton spent nearly 14 years studying the diversification of shrimp species along the Isthmus of Panama. She continues to dedicate her life to the conservation of coral reefs.

Continue Your Exploration

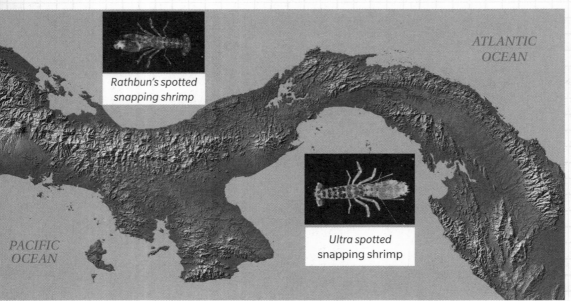

Rathbun's spotted
snapping shrimp

Ultra spotted
snapping shrimp

The Isthmus of
Panama is a narrow
strip of land that
connects North and
South America and
prevents the flow
of water between
the Atlantic and
Pacific Oceans.
Two shrimp species
separated by the
isthmus are shown
on the map.

2. The movement of Earth's plates caused the formation of the Isthmus of Panama
between 3.5–20 million years ago. Could the formation of the Isthmus of
Panama alone cause a shrimp population to diversify into distinct species? Explain
your reasoning.

3. To claim that the rise of the Isthmus of Panama contributed to the evolution of
different species of shrimp, would Dr. Knowlton need to establish that the east coast
and west coast shrimp species diverged before or after the rise of the isthmus?
Explain your reasoning.

4. **Collaborate** Rheas, emu, and ostrich are bird species that each live on different
continents, but they are more closely related to each other than to nearby bird
species. Work with a group to learn about their evolution from a common ancestor.
Write a report and present your findings to your classmates. Include photos or
drawings of each species in your report.

Can You Explain It?

Name: _____   Date: _____

How has the smell of rotting flesh become an adaptation for the rafflesia flower?

 EVIDENCE NOTEBOOK

Refer to the notes in your Evidence Notebook to help you construct an explanation for how the adaptations of the rafflesia flower are related to the process of natural selection.

1. State your claim. Make sure your claim fully explains how the smell of rotting flesh became an adaptation for the rafflesia flower.

2. Summarize the evidence you have gathered to support your claim and explain your reasoning.

Checkpoints

Answer the following questions to check your understanding of the lesson.

Use the table to answer Questions 3–4.

3. Which statements could be true based on the data shown in the table? Select all that apply.

    A. The B allele does not provide a survival advantage to the population.

    B. This population is evolving.

    C. The b allele does not provide a survival advantage to the population.

    D. The population is not evolving.

Generation	Allele Frequency of B	Allele Frequency of b
1	0.63	0.37
2	0.71	0.29
3	0.78	0.22
4	0.78	0.22
5	0.81	0.19

4. How might the migration of individuals in or out of the habitat affect the frequency of each allele in this population?

    A. Migration will change the frequency of only the B allele.

    B. Migration will not change the frequency of either allele.

    C. Migration will change the frequency of both alleles.

    D. Migration will change the frequency of only the b allele.

Use the photo to answer Question 5.

5. Which factors might cause a decrease in the size of hooks in the fish hook ant population over time? Select all that apply.

    A. Birds prefer to eat ants with smaller hooks.

    B. Ants with smaller hooks need less food to survive.

    C. Ant queens from colonies with smaller hook sizes are more likely to successfully mate and form new colonies.

    D. Small snakes cannot swallow ants with long hooks.

The fish hook ant has razor-sharp hooks to defend itself from predators.

6. Many species produce more offspring than can survive in their environment. How might this contribute to natural selection? Select all that apply.

    A. More offspring results in more competition for resources.

    B. Producing many offspring is a disadvantage.

    C. Helpful traits allow some individuals to outcompete others.

    D. Without competition, advantageous traits may have no effect on survival or reproduction.

Interactive Review

Complete this section to review the main concepts of the lesson.

Life on Earth is diverse because populations change over time through a process that happens now as it has happened in the past.

A. Explain how a single population of organisms can result in multiple different populations after many generations.

Natural selection is a process by which a population's environment determines which traits are beneficial and which are not.

B. Explain how genetic variation and the environment influence the distribution of traits.

Genetic variation causes differences in traits, and the distribution of traits in a population depends on environmental factors.

C. Describe the three factors required for natural selection to occur in a population.

Populations become better adapted to their current environments through natural selection.

D. Explain why adaptations are specific to the current environment of a population.

Natural Selection Requires Genetic Variation

The black color of this jaguar is the result of a gene that controls the dark pigment in the jaguar's fur.

Explore First

Changing Instructions Write a how-to procedure for an easy task, such as folding a paper airplane. Pair up and perform each other's tasks. Then alter your how-to procedure by adding, removing, or revising a step. Is your partner still able to perform your task? What is the relationship between instructions and a final product?

Go online to view the digital version of
the Hands-On Lab for this lesson and to
download additional lab resources.

CAN YOU EXPLAIN IT?

How can a change to just one gene cause a lobster to be blue?

Only 1 in about 2 million lobsters is blue. The blue color is the result of a rare genetic mutation.

1. Identify at least three other body features of these lobsters. What do you think
   determines these traits in the lobsters? How could these traits change?

EVIDENCE NOTEBOOK As you explore the lesson, gather evidence to help
explain how a change to a gene can result in a blue lobster.

Describing the Relationship between Genes and Traits

Observe the students in your classroom. They share many traits, but they do not look identical. Some traits can be inherited, such as eye color and face shape. Inherited traits are passed on from parents to offspring by genetic material. Other traits, such as language and musical taste, are determined by the environment. However, most traits are influenced by both genetic and environmental factors, and every person has a unique combination of many traits.

The differences in eye colors, face shapes, and smiles of these students are due to differences in traits.

DNA Is the Genetic Material Stored in Cells

The genetic material that determines traits in organisms is **DNA**. It is a double-stranded molecule organized into structures called *chromosomes*. In organisms that reproduce sexually, cells have pairs of chromosomes. For each pair, the offspring receives one chromosome from each of the two parents. DNA molecules contain the information that determines the traits that an organism inherits. DNA also contains the instructions for an organism's growth and development.

2. **Discuss** How might an inherited trait, such as height, be influenced by both genetic and environmental factors?

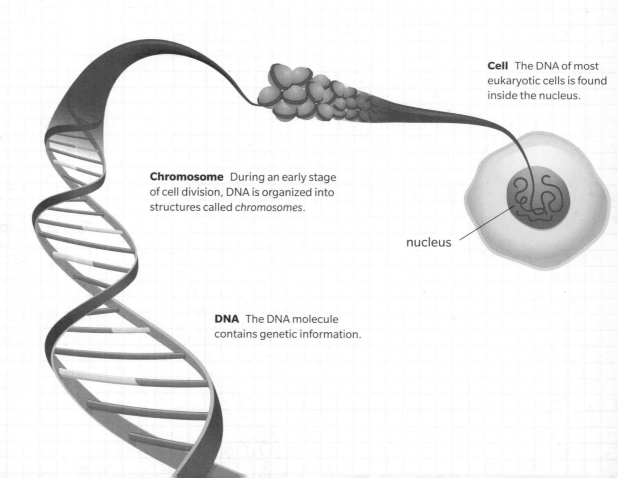

Cell The DNA of most eukaryotic cells is found inside the nucleus.

Chromosome During an early stage of cell division, DNA is organized into structures called *chromosomes*.

nucleus

DNA The DNA molecule contains genetic information.

Genes Are Segments of DNA

Each side, or strand, of DNA is a chain of building blocks called *nucleotides*. These repeating chemical units join together to form a DNA molecule. One part of a nucleotide is called the *base*. There are four different nucleotides in DNA, which are identified by their bases: adenine (A), guanine (G), cytosine (C), and thymine (T). Where the two strands connect, A pairs with T and G pairs with C. These paired bases fit together like the pieces of a puzzle.

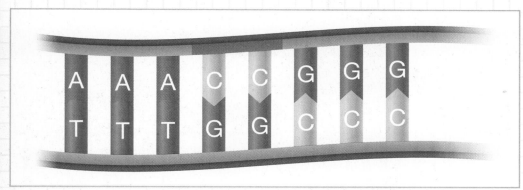

Nucleotides line up so that the DNA backbone is like the handrail of a ladder. The bases—A, T, C, and G—join to make the rungs of the ladder.

Combinations of alphabet letters make meaningful words. Likewise, combinations of DNA base pairs make "genetic words" called *genes*. A **gene** is a specific segment of DNA that provides instructions for an inherited trait. Each gene has a starting point and an ending point. DNA is read in one direction, just as you read words from left to right. Genes are responsible for the inherited traits of an organism. Organisms that reproduce sexually have two versions of the same gene for every trait—one version from each parent.

3. Complete the DNA sequence by adding complementary bases to the DNA strand. You may draw using colors or write letters to represent the nucleotide bases.

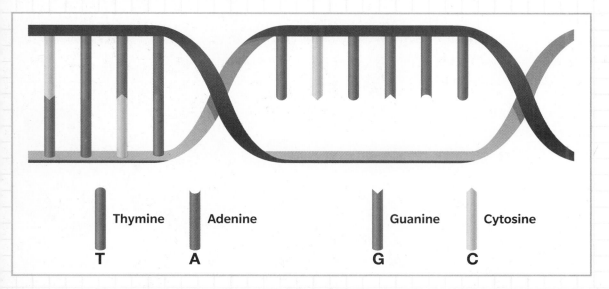

Thymine — T   Adenine — A   Guanine — G   Cytosine — C

Genes Code for Proteins

A **protein** is an important molecule that is necessary for building and repairing body structures and controlling processes in the body. Proteins are composed of smaller molecules called *amino acids*. About 20 different types of amino acids combine to make proteins. A specific sequence of three bases on a gene codes for a specific amino acid. These sequences are called *triplets*. The chain of amino acids produced by a gene depends on the order of the triplets. In this way, the genes of a chromosome carry the instructions for the proteins that are produced by cells.

Relate DNA Code to Protein Production

4. The diagram on the left shows the triplet order for six amino acids. Use the diagram to complete the triplets and amino acids on the right.

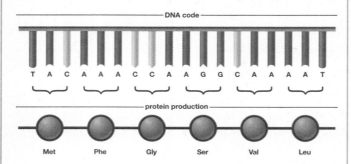 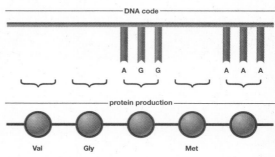

Once built, the amino acid chain twists and folds to form the protein's three-dimensional shape. A protein's shape is linked to its function. For example, collagen is a protein that folds into a long, fiber-like chain and strengthens skin. Other proteins, called *hormones*, deliver messages to cells by fitting into specific locations on target cells like a key in a lock.

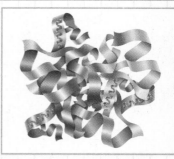

5. Some triplets code for the same amino acid. Sometimes, a DNA triplet is exchanged for another one that codes for the same amino acid. The function of the resulting protein will / will not be affected. If the DNA triplet codes for a different amino acid, the function of the protein will / will not be affected.

Amino acid chains fold and link together to form the 3D structure of a protein.

6. *Enzymes* are proteins that help speed up chemical reactions in the body. They often work by binding to target molecules. How do you think the sequence of amino acids in an enzyme relates to its ability to bind to a specific target molecule?

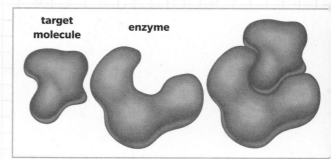

The active site of an enzyme has just the right shape to bind to the target molecule.

Model Protein Folding

You will use paper strips to model protein folding.

    Amino acid chains fold or twist when one region of the chain is attracted to, or repelled by, another region. This folding or twisting depends on the chemical structure of each amino acid, as well as how close they are together in the chain.

MATERIALS
- colored pencils, red, blue, green
- paper strips, white, 1 inch wide and 12 inches long (2)
- ruler

Procedure

STEP 1 Consider the amino acid sequence below. On the strip of white paper, draw colored dots indicated by the sequence using corresponding colors—red, blue, or green. Use the ruler to help you leave a 1 cm space between each dot.

Amino acid sequence 1:

His – Lys – Ser – Gly – Ala – Gly – Cys – Pro – Ser – Asp – Val – Leu – Met – Gly – Thr – Pro – Gly – Ala – Cys – Asp – Met

STEP 2 Fold your amino acid chain into a three-dimensional protein by following the guidelines below. Work from one end of the white paper strip to the other. Try to fold halfway between the relevant colored dots when folding.

- Same color next to each other—no fold
- **Red** next to **green**—90° fold down
- **Red** next to **blue**—90° fold up (dotted sides of strip come together)
- **Blue** next to **green**—45° airplane fold (colored dots come together with a diagonal crease)

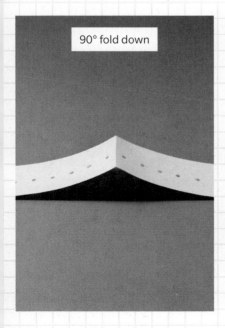

90° fold down

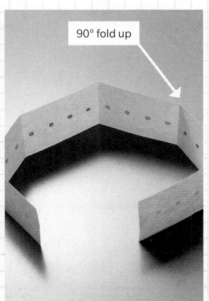

90° fold up

45° airplane fold

Analysis

STEP 3 Once you have folded your protein, observe its shape. Then set it aside to compare with other proteins you will make.

STEP 4 Now, consider the next amino acid sequence. Following the same procedure as you did for the first sequence, complete the three-dimensional protein.

Amino acid sequence 2:

His – Lys – Ser – Gly – Ala – Gly – Cys – Pro – Ser – Asp – His – Leu – Met – Gly – Thr – Pro – Gly – Ala – Cys – Asp – Met

STEP 5 Compare the two amino acid sequences. What is the difference between the composition of the two sequences? How does the shape of the proteins differ?

STEP 6 How did the alteration in the amino acid sequence affect protein structure?

STEP 7 Do you think the proteins formed by the different amino acid sequences can still perform the same function?

 EVIDENCE NOTEBOOK

7. How might the alteration in the folding pattern of the paper strip proteins relate to the genetic change that causes a lobster to be blue? Record your evidence.

Proteins Affect Traits

Different versions of the same gene can result in proteins with different structures and properties. Proteins perform much of the chemical work inside cells, so they are largely responsible for traits. The variety in proteins results in the variety of traits we observe in organisms. For example, Labrador Retrievers are dogs that exhibit a variety of coat colors. The coat will be brown or black depending on which protein is coded for in the pigment gene. When a different protein inactivates the brown or black coat pigment gene, Labradors have yellow coats.

Language SmArts
Illustrate the Flow of Genetic Information

Scientists have modified tomato plant genes to produce the same pigments that give blackberries their dark color and health benefits. The result—purple tomatoes!

8. **Draw** Use the terms protein, gene, trait, and amino acids to make a diagram or concept map that shows the flow of genetic information that causes purple tomatoes.

9. Use your completed diagram and evidence from the text to write a summary of the relationship between genes, proteins, and traits.

_____

_____

_____

_____

_____

_____

Exploring the Causes of Genetic Change

Leaf-like scales distinguish the bush viper from its smooth-skinned snake relatives. Keratin proteins shape scales. They arrange in ridges instead of smooth rows to help the viper blend in with leaves. What caused this new trait to appear in bush vipers? The ridged scale pattern in bush vipers is due to genetic changes that result in altered proteins.

The African bush viper lives in tropical forests. Its scales help it camouflage within the bright green foliage.

10. Which of the following outcomes could result from a change in one of the bush viper's genes? Select all that apply.

    A. no effect on traits

    B. a genetic disease

    C. a new skin color

Mutations

A change in the base-pair sequence of a gene is called a **mutation**. Most mutations occur when a cell copies its DNA for cell division. As the DNA is copied, base pairs may be added, deleted, or substituted. These chance mutations may be beneficial, neutral, or harmful to organisms. For example, a mutation that results in longer fangs may be beneficial if it helps the bush viper seize prey. Mutations can also occur when DNA is exposed to *mutagens*, or substances that cause genetic mutations, such as UV radiation and toxic chemicals.

11. Study the DNA base sequences. On the line provided, record whether the mutation is an addition, substitution, or deletion.

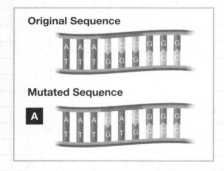

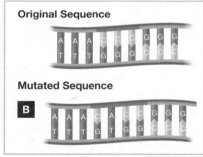

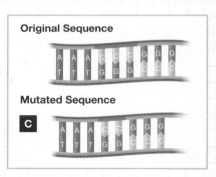

A. _____ **B.** _____ **C.** _____

12. **Collaborate** With a partner or group, consider the relationship between DNA and proteins. Which DNA mutation types might have the biggest effect on protein structure? Develop a model to help explain your answer and share your model with your class.

13. Look again at the enzyme diagram and its target molecule. How might a mutation affect the interaction between the enzyme and its target and the function of the enzyme in the organism?

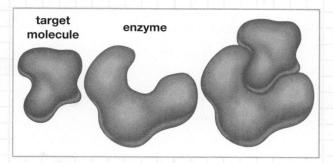

target molecule   enzyme

The target molecule and the enzyme are both proteins. Their 3D shapes are determined by the order of their amino acids.

Body Cells and Reproductive Cells

Mutations can occur in the DNA of body cells or in the DNA of reproductive cells—eggs and sperm. When cells divide, mutations are passed on with the genetic material into the new cell. Only mutations that occur in the DNA of reproductive cells can be passed on from parent to offspring.

Do the Math
Calculate Mutation Rate

Organisms must copy their DNA to reproduce, and mutations can occur any time DNA is copied. Many of these mutations are corrected by cells, but sometimes a mutation is not corrected and it becomes part of the genetic code of a species.

DNA Mutations Over Time		
Mutations (shown in black) accumulate at a fairly constant rate in the DNA of a particular species.	**Original DNA sequence**	GAACGTATTCAGGTCT
	5 million years later	GAACGTATTCAGGTCT
	10 million years later	GTACGTATTCAGGTCT
	15 million years later	GTAAGTATTCACGTCT
	20 million years later	GTAAGTATTCACGTCT
	25 million years later	GTAAGAATTCACGTCT

14. How many mutations accumulated in this DNA sequence over 25 million years?

15. Based on these data, estimate the mutation rate for this DNA sequence over 100 million years.

16. What are the connections between mutation, protein structure and function, and the lobster's blue color? Record your evidence.

Sexual Reproduction

Sexual reproduction, like mutation, is a source of genetic change. One or more genes can get reshuffled among chromosomes when the egg and sperm form. Since the shuffling of genes is random, each egg or sperm will carry a different combination of chromosomes. This explains differences among offspring that come from the same parents.

Chromosomes can "cross over" during egg or sperm formation, allowing large segments of DNA to swap locations and providing additional combinations of genes in offspring.

17. When DNA segments switch places during egg or sperm formation, it can affect only one / several gene(s).

Engineer It
Identify Design Solution Constraints

Earth's atmosphere includes a thin layer of *ozone*, a compound that absorbs UV rays emitted by the sun. UV light can initiate mutations in DNA by causing neighboring thymine bases on the same strand to break their bonds with adenine and bond with each other instead. Human-generated pollutants break down ozone in the atmosphere, putting people at higher risk of sunburn and skin cancer.

Earth's ozone layer can be seen from space. It lies within the thin blue band of the outer atmosphere .

18. According to the paragraph, pollution causes the ozone layer to thin / expand. As a result, living organisms have a higher / lower risk of UV damage. This represents an engineering problem for which a solution / an experiment can be designed to help reduce ozone depletion.

19. Which of the following are constraints that should be considered in designing solutions to this problem? Select all that apply.

   A. The solution must result in a cure for skin cancer.

   B. The solution must not cause harm to living organisms.

   C. The solution must prevent thymine-adenine bonds from breaking.

   D. The solution must not cause an imbalance of other atmospheric gases.

Explaining the Relationship between Genetic Change and Natural Selection

The star-nosed mole has a ring of twenty-two finger-like projections around its snout which helps the mole to detect and capture prey in a fraction of a second. Long ago, genetic change that caused nose segments to remain separated was passed from one mole to its offspring. The offspring were able to locate prey better than other moles in the population. These offspring reproduced successfully, passing the mutation to their offspring as well. Over many generations, this segmented structure became more common in the population.

20. Do you think the genetic change that resulted in the segmented nose occurred in the DNA of body cells or the DNA of reproductive cells? Why?

Star-nosed moles mostly eat earthworms and aquatic insects.

Genetic Change and Adaptation

Genetic changes resulting from mutation and sexual reproduction lead to different traits in the individuals of a population. Traits that help organisms survive and reproduce in their current environment are called **adaptations**. An adaptation can be a structure, a function, or a behavior. For example, the structure of the star-nosed mole's nose allows it to locate prey more effectively than a rounded nose. Specialized nervous system function allows the moles to process information from their environment very rapidly. When star-nosed moles search for food, they constantly touch the environment with the star—between 10 and 15 places every second. This behavior helps them to rapidly detect and capture small prey. The adaptations of the star-nosed mole are the result of evolution through natural selection, which requires genetic variation to act on a trait.

EVIDENCE NOTEBOOK

21. Do you think that the mutation that causes the blue color of the lobster is an adaptation? Record your evidence.

22. Read the description of each organism. In the space provided, list one structure, function, or behavior that you think is an adaptation. Then briefly explain how this adaptation benefits the organism.

The barrel cactus lives in dry, hot deserts. It has a round stem covered with spines. The flowers bloom when temperatures drop and pollinators are plentiful.

The scorpion has a tough exoskeleton and poison in its curled tail. It is well armed for life in the desert, and will burrow in the sand to escape the scorching heat.

The ocelot hunts a variety of prey, including rodents, iguanas, and monkeys. It has a unique patterned coat, visual acuity, and sharp teeth. The ocelot is nocturnal, meaning it is active mostly at night.

Relate Change to Natural Selection

The mountain goat is well-adapted to its current environment. It has a compact body covered in thick fur, split hooves, strong rear legs, and a narrow snout. It lives on steep, rocky slopes where temperatures can drop well below zero. Plants on these slopes grow only a few inches tall in the shallow, nutrient-poor soil.

23. Draw Suppose climate change affects the mountain goat's environment. Hot summers and more rainfall allow plants to grow tall and cover rocks. What variations in a population might help mountain goats survive these new conditions? Sketch a mountain goat with an adaptation and explain how this trait could increase in the population due to natural selection.

The mountain goat's round, compact body helps it to retain water and heat.

Continue Your Exploration

Name: _____   Date: _____

Check out the path below or go online to choose one of the other paths shown.

| Evolution of Drug-Resistant Bacteria | • **Mutation and Phenotype** • **Hands-On Labs** 🖐 • **Propose Your Own Path** | *Go online to choose one of these other paths.* |

A bacterial cell may have an allele that results in resistance to an antibiotic medicine. This cell may survive antibiotic treatment and pass the beneficial allele to its offspring, or to other bacterial cells in the medium in which they live. Scientists identified bacterial strains resistant to penicillin within 20 years of the first use of the antibiotic in humans. Bacterial resistance to levofloxacin, an antibiotic used to treat pneumonia and other life-threatening infections, evolved within just one year. Scientists observed two contrasting trends. The number of antibiotic-resistant bacteria was increasing, while the development of new antibiotic medicines was decreasing.

1. What is needed for a population of bacteria to develop resistance to antibiotics? Select all that apply.

   A. the existence of resistance genes in the population

   B. the presence of antibiotics in the bacteria's environment

   C. competition between bacterial species

   D. transfer of alleles from one generation to the next

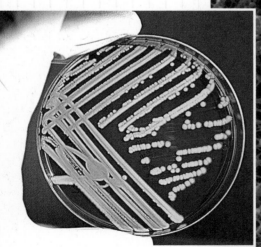

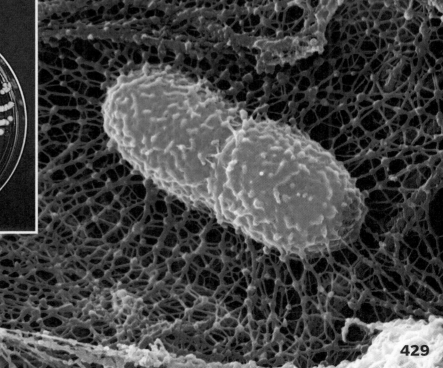

"Superbugs," like *Klebsiella pneumoniae*, the bacteria growing on the petri dish, resist almost all antibiotics. The colored micrograph (right) shows the bacterium trapped by a white blood cell.

Continue Your Exploration

Antibiotic Resistance in *K. pneumoniae,* United States 1998–2010

Klebsiella pneumoniae is a bacteria that causes infections of the respiratory and urinary systems. The graph shows the percentage of *K. pneumoniae* that are resistant to certain antibiotics. Each line represents a different antibiotic.

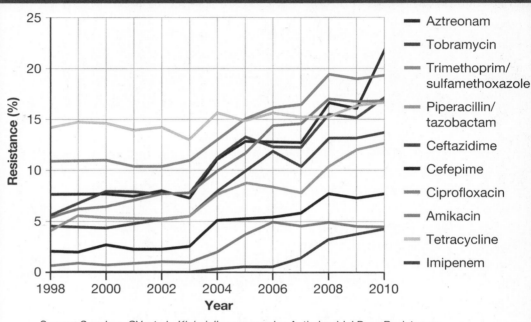

Legend:
- Aztreonam
- Tobramycin
- Trimethoprim/sulfamethoxazole
- Piperacillin/tazobactam
- Ceftazidime
- Cefepime
- Ciprofloxacin
- Amikacin
- Tetracycline
- Imipenem

Source: Sanchez, GV, et al., *Klebsiella pneumoniae* Antimicrobial Drug Resistance, United States, 1998–2010, *Emerging Infectious Diseases,* 2013, 19(1): 133–136

2. Describe the pattern of antibiotic resistance shown in the graph. How many years of data are shown in the graph? What does the percentage of resistance at the beginning of the study tell you about each antibiotic?

3. How do you think the growth and spread of human populations and the use of antibiotics has affected the frequency of the antibiotic resistant allele in populations of *K. pneumoniae*?

4. **Collaborate** Work with a classmate to research other examples of natural selection that have been observed and measured by scientists. Prepare an oral presentation or short play for each example. Identify the variation of traits in the population, describe the environmental change, and explain why certain traits are increasing or decreasing in the population due to natural selection. Be prepared to ask and answer questions at the end of each presentation.

Can You Explain It?

Name:

Date:

How can a change to just one gene cause a lobster to be blue?

EVIDENCE NOTEBOOK

Refer to the notes in your Evidence Notebook to help you construct an explanation for how a change to a single gene can cause a lobster to be blue.

1. State your claim. Make sure your claim fully explains how a change to one gene can cause the blue color in lobsters.

2. Summarize the evidence you have gathered to support your claim and explain your reasoning.

Checkpoints

Answer the following questions to check your understanding of the lesson.

Use the photo of the betta fish to answer Question 3.

3. A gene mutation in the betta fish results in a double-tail. In this example, the mutation results in a change to a physical trait / behavior. This change is desirable by fish breeders but does not provide a survival advantage for the fish, so it is / is not considered an adaptation.

4. Which sequence best explains the relationship between DNA and protein structure and function?

   A. DNA → gene → protein → trait

   B. DNA → amino acid triplets → protein → trait

   C. DNA base triplets → amino acid sequence → protein folding pattern → protein shape and function

   D. DNA shape → amino acid sequence → protein shape and function

Use the photo of the bee-eater to answer Questions 5–6.

5. Bee-eaters are birds that eat insects, especially bees and wasps. They grab flying prey from the air with their beaks. Long ago, genetic changes that resulted in shorter / longer beaks were advantageous for the bee-eater.

6. Which statement correctly connects the bee-eater's adaptations with its environment?

   A. The environment determines which bee-eater traits are adaptive.

   B. The bee-eater's traits influence the environment it chooses to live in.

   C. The bee-eater's adaptive traits will not change as the environment changes.

   D. The environment has no relationship to the bee-eater's adaptive traits.

Interactive Review

Complete this section to review the main concepts of the lesson.

Genes in DNA code for proteins that determine an organism's traits.

A. Describe how genes are related to the structure and function of proteins.

Mutations and sexual reproduction are causes of genetic change.

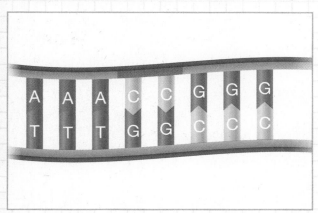

B. Explain how mutations to genes can affect traits in organisms.

Traits that help organisms survive or reproduce in their current environment are called adaptations.

C. Explain the relationship between genetic change and adaptation.

Artificial Selection Influences Traits in Organisms

Dogs have many different traits that humans may find valuable, such as size, shape, or coat color of the dog.

 Explore First

Analyzing Dog Breeds In a group, brainstorm as many dog breeds as you can. For each breed, include a list of characteristics. For example, a Dalmatian is a large dog with a spotted coat. What causes differences between the dog breeds?

CAN YOU EXPLAIN IT?

How did humans cause alpacas to become different from vicuñas over time?

vicuña

alpaca

Vicuñas are shy, fast animals. They feed on short, tough grasses in the Andes Mountains. Alpacas are their relatives. They are gentle and curious. Alpacas are raised by humans for their warm wool.

1. Compare the way the alpaca and the vicuña look. How are they alike or different?

2. Do you think alpacas or vicuñas are more useful to humans? Explain your answer.

 EVIDENCE NOTEBOOK As you explore the lesson, gather evidence to help explain how humans influenced the development of alpaca populations from vicuñas.

Analyzing Human Influence on the Inheritance of Traits

Humans have been influencing the traits of certain plants and animals for thousands of years. For example, people may breed horses to race, or grow fruits that taste a certain way. People grow plants and keep animals for the products or services they provide. They isolate these organisms from their wild populations, which affects the possible traits in the isolated population. Over time, domesticated populations may become very different from their wild relatives.

People at the market may want to buy these tomatoes because of the colors and shapes.

3. **Discuss** What traits make each tomato type unique? Why might farmers want to grow tomatoes with so many different traits?

Traits Are Passed from Parents to Offspring

The Saint Bernard pass lies high in the Alps, a European mountain system. During the 1700s, a single monastery near the pass kept a population of large dogs with thick fur. The dogs helped the monks avoid avalanches and detect people trapped in the snow. The monks depended on the dogs for survival, and they bred only the most gentle and snow-wise dogs. Over time, these traits became common in the population of dogs. Even now, St. Bernard dogs will instinctively help people lying or trapped in the snow.

The monks had little understanding of the biology behind inheritance. Yet, they knew that traits pass from parents to their young. They used this understanding to influence the dogs' traits through *selective breeding*, or the breeding of specific organisms based on preferred traits. More than 100 years later, scientists began to understand the way inheritance works.

Scientific Understanding of Inheritance

Factors That Influence the Frequency of Traits Charles Darwin was an English naturalist who studied the inheritance of traits in living things. He loved raising pigeons. Darwin bred the birds to have certain features. He realized that nature, like humans, might influence the traits of living things. Darwin applied this thinking to data he collected from living and fossil organisms. He observed that traits that provide a benefit in a certain environment become more common in populations over time.

Inheritance Follows Patterns Gregor Mendel was an Austrian monk who studied traits in pea plants. He carefully bred peas and learned that some traits follow a simple pattern when passed from parent to offspring. Dominant traits appear in offspring when present and recessive traits might be present, but masked. Mendel explained that there are two "factors" that can be inherited for each trait—one from each parent. These "factors" are now known as *alleles*. Modern genetics is based on Mendel's work.

Inheritance Patterns Can Be Predicted Reginald Punnett was a geneticist who built on Mendel's work by studying more complex patterns of inheritance. Punnett developed a simple calculation table to predict the likelihood that offspring would inherit certain traits from parents. This table is called a *Punnett square*. Punnett used this table to demonstrate that certain feather colors in chickens are linked to being male.

4. By observing inheritance patterns, Darwin, Mendel, and Punnett developed the foundation for understanding how breeding influences traits in a population. They worked *before / after* scientists understood the relationship between traits and genetic material. Society can use inheritance patterns to meet various needs because the patterns are *unpredictable / predictable*.

Analyze Selected Traits in Vegetables

You will compare vegetable plants bred from wild *Brassica oleracea*. You will analyze traits to describe how each vegetable could develop from the wild type by selective breeding.

MATERIALS
- colored pencils
- samples of fresh vegetables cultivated from wild *Brassica oleracea*, including broccoli, cauliflower, Brussels sprouts, kohlrabi, and kale

Procedure and Analysis

STEP 1 Study the diagram of wild *Brassica oleracea*.

Anatomy of Wild *Brassica oleracea*

Many types of vegetables were cultivated from the wild type of this plant, shown below. Some traits were encouraged and other traits were suppressed.

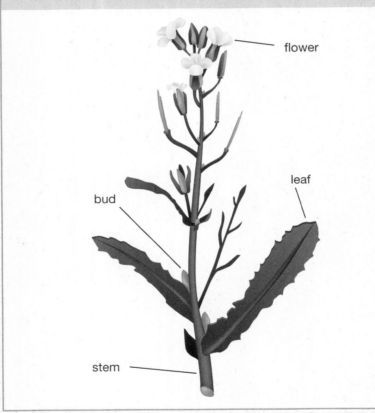

flower

leaf

bud

stem

STEP 2 Choose your first vegetable. Describe it in the table. Sketch the vegetable on a separate sheet of paper.

STEP 3 In your observations, circle specific traits the vegetable has in common with the wild-type plant and note these in the table.

STEP 4 Repeat Steps 2 and 3 for each vegetable.

Vegetable	Observations

STEP 5 Which vegetables are the most and least similar to the wild-type plant? What does this tell you about the selective breeding process for each vegetable?

STEP 6 Choose one of the vegetables from the table. Explain how it might have developed from wild *Brassica oleracea* through selective breeding.

Artificial Selection

The human control of reproduction in order to influence the traits present in offspring is called **artificial selection**. For example, dairy cows are bred for the amount of milk they produce, the milk fat level, and their pregnancy success. Artificial selection can encourage traits in a population that people want. It can also discourage traits that people do not want. Science can help describe the impact of artificial selection on populations. Society must then decide how to apply this knowledge.

The traits present in a population are different when humans are the selective pressure instead of environmental factors. The traits people choose may not improve an organism's chance for survival or reproduction. This is one way artificial selection is very different from natural selection. Yet, natural and artificial selection do follow some of the same rules. Both can only affect traits that are present in a population. Also, both selection types alter the frequency of *phenotypes* (traits) and *genotypes* (gene combinations) in a population.

5. Which of these factors make dairy cows a good choice for artificial selection? Select all that apply.

   A. The cows vary in the amount of milk they make.

   B. The amount of milk cows make is affected by diet.

   C. The amount of milk cows make is an inherited trait.

   D. Many people want to drink milk or cook with milk.

 EVIDENCE NOTEBOOK

   6. What traits might have been selected for in alpacas? Record your evidence.

Predict the Outcome of Artificial Selection

Guppies are a popular fish for home aquariums. They have bright colors, broad tails, and spotted patterns. People who sell fish use selective breeding to emphasize certain traits in offspring. As a result, there are many types of guppies. For example, the half-black yellow guppy has a half-black body and a broad yellow tail. Every part of the albino red guppy is a striking scarlet color, even its eyes.

The color, spot pattern, shape, and size of guppies in a population can be influenced through artificial selection.

7. **Draw** Choose one trait of the guppies in the photo. Draw what a guppy might look like if people selected for this trait over ten generations. Include a caption that explains the process.

Modeling the Genetic Basis for Artificial Selection

Humans raised dogs long before they farmed land or raised chickens and sheep. Dogs were the first animals bred by people, beginning between 10,000 and 40,000 years ago. Dogs are different from wolves because of selective breeding. Dogs have smaller skulls, paws, and teeth. Their ears flop forward, they are more friendly than fierce, and dogs can sense some human emotions.

Wolves have traits that help them survive in the places they live.

8. How might humans have influenced the inheritance of traits they found desirable in wolves?

Artificial Selection Acts on Inherited Traits

In the early 1900s, experiments confirmed Mendel's idea that traits are controlled by factors inherited from each parent. Over time, new technologies and discoveries linked traits to DNA. *DNA* is genetic material in cells that is transferred from parent to offspring during reproduction. *Genes* are segments of DNA that produce specific traits. As understanding of inheritance advances, so do the ways humans affect the traits in organisms.

The Shar-Pei on the left has many more wrinkles than the Shar-Pei on the right.

9. A single gene determines if Chinese Shar-Peis will have normal skin or excessively wrinkled skin. Two Shar-Peis that differ in skin type have different genotypes / phenotypes / genotypes and phenotypes . Breeding Shar-Peis so that they are more likely to have wrinkled skin is an example of natural / artificial selection. It requires traits that are / are not inherited from parents.

   Dog breeders cannot make new traits, but they can cause traits that dogs already have to become more or less common in a population. They do this by deciding which dogs mate. Puppies are more likely to have desired traits if both of their parents have those traits. Artificial selection directs change in populations that can occur more quickly than with natural selection. Artificial selection outcomes are also more predictable than those of natural selection because people control which individuals reproduce. Reproduction in nature may cause different traits to become more common in the population.

EVIDENCE NOTEBOOK

10. How do artificial selection and heritable traits relate to the development of alpaca populations from vicuñas? Record your evidence.

Model Artificial Selection

A *Punnett square* models the transfer of genes from parents to offspring during sexual reproduction. The gene versions (or *alleles*) for an inherited characteristic from one parent are listed above each column as letters. The alleles from the other parent are listed next to each row. Capital letters are used for dominant alleles and lowercase letters are used for recessive alleles.

To complete the Punnett square, the parent alleles are combined in each cell. In this diagram, the allele for short hair, *H*, is dominant to the allele for long hair, *h*. Having at least one dominant allele will produce short hair, the dominant phenotype. The top parent has an *HH* genotype and the parent to

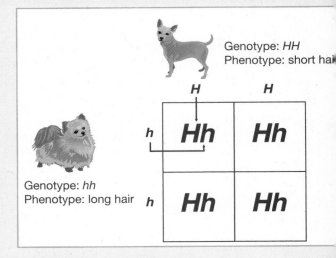

Genotype: *HH*
Phenotype: short hair

Genotype: *hh*
Phenotype: long hair

the left has an *hh* genotype. In this example, the predicted ratio of short-haired dogs in a litter of four is 4:4. In other words, you could expect 100% of the dogs to have short hair.

11. A breeder crosses two *Hh* Chihuahuas. Complete the Punnett square that models this cross.

12. Based on the Punnett square modeling the cross of two *Hh* Chihuahuas, what percentage of Chihuahua puppies should the breeder expect to have long hair?

Short-Haired Chihuahua

H   h

Short-Haired Chihuahua

H   HH

h

13. What is the predicted ratio of short-haired to long-haired offspring?

14. Which other crosses have a greater probability of producing Chihuahuas with the long-hair trait than the *Hh* x *Hh* cross? Circle all that apply.

A. *HH* x *Hh*

B. *hh* x *hh*

C. *Hh* x *hh*

D. None of these crosses

Artificial Selection Does Not Modify Genes

Advances in the scientific understanding of genes and inheritance improved selective breeding programs. For example, recessive traits are not always visible in an organism. Understanding inheritance patterns can assist breeders in making recessive traits more or less common in a population, even if the traits cannot be seen in the parents. Humans are still finding new methods to influence desired traits in living things. Biologists now understand how to change genes directly using molecular tools. The process of changing genes directly is called *genetic engineering*. Artificial selection influences how common existing traits are in a population, but it does not alter genes.

Language SmArts

Compare Mechanisms of Change in Species

15. Read the text for each photo to decide if humans or environmental factors are influencing traits. Identify each example as natural selection, artificial selection, or genetic engineering. Use evidence from the lesson to support your choices.

Example	Mechanism and evidence
Neon-colored zebra fish are produced when DNA from sea anemones, coral, or jellyfish is inserted into the genetic material of wild-type zebra fish.	
Dutch farmers carefully bred the pineberry, or "reverse strawberry," over several years. Cultivation begins with crossing a nearly extinct white strawberry plant with a red strawberry plant.	
Farmers want dairy cows to produce as much high-fat milk as possible. The DNA of beef and dairy cows have differences in genes that control milk production.	
This hummingbird's bill is long and curved. Its food source is nectar, which is found deep in flowers. Some flowers have long tube shapes.	

Applying Artificial Selection to Solve Problems

Artificial Selection as a Biotechnology

Artificial selection is a type of **biotechnology**—the use of biological understanding to solve practical problems. The root word, *technology*, implies that people use creativity to design and implement biological solutions. Using yeast to produce bread and cheese is biotechnology. Other examples are using bacteria to make antibiotics, to break down sewage, or to clean up oil spills. In each case, people use advances in the scientific understanding of a biological process to solve a problem or improve the quality of life.

16. Is natural selection considered a biotechnology? Why or why not?

Case Study: Artificial Selection of Corals

In 2005, the Caribbean lost 50% of its coral reefs due to a rise in the area's ocean temperatures. Warm water causes corals to get rid of the algae living in their tissues. This process is called *bleaching*. The bleached corals become weaker and some corals may die from lack of food without the photosynthetic algae to provide nutrients.

Artificial selection might help corals become more tolerant of warm temperatures. Coral species from Australia have adapted to warmer waters. Breeding corals from Australia with ones found in colder regions introduces warmth-tolerance genes into more coral species. Scientists can continue selective breeding to increase the total number of corals with these genes.

These tanks are full of corals from different world regions. Selectively breeding coral types might help improve a coral species' ability to resist threats in its environment.

Meeting Needs and Desires

When humans use artificial selection to protect corals, they are helping meet a variety of human needs and desires. Coral reefs are beautiful. This makes them a favorite spot for tourists to visit. Companies around reefs, such as ecotourism companies, hotels, restaurants, and local fisheries, provide many jobs. Coral reefs are also areas of high biodiversity. Therefore, there are many species and many individuals present. Ocean algae that live among reef systems provide a large percentage of the oxygen in Earth's air. Some medicines also come from coral reefs. For example, an enzyme used by corals to fight disease is an ingredient in medicines used to treat asthma and arthritis. Protecting reefs through artificial selection will also protect these valuable resources.

Healthy reef systems support nearly 4,000 species of fish. Scientists think there may be over a million undiscovered species that also live among the world's coral reefs.

---

17. What criteria must be met for artificial selection to be a successful solution to coral bleaching and the long-term success of coral reefs? Select all that apply.

   A. Corals must have variation in their ability to survive changing temperatures.

   B. The trait being influenced in corals must be beneficial to humans.

   C. The offspring of corals must be able to reproduce in nature.

   D. The ability to survive changing temperatures must involve heritable traits.

   E. The artificial selection process must not harm healthy coral reefs.

EVIDENCE NOTEBOOK

   18. What human needs or desires were met through the development of alpaca populations? Record your evidence.

Engineer It | Evaluate Uses of Artificial Selection Ocean water is becoming more acidic. Higher acidity prevents corals from using carbonate to build their skeletons. An effective artificial selection solution will help corals hold on to algae. It will also increase the amount of carbonate corals take up in increasingly warm and acidic ocean water. Two proposed solutions are provided in the table.

Proposed solution	Description
Farming corals in several conditions	Corals are grown in different acidity levels and with different algae in order to detect and breed the healthiest combination.
Exposing lab-raised corals to stress	Scientists think that the DNA of stressed corals changes in a way that makes them better able to withstand the same stress when it occurs again. Corals that can best tolerate stress are chosen for breeding programs.

19. What do the proposed solutions for reducing coral bleaching have in common? Circle all that apply.

    A. They both include identifying variation in traits.

    B. They both include selectively breeding corals for desirable traits.

    C. They both include selectively breeding algae for desirable traits.

    D. They both depend on environmental factors to alter coral DNA.

20. Choose one of the solutions. Explain how it could be improved or expanded to help solve the problem of coral bleaching.

Analyze the Impacts of Artificial Selection on Society

Today's juicy corn is the result of thousands of years of selective breeding. Just five gene locations cause the differences between corn and teosinte, corn's ancestor. Farmers selected plants with more or larger kernels. Now, advances in genetics allow farmers to encourage pest and drought resistance in corn. Corn has become a *super crop*, grown in large amounts to meet many needs.

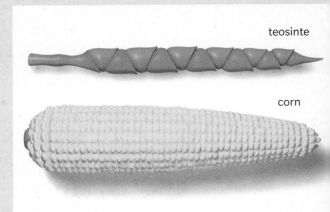

teosinte

corn

21. Describe how important crops that have been highly influenced by selective breeding, such as corn, have affected society.

_____

_____

_____

_____

Continue Your Exploration

Name: _____   Date: _____

Check out the path below or go online to choose one of the other paths shown.

Breeding Bacteria

- **Accidental Selection**
- **Hands-On Labs** 🖐
- **Propose Your Own Path**

Go online to choose one of these other paths.

Plants often depend on bacteria to help them obtain nutrients, fight disease, and resist environmental stress. Humans use plants in many ways, such as for food. Using artificial selection to encourage plant-helping traits in bacteria can help meet human needs. For example, scientists have learned that some bacteria help rice plants survive in locations with high temperatures and acidic soil. Scientists are testing the use of these bacteria to help corals as oceans becomes warmer and more acidic! Using safe bacteria to promote plant health also reduces the need for fertilizers and pesticides that cause pollution.

Bacteria can help plants in many ways. Scientists use the procedures below to identify and choose plant-helping bacteria.

STEP 1 Grow plants in soils treated with different types of plant-helping bacteria.

STEP 2 Compare the plants to determine which bacteria help them the most.

STEP 3 Collect bacteria from the healthiest plants for selective breeding.

STEP 4 Test the offspring bacteria in fresh soil with new plants.

STEP 5 Repeat Steps 1–4 to optimize the effects.

Once this process is complete, the selectively bred plant-helping bacteria can be sold to farmers to improve crop harvests.

These root nodules are the result of a plant-bacteria symbiosis. The bacteria help plants obtain nitrogen and the plants give the bacteria energy-rich sugars.

447

Continue Your Exploration

1. How might the artificial selection of plant-helping bacteria affect society? Select all that apply.

    A. It boosts the economy by increasing farmer profits.

    B. It increases pollution due to pesticide use.

    C. It encourages partnerships between scientists and industry leaders.

    D. It reduces pollution from artificial fertilizers.

2. Is the process used to isolate and increase plant-helping bacteria an engineering solution? Use evidence from the passage to support your answer.

3. Scientists use genetic testing to identify specific genes present in organisms, including bacteria. How might this technology make it easier to breed plant-helping bacteria using artificial selection?

4. **Collaborate** Genetic engineering could also be used to increase plant-helping traits in bacteria. What advantages does the use of artificial selection provide compared to genetic engineering? Make a list of possible advantages to discuss with your class.

Can You Explain It?

Name: _____   **Date:** _____

How did humans cause alpacas to become different from vicuñas over time?

vicuña

alpaca

EVIDENCE NOTEBOOK

Refer to the notes in your Evidence Notebook to help you construct an explanation for how humans influenced the development of alpaca populations from vicuñas.

1. State your claim. Make sure your claim fully explains how humans influenced the development of alpaca populations.

2. Summarize the evidence you have gathered to support your claim and explain your reasoning.

Checkpoints

Answer the following questions to check your understanding of the lesson.

Use the Punnett square to answer Questions 3–4.

3. What is the probability that these parents will produce a short-haired Chihuahua?

    A. 0%

    B. 25%

    C. 50%

    D. 100%

4. Which two individuals should be bred to produce the highest probability of having a long-haired Chihuahua?

    A. *HH* and *hh*

    B. *Hh* and *Hh*

    C. *Hh* and *hh*

    D. *HH* and *Hh*

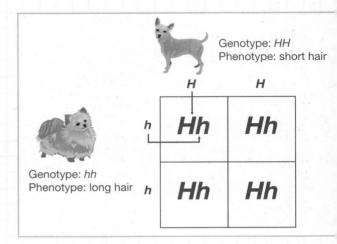

Genotype: *HH*
Phenotype: short hair

Genotype: *hh*
Phenotype: long hair

	H	*H*
h	*Hh*	*Hh*
h	*Hh*	*Hh*

Use the photograph to answer Question 5.

5. What evidence in the photo suggests that roses have been influenced by artificial selection?

    A. The roses all have very soft petals.

    B. The roses display variety in only one trait.

    C. The roses display traits that appeal to humans.

    D. Some roses have more stripes or flecks than others.

6. How does artificial selection differ from natural selection? Circle all that apply.

    A. During artificial selection, the mating pairs are selected by humans, not the organisms.

    B. The outcomes of artificial selection are predictable.

    C. Artificial selection requires variety in a population.

    D. Artificial selection does not help a population adapt to its environment.

7. How are genetic engineering and artificial selection similar? Circle all that apply.

    A. They influence traits in organisms.

    B. They involve altering DNA sequences.

    C. They attempt to meet human needs or desires.

    D. They expand as scientific understanding of inheritance improves.

Interactive Review

Complete this section to review the main concepts of the lesson.

People have used artificial selection for thousands of years to influence the inheritance of desired traits in living things.

A. What is required for artificial selection? Is an advanced understanding of genes needed?

Artificial selection influences the genotypes and phenotypes of populations.

B. How do Punnett squares help predict the outcomes of artificial selection?

Artificial selection helps meet the needs and desires of humans.

C. Use an example to explain how artificial selection can help solve human problems.

Genetic Engineering Influences Traits in Organisms

This cat is producing proteins that cause it to glow green under certain types of light.

Explore First

Evaluating Genetic Engineering Make a list of the benefits and drawbacks of directly modifying an organism's DNA through genetic engineering. Do you think it's okay for scientists to directly modify the DNA of plants? Of animals? Of humans? Use evidence from your list to support your answer.

Go online to view the digital version of the Hands-On Lab for this lesson and to download additional lab resources.

CAN YOU EXPLAIN IT?

How can goats produce spider silk proteins?

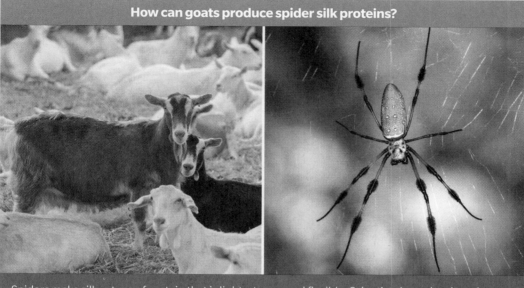

Spiders make silk, a type of protein that is light, strong, and flexible. Scientists have developed goats that produce spider silk proteins in their milk. The spider silk protein can be separated from the milk for human use. Potential uses include protective clothing and wound dressings or sutures.

1. What are the advantages of getting spider silk from goats instead of spiders?

2. Do you think people could breed goats to produce spider silk proteins? Explain your answer.

 EVIDENCE NOTEBOOK As you explore the lesson, gather evidence to help explain what can cause goats to produce spider silk proteins.

Exploring Genetic Engineering Techniques

You may have friends with blue, green, or brown eyes. Eye color is an inherited *trait* that is passed from parents to offspring. Traits are controlled by genes. *Genes* are segments of DNA on chromosomes. Genes code for proteins that cause specific traits in an organism, such as eye color. Scientists can change genes to influence traits in organisms.

Inheritance of Eye Color

3. Eye color is a trait influenced by several genes. The *OCA2* and *HERC2* genes determine how much melanin pigment is produced in iris cells. More melanin leads to brown eyes. Less melanin leads to blue eyes. Complete the diagram using terms in the word bank.

WORD BANK
proteins
DNA
traits
genes

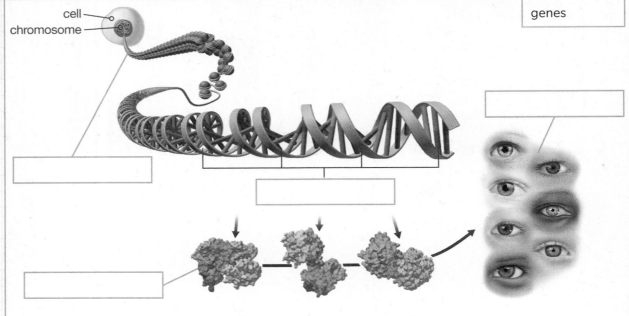

cell
chromosome

Genetic Engineering as Biotechnology

As scientists improve their understanding of the biological processes that connect genes to traits, they develop technologies to study and influence desired traits in organisms. **Genetic engineering** is the process of modifying DNA for practical purposes. Scientists might modify DNA for use in research, medicine, or agriculture. For example, soybean plants are important for oils and livestock feed. Soybeans are a genetically modified crop. Soybean crop health improved after scientists inserted genes for pest resistance into soybean seeds. Gene insertion is just one biotechnology used by genetic engineers. Other genetic engineering technologies encourage the production of specific proteins, or change genes to modify traits in organisms.

A caterpillar chewed holes in the leaves of this soybean plant. Inserting a pest resistance gene into soybeans can decrease damage due to pests.

Comparing Genetic Engineering and Artificial Selection

Humans have influenced the traits of organisms for thousands of years through artificial selection. *Artificial selection* is the process of breeding organisms to increase the frequency of desired traits in a population. Both artificial selection and genetic engineering influence the traits present in a population. For example, humans can improve pest resistance in soybeans by breeding plants that show increased resistance to pests *or* by inserting a pest-resistance gene. Influencing traits through genetic engineering can be more precise and faster than using artificial selection. In some cases, genetic engineering allows scientists to make changes to the traits of an organism that would not be possible through artificial selection.

Inserting a Gene into a Bacterium

Segments of DNA from one organism may be integrated into the DNA of a different organism. The simple structure of bacterial cells makes them good candidates for genetic engineering.

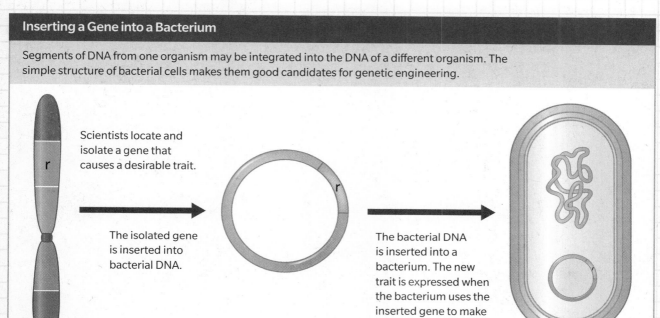

Scientists locate and isolate a gene that causes a desirable trait.

The isolated gene is inserted into bacterial DNA.

The bacterial DNA is inserted into a bacterium. The new trait is expressed when the bacterium uses the inserted gene to make proteins.

4. What is required to insert a new gene into a bacterium and for the bacterium to show the new trait? Select all that apply.

   A. proteins

   B. biotechnology

   C. cellular processes

   D. a breeding program

5. **Discuss** When inserting a new gene into an organism, the gene could come from the same species or it could come from a different species. Generate at least three questions you could research about each of these scenarios.

Milestones in Genetic Engineering

Rapid advancements in genetic engineering began in the early 1970s. Biologists saw that bacteria use special enzymes to repair their DNA. For example, bacteria use enzymes to cut and remove DNA that was inserted by a virus. *Viruses* are small particles that insert viral genetic information into host cells. The discovery about how bacteria use "cut and paste" enzymes inspired scientists to investigate how these enzymes could be used to solve human problems. Developments in genetic engineering reflect scientific progress. Scientists use creativity and existing technology to make new discoveries. This leads to increased understanding and chances for more exploration.

Recombination Technology

When a new gene is inserted into DNA, the DNA is called *recombinant DNA*. Recombinant DNA began by using *plasmids*, or small circles of bacterial DNA.

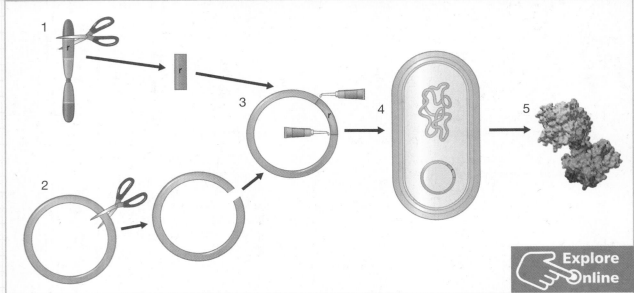

Explore Online

| **Step 1** The gene that controls a trait is located and cut from the chromosome. | **Step 2** The plasmid is opened using "cut" enzymes. | **Step 3** The new gene is added to the plasmid using "paste" enzymes. | **Step 4** The plasmid with the new gene is inserted into a bacterium. | **Step 5** The bacterium produces the new protein. |

6. Number the milestones of genetic engineering to show the progression of science.

   _____ Foreign DNA is successfully inserted into the DNA of bacteria.

   _____ Scientists confirm that the new genes give the bacteria new traits.

   _____ "Cut and paste" enzymes are discovered by observing how bacteria use enzymes to destroy the DNA of invading viruses.

   _____ Bacteria use inserted genes to make proteins, just as they do with their own genes.

Hands-On Lab
Model the Modification of Bacteria

You will model genetic modification of a bacterium using "cut and paste" enzymes. You will also analyze how genetic modification of bacteria can help humans.

Bacteria are unicellular organisms. Bacteria do not have nuclei. Instead, most of the genes are in a single, circular chromosome in the cytoplasm. The simple structure and rapid reproduction of bacteria make them a good choice for scientific research.

MATERIALS
- colored beads (to fit on chenille stem)
- colored pencils
- chenille stems
- scissors

Procedure

STEP 1 Locate the circular chromosome and the plasmids in the diagram. Use evidence from the diagram to make a list of traits controlled by the bacterium's DNA.

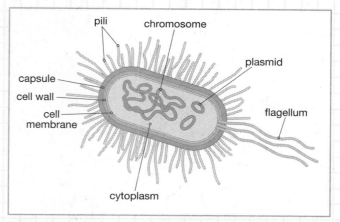

This bacterium has a single large chromosome and several smaller circles of DNA called plasmids. The plasmids contain few genes. They are not essential for the bacterium's survival.

STEP 2 Build a chenille stem plasmid to model a circular plasmid in the bacterium. To model DNA bases, use beads similar in color to the letters in the sequence given. Add the correct sequence of DNA "bases" to the chenille stem and then twist the free ends together.

DNA sequence: TTGAGCGCATTGCGT

STEP 3 The "cut" enzyme cuts the plasmid between an ATT sequence and a GCG sequence. Cut your plasmid in the correct location. The scissors model the enzyme in this step.

STEP 4 Choose one of the genes from the table to insert into your plasmid. Add the correct sequences of bases. Then "paste" (twist) the free ends together.

Function of protein encoded by gene	DNA sequence of gene
stops the bacterium from building pili that help the bacterium infect cells	TTGAA
causes bacterium to burst	GCGTA
increases production of a protein used in livestock feed	ATTTA

Analysis

STEP 5 Draw the modified bacterium with its new trait.

STEP 6 How might a population of bacteria with this new trait be helpful for people?

Influencing Traits in a Population

Engineers can insert genes that cause desirable traits in an organism. In order to be heritable, the modification must be made to cells passed to offspring. This is easy in bacteria. Bacteria divide in half and pass a complete copy of their DNA to their offspring. In sexually reproducing organisms, genetic modification will only be heritable if it occurs in reproductive cells—egg or sperm—or in early embryos. This makes it more difficult to use genetic engineering to influence traits in a population of organisms that reproduce sexually compared to bacteria.

The cells in early embryos can still develop into any cell type. They pass an identical copy of their DNA to every offspring cell, including any genetic modifications. During the process of *cell differentiation*, cells become specialized for a specific function. Once cells differentiate into various types, such as muscle cells or blood cells, genetic modifications made to the cells will only pass to the offspring cells of that cell type.

Cell Differentiation in Embryos

Early embryo cells differentiate into the different cell types found in an organism. This diagram shows three examples of specialized cell types.

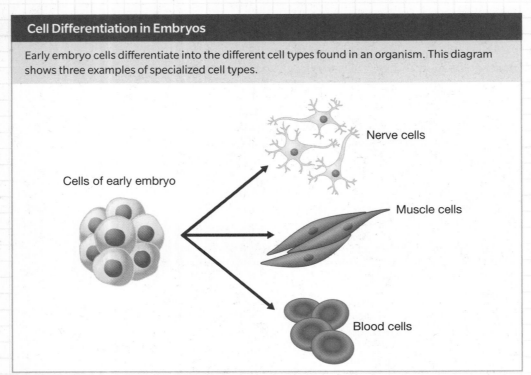

Nerve cells

Cells of early embryo

Muscle cells

Blood cells

7. Do the Math If all of a poisonous frog's eggs are genetically engineered right after fertilization to include a gene that prevents poison production, what is the ratio of poisonous to non-poisonous frogs in the offspring?

A. 1:0

B. 1:2

C. 0:1

D. 1:1

EVIDENCE NOTEBOOK

8. How could genetic engineering cause goats to produce a new protein? Record your evidence.

Genetic Modification of Bacteria

Genetic engineering can be used to help solve human problems. People with diabetes need a dependable supply of insulin. Insulin is a protein that helps regulate blood sugar. Scientists have modified bacteria to produce insulin for human use. Large numbers of the modified bacteria can be farmed to produce large amounts of insulin.

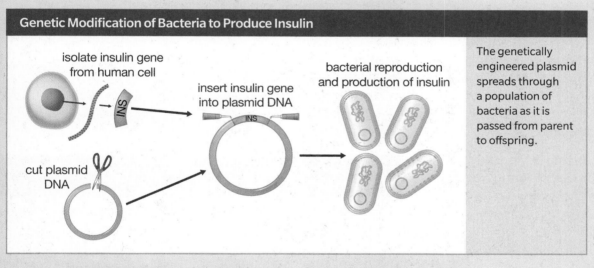

Genetic Modification of Bacteria to Produce Insulin

isolate insulin gene from human cell

insert insulin gene into plasmid DNA

INS

cut plasmid DNA

bacterial reproduction and production of insulin

The genetically engineered plasmid spreads through a population of bacteria as it is passed from parent to offspring.

9. Based on your knowledge of recombinant DNA and the diagram above, explain why is it necessary to genetically engineer the bacteria to produce insulin instead of inserting the insulin gene in humans.

_____

_____

_____

_____

_____

_____

_____

_____

Evaluating Genetic Modification

Genetically engineered crops, especially those not intended for the human food supply, are common in the United States and other industrialized nations. For example, genetically modified soybean plants now make up more than 80% of all soybean crops around the world. Many of these soybeans are used for animal feed. The use of genetically modified crops is increasing. Some modified crops are hardier and more productive than non-modified crops.

These cotton plants contain genes to resist the herbicides that farmers use to kill weeds.

10. Why might farmers want to grow cotton plants that have been modified to be resistant to herbicides?

Genetically Modified Organisms

Inserting foreign DNA into an organism results in a **genetically modified organism**, or GMO. These organisms are often called *transgenic* because genetic modification allows genes to cross the normal barriers between species (*trans* means "across"). GMOs have applications in agriculture, scientific research, medicine, and other industries. For example, genetically modified soybeans provide oils for skin-care products and protein for food products. Many people are cautious about GMOs because they are unsure of potential side effects on humans and other species. This has limited the planting of genetically modified crops in some countries. Some GMO crops allow for reduced use of pesticides. Others require increased pesticide use for a successful harvest.

11. According to the graph, which crop was the first to reach 75% GMO-planted acres?

12. There may be more support for the genetic modification of a crop if it is not used for human food. What pattern in the graph might be explained by this statement?

A. the different adoption rates between cotton and soybeans

B. the different adoption rates between cotton and corn

C. the current adoption level of soybeans, cotton, and corn

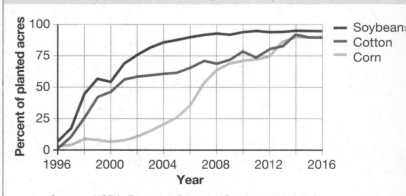

Adoption of Crops Genetically Engineered for Herbicide Tolerance (United States, 1996–2016)

The number of acres planted with genetically modified crops has increased since their introduction in the mid-1990s.

Sources: USDA, Economic Research Service using data from Fernandez-Comejo and McBride (2002) for the years 1996–99 and USDA, National Agricultural Statistics Service, June Agricultural Survey for the years 2000–16.

Case Study: Glowing Mosquitoes

Malaria and dengue fever are human diseases that are spread by mosquitoes. Scientists can insert a gene that causes mosquitoes to die if they do not receive a specific chemical. Scientists insert a fluorescent gene from jellyfish at the same time to track which mosquitoes have been successfully modified. Researchers release only modified male mosquitoes to the wild because male mosquitoes do not bite humans. When female mosquitoes in the wild mate with the modified males, the offspring inherit the modified gene and die without access to the chemical. This reduces mosquito populations and can slow the spread of some human diseases. However, the release of genetically modified mosquitoes into the wild raises concerns about the impact on birds and bats that may eat the GMOs.

These mosquito larvae glow. Their cells have genes from jellyfish that make fluorescent proteins.

The Impact of Genetically Modified Mosquitoes	
Effect on individuals	Human individuals experience reduced exposure to diseases carried by mosquitoes, including malaria and dengue fever.
Effect on society	Society benefits by saving lives and reducing health care costs associated with malaria and dengue fever. The money saved can be used for other beneficial projects in communities.
Effect on the environment	The release of genetically modified mosquitoes might have negative impacts on birds or bats that feed on mosquitoes.

Case Study: Research Mice

Some research mice are genetically modified for scientific research. *Knockout mice* have a gene in their DNA "knocked out" or disrupted. Scientists then observe the mice to see how their traits change. This helps scientists identify the gene's function. Humans and mice have similar DNA, so research with knockout mice can help scientists learn what human genes do. For example, knockout mice research has provided data about genes involved in cancer and anxiety in humans. However, knockout mice are not a perfect research tool. Knocking out an important gene can cause developmental problems in the mice. Also, data from knockout mice studies cannot always be applied to humans.

A gene has been "knocked out" in the mouse on the left. Scientists use knockout mice to learn what genes do.

13. Identify whether the impacts described in the table relate to individuals, society, or the environment.

The Impact of Genetically Modified Mice	
	Knockout mice stay in a lab to limit the chance of spreading modified genes to wild mice.
	Researchers use information from knockout mice to treat similar diseases in humans.
	Knockout mice might be hurt by changes made through genetic engineering.

Case Study: Pharmaceutical Chickens

In 2015, officials in the United States approved the farming of genetically engineered chickens. The chickens produce a special protein in their eggs that can be used to treat a human disorder. The protein is isolated from the eggs and given to people who lack the protein in their bodies. Without this protein, humans cannot break down fat molecules. The condition is fatal to infants and causes heart disease in adults. There is no other effective treatment for the disorder.

Plants, bacteria, and other organisms have been genetically modified for medical purposes. Goats can be modified to produce a chemical in their milk that breaks down blood clots in humans. Using mammals to produce pharmaceutical chemicals in their milk can be effective. Milk production is a natural process, and milking does not harm the animals.

Chickens can be genetically modified to produce a pharmaceutical protein in their eggs.

The Impact of Genetically Modified Chickens	
Effect on individuals	Humans with a protein disorder will experience fewer deaths and reduced illness by receiving replacement protein from the chicken eggs. Laying eggs is a natural process, so the chickens are not harmed.
Effect on society	Some medical chemicals need cellular processes for production. Using GMOs to produce these chemicals provides medicines that cannot be made in a laboratory.
Effect on the environment	The introduction of GMOs into communities can be risky. Scientists try to prevent the transfer of genetically modified DNA by isolating GMOs. Some people worry that modified genes will accidentally spread to wild species.

14. Which of the following are positive impacts that genetically modified chickens have on society? Circle all that apply.

   A. production of pharmaceuticals that cannot be manufactured

   B. improved medical care for humans

   C. increasing numbers of GMOs in communities

   D. production of proteins that cure all diseases

15. Discuss Scientific knowledge can describe the benefits and drawbacks of actions, but society makes decisions about how and when to act. For example, the use of animals in scientific research can help society by providing test subjects that are not humans. However, animals are often harmed during research studies and many people believe that the rights of the animals must be considered. How can you apply the concept of ethics to the subject of animal testing?

16. What evidence suggests that genetic modification is involved in goats that produce spider silk in their milk? Record your evidence.

Engineer It

Evaluate Impacts of Genetically Modified Crops

Bacillus thuringiensis (Bt) is a bacterium that makes proteins that kill pests. Scientists isolated the Bt gene and inserted it into the DNA of corn seeds. The result is Bt corn. Bt corn is a GMO that is resistant to leaf-eating caterpillars.

Corn can be genetically modified to protect the plants from caterpillar damage.

17. Complete the table to explain how genetically modified corn might impact individuals, society, and the environment.

The Impact of Genetically Modified Corn	
Effect on individuals	
Effect on society	
Effect on the environment	

18. Would you grow genetically modified corn if you were a farmer? Provide your reasoning.

_____

_____

_____

_____

_____

_____

Evaluating Gene Therapy

Genetic engineering is not limited to genetic modification using bacteria. Other microbes and molecules can also be used to insert or influence genes in similar ways. For example, viruses are used in genetic engineering. Viruses inject viral genes into a cell. The cell then produces viral proteins that are assembled into new viruses. Scientists can change viruses so that they inject desirable genes into cells instead of viral genes.

19. **Discuss** What might be some advantages and disadvantages of using viruses in genetic engineering to treat human diseases?

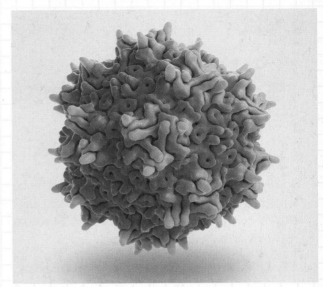

Scientists often choose *adenoviruses* to deliver genes to target cells. These viruses inject their genetic material into a cell's nucleus.

Gene Therapy

Advances in biotechnology allow scientists to treat certain diseases. **Gene therapy** is a technique that uses genes to treat or prevent disease. Gene therapy may be used to insert helpful genes or to remove harmful genes. It may also be used to insert "suicide genes" that cause cell death. This is a promising treatment for cancer.

Most gene therapies are still being tested and studied. To be successfully treated with gene therapy, a disease must have a genetic cause and scientists must know which genes cause the disease. Also, the disease should involve one or only a few genes. Finally, the affected genes must be accessible for treatment for gene therapy to be successful.

A gene therapy success story involves children born with immune cells that do not work. A single gene normally active in bone marrow causes severe combined immunodeficiency disorder. Therapy involves taking bone marrow cells from a patient, inserting the correct gene, and replacing diseased bone marrow cells with modified cells. Without treatment, children born with the disorder must live in germ-free plastic bubbles. Gene therapy allows these children to live healthy lives.

Types of Gene Therapy

Gene therapy can involve adding a functional gene, blocking a malfunctioning gene, or causing a malfunctioning cell to die.

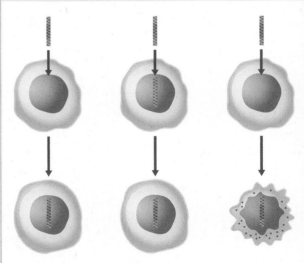

Addition of a therapeutic gene provides normal cell function.

Addition of a therapeutic gene blocks a malfunctioning gene, providing normal cell function.

Addition of a harmful gene produces a lethal substance and the targeted cell dies.

Methods of Gene Delivery

Gene therapy may involve direct or indirect delivery of therapeutic genes. In *direct gene delivery*, a therapeutic gene is inserted into a virus. Then the genetically modified virus is delivered directly to the target site. In *indirect gene delivery*, a therapeutic gene is inserted into a virus. Cells are extracted from the patient. The genetically modified virus is used to introduce the gene to the cells outside of the body. The genetically modified cells are delivered to the target site.

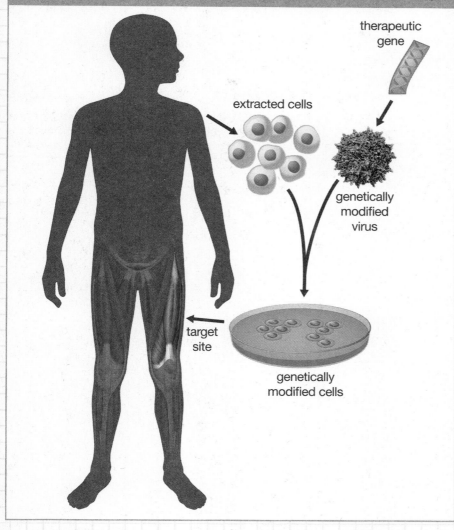

therapeutic gene

extracted cells

genetically modified virus

target site

genetically modified cells

Indirect Gene Delivery

1. **Identify Target Cells** Cells receiving therapeutic genes must be in an isolated area.

2. **Prepare Gene for Delivery** A therapeutic gene is inserted into a virus or other delivery mechanism.

3. **Remove Cells for Modification** Diseased cells are removed from a patient so they can be modified in a lab.

4. **Inject Virus into Extracted Cells** The virus carrying the therapeutic gene is injected into cells removed from the patient's body. Modified cells are grown in the lab.

5. **Deliver Modified Cells** Modified cells are delivered to the patient through injection at a target site.

20. Why might scientists choose indirect delivery instead of direct delivery for a gene therapy?

A. Indirect delivery methods take less time than direct delivery methods.

B. Direct gene delivery is only possible if the target area is accessible.

C. Genetically modified cells are easier to deliver to the target area than genetically modified viruses.

D. Indirect delivery allows scientists to make sure the cells have been correctly modified and are producing the protein.

21. Why are diseases involving many different genes poor candidates for gene therapy?

Impacts of Gene Therapy

Gene therapy has the potential to treat many diseases. The field of gene therapy is still new. Advances in biotechnology are improving gene delivery methods. While the future of gene therapy looks promising, it faces many challenges. Gene therapy raises many ethical concerns about whether human DNA should be changed. Genetic engineering is also costly. Gene therapy may not be available to poorer populations. Gene therapy can disrupt the function of healthy genes in target cells, and long-term effects are uncertain. New genes often result from natural mutations. Over time, evolutionary forces will minimize genes and traits with negative effects. New genes resulting from genetic engineering do not go through the same evolutionary process.

Cystic fibrosis is a genetic disease that causes persistent lung infections. Treatment includes inhaling medicine through a nebulizer. Gene therapies are being tested for this disease.

22. What are the requirements a disease must meet for gene therapy to be an effective option for treatment? Circle all that apply.

   A. It must have a genetic cause.

   B. It should involve many genes.

   C. Target cells must be accessible.

   D. Target cells must be found throughout the patient's body.

Language SmArts

Identify a Potential Disease for Gene Therapy Treatment

Consider what scientists know about these three diseases:

- The predisposition to have **heart disease** is inherited. The disease is influenced by other factors, including age, diet, high blood pressure, and smoking.

- A single gene causes **hemophilia.** Hemophilia results in a lack of clotting proteins in the blood. Clotting proteins are produced in the liver. The lack of clotting proteins can lead to severe bleeding and joint damage.

- People with **type I diabetes** produce little or no insulin. Insulin is needed to move sugar from the blood into cells. Type I diabetes involves multiple genes. It is triggered by environmental factors.

23. Which disease has the best potential for treatment with gene therapy? Defend your answer using evidence from the text and explain what criteria you used.

_____

_____

_____

_____

_____

Continue Your Exploration

Name: _____   Date: _____

Check out the path below or go online to choose one of the other paths shown.

People in Science

- **Careers in Science**
- **Applications of Cloning**
- **Hands-On Labs** 🖑
- **Propose Your Own Path**

Go online to choose one of these other paths.

Dr. Lydia Villa-Komaroff, Molecular Biologist

Dr. Lydia Villa-Komaroff has been a laboratory scientist, a university administrator, a company executive, and an advocate for diversity in STEM during her remarkable career in science. Villa-Komaroff has deep roots in the Southwest. Her mother's family is from the Basque region of Spain and came to America with the conquistadors. Her father's father came from Mexico during the Mexican revolution. She grew up in New Mexico and knew at an early age that she wanted to be a scientist. Education was important to her parents, both the first in their family to go to college.

Villa-Komaroff attended the University of Washington before transferring to Goucher College in Maryland. She had to study harder in college than she did in high school, but she persisted in pursuing science degrees. After studying microbiology and cell biology at MIT, Villa-Komaroff began postdoctoral research at Harvard involving recombinant DNA. Her project at Harvard could not continue when the city of Cambridge banned recombinant DNA research. Villa-Komaroff moved her project using recombinant DNA to study the genome of silk moths to a lab in a different city. Her project was doomed to failure because the tools available were not up to the job of dealing with a large genome; the silk moth genome is almost as large as the human genome. The ban on recombinant DNA research and the unsuccessful project provided valuable lessons about setbacks and learning from failure when working on the cutting edge of science and medicine.

Dr. Lydia Villa-Komaroff studies the structure, function, and interactions of molecules at the cellular level, a field known as molecular biology.

1. How do failures fit into the scientific method or the engineering design process?

Continue Your Exploration

Proinsulin Production in Bacteria

When the research ban was lifted, Dr. Villa-Komaroff returned to Harvard. She was the lead author in a groundbreaking study that explained how to produce proinsulin in bacterial cells by inserting the insulin gene into *E. coli* bacteria. She and her colleagues used rat insulin as a model and these results opened the door for the production of many medically useful proteins. Proinsulin is a precursor of insulin, an important hormone that regulates blood sugar levels. People with diabetes may not produce enough insulin or their bodies may not respond to the insulin that is produced. Eventually, scientists were able to mass produce insulin using bacteria, which decreased the cost and increased the availability of insulin for treating diabetes.

2. Before insulin was available from bacteria, it was taken from animals such as cattle or pigs. Brainstorm potential benefits of using bacteria instead of animals to produce insulin.

Neuroscience and Cell Biology

Dr. Villa-Komaroff also performed neuroscience and cell biology research. For example, Villa-Komaroff collaborated on an experiment that showed beta-amyloid is toxic to neuron cells similar to those found in the brain. The pieces of protein that make up beta-amyloid form plaques in brains affected by Alzheimer's disease. This progressive disease is characterized by dementia and loss of cognitive abilities. It was unclear whether beta-amyloid caused neuron cell death or was a byproduct of the cell death. In the experiment, the gene for the beta-amyloid protein was inserted into neuronal cells. The researchers could turn the gene on and off. When the gene was turned on, the protein was expressed and the cells died, indicating that beta-amyloid was indeed toxic to cells.

3. What aspect of this experiment represents an advancement over the experiment performed to produce proinsulin in bacteria?

   A. cells died

   B. a gene was inserted

   C. a protein was expressed

   D. the gene was turned on or off

4. **Collaborate** Dr. Villa-Komaroff was a co-founding member of the Society for Advancement of Chicanos and Native Americans in Science (SACNAS). Diversity in STEM has been important to Villa-Komaroff throughout her career. Implicit bias and opportunity are two of the major roadblocks to having diverse STEM fields. Select a current, credible research paper that explores one of these topics and summarize the research in a short presentation to the class. Be sure to explain what diversity is and why it is important for STEM.

Can You Explain It?

Name: Date:

How can goats produce spider silk proteins?

EVIDENCE NOTEBOOK

Refer to the notes in your Evidence Notebook to help you construct an explanation for what can cause goats to produce spider silk proteins.

1. State your claim. Make sure your claim fully explains how genetic changes allow goats to produce spider silk proteins.

2. Summarize the evidence you have gathered to support your claim and explain your reasoning.

Checkpoints

Answer the following questions to check your understanding of the lesson.

Use the photo of weeds in a cotton field to answer Question 3.

3. This field was sprayed with an herbicide and specific plants survived. What might cause herbicide resistance in the cotton plants or weeds in this field? Select all that apply.

A. Scientists modified the cotton DNA to resist the herbicide.

B. Some weeds naturally resist herbicide better than others.

C. Cotton became herbicide resistant over thousands of years.

D. Bees transferred herbicide resistance from cotton to weeds.

4. Why are viruses used to deliver therapeutic genes to target cells? Circle all that apply.

A. scientists can modify viral DNA

B. viruses carry many beneficial genes

C. viruses can direct cells to make specific proteins

D. viruses can be injected directly into cells

5. Some cause-and-effect relationships can only be explained using probability, such as the likelihood that an offspring will inherit a particular trait from one of its parents. Artificial selection *increases / decreases* the likelihood that offspring will inherit a desirable trait. Genetic engineering *can / cannot* bring the likelihood of inheritance of a desirable trait to 100%.

6. What is an advantage of using genetically modified mammals to produce desirable proteins in their milk?

A. It is easy to genetically modify mammals.

B. It is difficult to isolate the desirable proteins.

C. Milk production is a natural process, so there are few negative impacts to the mammals.

D. Genetic modification of mammals raises few ethical concerns.

Use the eye diagram to answer Question 7.

7. Why is wet macular degeneration a good candidate for gene therapy? Circle all that apply.

A. The gene therapy is delivered by injection.

B. The gene therapy makes a single protein that blocks new blood vessels causing the eye disease.

C. The target cells in the eye are easily accessible.

D. The modified cell produces new proteins.

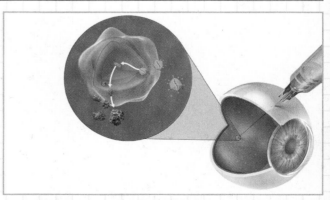

Wet macular degeneration is an eye disease caused by leaking blood vessels. A gene therapy has been made that produces a protein that blocks the production of new blood vessels.

Interactive Review

Complete this section to review the main concepts of the lesson.

Genetic engineering involves the modification of genes for practical purposes.

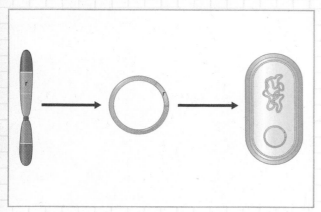

A. Describe the process genetic engineers use to insert genes into a bacterium's DNA so that it produces new proteins.

Inserting a new gene into an organism results in a genetically modified organism (GMO). The introduction of GMOs impacts individuals, society, and the environment.

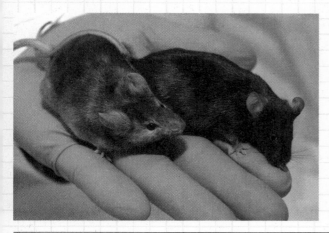

B. What are some impacts of genetically modified organisms on society?

Gene therapy is an experimental technique that uses genes to treat or prevent disease.

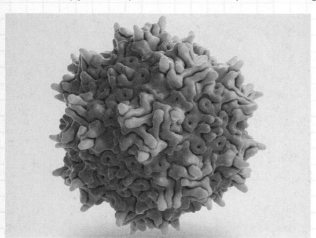

C. Explain the different techniques used to deliver therapeutic genes to target cells.

Choose one of the activities to explore how this unit connects to other topics.

☐ People in Science

Dr. Vanessa Koelling, Evolutionary Biologist
Interest in nature and Earth's history inspired Koelling to become a scientist. Dr. Koelling has Morquio Syndrome, a genetic disease of metabolism that causes physical disability. She has been part of the battle to include people with disabilities in the sciences. Dr. Koelling studies how populations adapt and change, a field known as *population genetics*. She identifies genes involved in adaptations in plant populations.

Research population genetics. Create an infographic that explains this field and highlights five skills or subdisciplines that researchers may use in population genetics, such as mathematical modeling.

☐ Art Connection

Art and Extinction The purpose of extinction art is to raise awareness of endangered species, and species that have already become extinct. This branch of art can also help to relate human impacts on the environment to the risk of losing certain species.

Research an extinct species such as the great auk, shown here, the Wake Island rail, the small Mauritian flying fox, the desert bandicoot, or the Round Island burrowing boa. Find out when and where the species lived and how it went extinct. Create a drawing of your species. Then summarize your research in a short paragraph.

☐ Social Studies Connection

Artificial Selection and Chinese Culture Goldfish were first domesticated in China over 1,000 years ago during the Tang dynasty. People began to breed the gold variety as a sign of wealth. Over the years, more varieties of goldfish have been bred, such as the bubble-eyed goldfish, first bred in 1908. This fish has enlarged fluid-filled sacs beneath its eyes.

Research another example of an animal or plant that has been influenced genetically over time by Chinese culture. Explain the connection between culture and the desired traits. Present your findings in a multimedia presentation.

Name: _____   Date: _____

Complete this review to check your understanding of the unit.

Use the photos to answer Questions 1-4.

This corn has been influenced by artificial selection and genetic modification.

This wheat has been influenced only by artificial selection.

1. Describe the types of traits that can be influenced in these food crops.

2. How are these examples of human influence on traits similar?

3. How are these examples of human influence on traits different?

4. Which is associated with a greater risk for negative impacts on the environment? Use evidence and reasoning to justify your answer.

Name: _____   Date: _____

Use the graph to answer Questions 5–8.

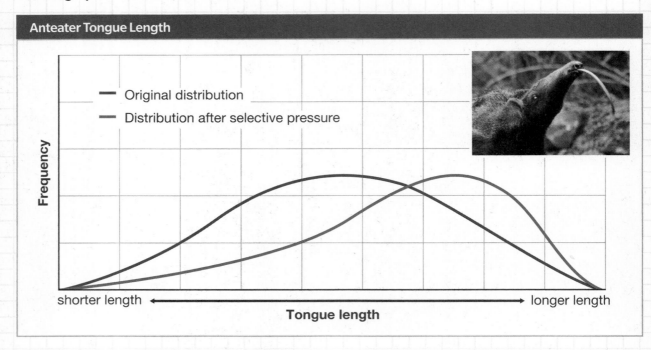

Anteater Tongue Length

— Original distribution
— Distribution after selective pressure

Frequency

shorter length ⟵ ⟶ longer length

Tongue length

5. What variation of traits is shown in this graph?

6. Explain the connection between genes, proteins, and this variation of traits.

7. Compare and contrast the original distribution of traits prior to selective pressure to the most recent distribution.

8. An anteater's main food source is termites, which live underground. Propose an explanation for how selective pressure could have resulted in the change in traits within the anteater population shown in the graph.

Name: Date:

How does the use of insecticides lead to insecticide resistance?

A single genetic mutation causes resistance to the insecticide DDT. This research is key to helping scientists improve malaria-control strategies related to mosquitoes. Research how certain insect species have become resistant to different insecticides over time. What types of variation exist in insect populations that have allowed insect populations to become resistant?

Explain why it is important to minimize the use of harmful insecticides. Create a public education poster using the concept of natural selection to explain the issue of increasing insecticide resistance in insects.

Insecticide Resistance between 1940 and 1990						
	Approximate number of species resistant to each insecticide					Total number of resistant insect species
Year	Cyclodienes	DD1	Organophosphates	Carbamates	Pyrethroids	
1940	<5	<5	<5	<5	<5	<5
1950	25	30	10	<5	<5	45
1960	75	75	40	<5	<5	125
1970	155	125	70	<5	10	235
1980	320	255	215	65	40	435
1990	365	300	305	120	80	505

Source: Metcalfe, R.L., and W.H. Luckmann, eds, *Introduction to Insect Pest Management*, Third Edition, 1994, John Wiley and Sons, N.Y., as quoted by "DDT, Junk Science, Malaria, and insecticide resistance," Bug Gwen, Gwen Pearson, 2007

The steps below will help guide your research and develop your recommendation.

1. **Define the Problem** Write a statement defining the problem you have been asked to solve.

2. **Conduct Research** How have insects become resistant to insecticides over time? During your research, use information from credible and accurate sources, analyze studies for potential bias in methods, and make sure the information you use is supported by evidence.

3. **Analyze the Data** Use the insecticide resistance data to analyze how the resistance to insecticides has changed over time. Then make predictions about how insecticide resistance might change in the future.

4. **Identify and Recommend Solutions** How can the incidence of insecticide resistance be managed? Make a recommendation based on your knowledge of natural selection and your research. Explain your reasoning.

5. **Communicate** Present your findings with a public education poster. Use the concept of natural selection to explain the issue of increasing insecticide resistance, and explain how your solution would help address the problem. Include a graph or other mathematical model to support your conclusions and solution.

✓ **Self-Check**

		I researched how insect species have become resistant to insecticides.
		I analyzed data to describe how resistance to insecticides has changed over time and to predict how it might change in the future.
		I used knowledge of natural selection to make a recommendation about how to manage insecticide resistance.
		My findings and recommendation were clearly communicated to others.

Go online to access the **Interactive Glossary**. *You can use this online tool to look up definitions for all the vocabulary terms in this book.*

Pronunciation Key

Sound	Symbol	Example	Respelling	Sound	Symbol	Example	Respelling
ă	a	pat	PAT	ŏ	ah	bottle	BAHT'l
ā	ay	pay	PAY	ō	oh	toe	TOH
âr	air	care	KAIR	ô	aw	caught	KAWT
ä	ah	father	FAH•ther	ôr	ohr	roar	ROHR
är	ar	argue	AR•gyoo	oi	oy	noisy	NOYZ•ee
ch	ch	chase	CHAYS	o͞o	u	book	BUK
ĕ	e	pet	PET	o͞o	oo	boot	BOOT
ĕ (at end of a syllable)	eh	settee lessee	seh•TEE leh•SEE	ou	ow	pound	POWND
ĕr	ehr	merry	MEHR•ee	s	s	center	SEN•ter
ē	ee	beach	BEECH	sh	sh	cache	CASH
g	g	gas	GAS	ŭ	uh	flood	FLUHD
ĭ	i	pit	PIT	ûr	er	bird	BERD
ĭ (at end of a syllable)	ih	guitar	gih•TAR	z	z	xylophone	ZY•luh•fohn
ī	y eye (only for a complete syllable)	pie island	PY EYE•luhnd	z	z	bags	BAGZ
îr	ir	hear	HIR	zh	zh	decision	dih•SIZH•uhn
j	j	germ	JERM	ə	uh	around broken focus	uh•ROWND BROH•kuhn FOH•kuhs
k	k	kick	KIK	ər	er	winner	WIN•er
ng	ng	thing	THING	th	th	thin they	THIN THAY
ngk	ngk	bank	BANGK	w	w	one	WUHN
				wh	hw	whether	HWETH•er

Index

Page numbers for key terms are in **boldface** type.
Page numbers in *italic* type indicate illustrative material, such as photographs, graphs, charts, and maps.

A

Abell-370 galaxy cluster, *291*
absolute age, 16, 320–322, 348
absolute dating, 320, 322
absorption, 505
absorption of wave, 505–506, 507
acanthostega, 352
acceleration, 55
    effect of collision during, 106
    friction effect on, 79, 84
    rate of velocity changes, 76
    in relationship to mass, 81–85
    speed's relationship to, 55
    unbalanced forces changing, 77–80, 97, *97*
acid rain, 603
acoustic panel, 512, *512*
acquired trait, 396
Act, 9, 79, 217, 241, 246, 532, 643
action force, 86–88, 96
adaptations, 427
    of cactus and their predator, 409, *409*
    evolution of, 398
    identifying, 428, *428*
    of manta rays, 394, *394*
    of predator, 399–403, 409, *409*
    of rafflesia flowers, *395*
    traits for organism survival, 427–428
adenine (A), 419, *419*
adenoviruses, 464, *464*
African elephant, 378–379, *378*
agriculture
    changes in land used for, 608, *608*
    population growth rate affected by, 573, *573*
air, light traveling through, 518–519
airbag, 80, *80*
airplane, 478, *478*
air resistance, 193, 196
algae, 391
allele, 437, *437*, 442, *442*

allele frequency, 405
alpaca, 435, *435*, 449, *449*, 576, *576*, 589, *589*
alphadon, 357, *357*
Altamira, Brazil, 592, *592*
Alvarez, Luis, 8, *8*, 11
Alvarez, Walter, 8, *8*, 11, 15
amber, 336, *336*
ambulocetus natans, 353, *353*, 370, *370*
American badger, 308, *308*
amino acid chain, 420, *420*, 421, *421*
ammonites
    in ancient sea, 311, *311*, 325, *325*
    index fossil of, 318
amphibian, evolution of, 352, *352*
amplitude, 489
amplitude of waves
    energy of partial reflection and, *508*
    of light wave, 522, *522*, 539
    modulating, 626, *626*
    volume relating to, 506, *506*
    as wave property, 489–492
    wave size affected by, 504–506, 515, *515*
anacus, *379*
analog information, 622, *622*
analog signal, 623
    analyzing, 621–625
    compared to digital signal, 565
    continuous information, 623–624, *623*, 637
    converting to digital, 628
    modulating, 626–627
    noise affecting, *629*, 631, *631*, 637, 644
    storage of, 632, *632*
analysis
    of apparent motion of the sun, 217
    of correlation, 20
    of Earth, moon, and sun system, 242

    of Earth's tilt, 550
    of Earth-Sun model, 549–554
    of electrical force, 127, 129, 130–131
    of electromagnet, 153
    of encoding messages, 617
    of energy, 28–31
    of energy in systems, 43–44
    of extinction and land use, 608
    of extinction data, 356
    of factors in resource use, 580
    of falling objects, 186
    of forces, 58–61, 83
    of fossil record, 358–359
    of fossil to describe Earth's past, 314
    of gravitational forces, 188
    of growth curve data, 376, *376*
    of impact of water use, 598
    of inferences from evidence, 377
    of kinetic and potential energy, 35–38
    of law of universal gravitation, 258
    of light transmission, 531
    of longitudinal and transverse waves, 487
    of magnets, 143, 144–145, 146–147
    of mechanical waves generation, 501
    of the moon's craters, 16
    of motion of falling objects, 195
    of observations, 289
    of other galaxies, 291–296
    of packing materials, 103–104
    of parallax, 224
    of population growth and resource use, 577–578
    of protein folding, 422
    of rock layers, 317, 334
    of salamander species distribution, 401–402
    of selected traits in vegetables, 438–439
    of signal, 630
    of solar system model, 281–282

F

M

Y

Z